SAYING YES TO LIFE

An autobiography

SAYING YES
TO LIFE

An autobiography

by

General John Larsson

Crest Books
Salvation Army National Publications
615 Slaters Lane
Alexandria, Virginia 22313

Published by Crest Books
The Salvation Army National Headquarters
615 Slaters Lane, Alexandria, VA 22313
Major Ed Forster, Editor in Chief for National Publications and National Literary Secretary
Phone: 703/684-5523
Fax: 703/684-5539

Available from The Salvation Army Supplies and Purchasing Departments
    Des Plaines, IL – (800) 937-8896
    West Nyack, NY – (888) 488-4882
    Atlanta, GA – (800) 786-7372
    Long Beach, CA – (800) 937-8896

Printed in the United States of America

Library of Congress Control Number: 2007924470

Cover design by Berni Georges

ISBN-13: 978-0-9792266-0-1

ISBN-10: 0-9792266-00

Contents

		Page
Chapter One	An International Gene	1
Chapter Two	South American Youth	19
Chapter Three	At the Battle School	35
Chapter Four	Early Officer Years	49
Chapter Five	Corps, Musicals and Marriage	69
Chapter Six	Youth, Musicals and More	93
Chapter Seven	Return to Chile and Denmark Hill	111
Chapter Eight	Resolving a Conundrum	131
Chapter Nine	Three Diverse Territories	157
Chapter Ten	Gowans and Larsson – Again	181
Chapter Eleven	What's the General For?	203
Chapter Twelve	Culminating Events	227
Index		251

Preface

Life has been good to me. With the psalmist I can say that 'the boundary lines have fallen for me in pleasant places' (Psalm 16:6, *New International Version*). And a main purpose for telling the story of my life is to give praise and thanks to God for the blessings that have been mine.

Life for me has been a quest, a continual and often exhilarating exploration that has led to great and often unexpected discoveries along the way. From my earliest days I seem to have grasped intuitively that the key to abundant living is to say yes to God and yes to all that is good in life. If I dare call this account *Saying Yes to Life* it is not because I have always succeeded, but because saying yes to life has been my aim.

Life is multidimensional, and saying yes to life means saying yes to it in all of its diversity, richness and fullness. I have therefore not wanted the telling of my story to be just an extended version of my officer service record. My ministry as a Salvation Army officer has been central to my life for nearly 50 years and I therefore use the various appointments I have held as useful time markers for my chapter divisions. But within each chapter I roam widely in my observations and reflections, for life has been much more than a series of appointments.

So in these pages I tell the story of the musicals and my other writings, tell of the precious ones the Lord has given me, and tell of my love for music and yearning for wild nature. I also touch on events in Army history that I have lived through or with which I am in some way linked. In addition I leave the door ajar to the hinterland of heart, mind and spirit where I find my inspiration, and also share something of the deep convictions which have become the passions of my life.

I pray that this record of my life may not only be of interest, but that it may also be of encouragement and inspiration.

John Larsson

Chapter One

AN INTERNATIONAL GENE

THAT the 2006 High Council summoned to elect my successor as General of The Salvation Army had to meet in the dead of winter – the first winter High Council since 1929 – was entirely due to the fact that I was born in April. I was to retire on my 68th birthday in that month so the Council had to meet in January.

It was on the second day of April 1938 that I arrived in this world. The place was Malmö, a town in the south of Sweden, where my parents, Captain and Mrs Sture and Flora Larsson, were the divisional youth leaders. I was the second-born, my brother David having been born in England two years previously. My father was Swedish and my mother British.

I didn't know it then, but I had been born into an international family with no fixed abode. For two generations both sides of the family had been moving from country to country in the service of the Lord and of the Army. Malmö was but a staging post *en route*. For me it was the starting point for the same kind of life. My DNA includes an international gene.

The Larsson heritage

My paternal grandfather, Commissioner Karl Larsson, was the territorial commander in Sweden when I was born. The Salvation Army there was at its peak in those years. With more than 1,500 active officers it was the second-largest territorial command in the Army world, next only to the then British Territory.

Karl Larsson turned 70 the year I was born and he and my grandmother Anna should have retired from active service. But General Evangeline Booth asked them to continue for a further year. During that year war broke out, so they were requested to extend their service even further. With the Second World War lasting until 1945, my grandfather did not retire until he was 77. By

1

that time he had been a territorial commander for more than 30 years.

Karl Larsson was a remarkable character, a true Viking warrior, an ardent evangelist, a visionary, a born leader and man of action endued with seemingly boundless energy, a giant of a man.

He was the son of a railway worker and his parents and their nine children lived in a small cottage next to the railway line in the woods near Bodafors in southern Sweden. This two-roomed cottage has now been turned into a museum to honour his memory, and when Freda, my wife, and I visited it some years ago, we could not help wondering how 11 people could have fitted into that minute space. But they did.

Karl met The Salvation Army and was converted at the age of 21 in Jönköping. There must already have been signs of his leadership qualities, for the corps officer appointed him as a sergeant before he had even become a soldier! He soon became an officer, and following corps and literary appointments – and marriage to Captain Anna Dahlbom – he quickly became a divisional commander, then – successively – training principal, field secretary and chief secretary. It was in 1912 that life as international nomads began for Karl and Anna Larsson and their seven children. In the course of one 10-year period the family was to live in eight different countries!

Karl Larsson was appointed territorial commander for Finland. Finland was then part of the Russian empire, and from his Helsinki base Karl Larsson helped to pioneer and establish the Army's work in Russia, a venture that was to last from 1913 to 1923.

In 1918 he was formally appointed in charge of the work in Russia, and the family moved to St Petersburg. The country had been in political turmoil for some time but new possibilities seemed suddenly to be opening up. However, within months the communists launched their revolution and civil war raged. My father was then a boy of 12 and in later life would sometimes recall seeing the fighting in the streets – and the hunger which was a permanent feature of their lives.

When all foreigners were expelled, the Larsson family had to flee the country. Karl Larsson later told the story of those years in his book *Ten Years in Russia*. So meticulous was his recording that, when the Army was seeking to re-establish itself in Russia in the

1990s, some exact reference details he had included helped to locate documents that persuaded the authorities that the Army had indeed worked in Russia previously.

Karl Larsson's next appointment, in 1919, was to pioneer the Army's work in Czechoslovakia, and the family soon followed him to Prague. His appointment after that was as leader of the South America Territory, which in those days comprised the countries of Argentina, Uruguay, Paraguay, Chile, Peru and Bolivia. The territorial headquarters was in Buenos Aires.

My father, having reached the age of 16, did not accompany the family to South America but moved to London, where Lieut-Colonel and Mrs Alfred and Mathilda Benwell opened their home to him. They had a daughter named Flora, and she will re-appear in this story!

Following the years in South America, Karl Larsson was appointed to International Headquarters for 18 months, then as territorial commander to Finland for a second time, then to Norway for seven years, and finally back to his own country of Sweden for the last 10 years of his active service.

As noted, Karl Larsson's leadership in Sweden coincided with the Second World War. Following the 1939 High Council, as members were preparing to return quickly to their appointments because of the threat of war, General-elect George Carpenter had a quiet word with Karl Larsson. On the assumption that Sweden would remain neutral, the General-elect asked Karl Larsson to oversee and assist the Army in European countries should International Headquarters find itself unable to do so.

Soon afterwards General Carpenter appointed Adjutant – later General – Erik Wickberg to be Karl Larsson's right-hand man for that task. The Wickbergs at that time were stationed at International Headquarters and, with only a few hours of warning, caught the last boat from England to Sweden before war broke out.

When the war made it impossible for International Headquarters to communicate with the European territories, Karl Larsson began a ministry of support that in the end extended not only to the rest of Europe but as far as China and The Philippines.

But the continuing link between The Salvation Army in Sweden and International Headquarters in England began to be questioned by Nazi authorities in neighbouring occupied countries. At times a Nazi invasion of Sweden also seemed imminent. This would inevitably reveal the link with International Headquarters, and would put at risk not only the support programme but the Army's right to exist in some of the occupied countries. With these considerations weighing on his mind, Karl Larsson consulted with his territorial leadership team and decided in May 1941 that it would be in the greater interests of the Army for him to cut off all contact with International Headquarters – and, in effect, take over command of The Salvation Army in the whole of continental Europe.

There was consternation at International headquarters when the decision was communicated. 'Bombshell cable from Larsson severing connection with IHQ,' wrote General Carpenter in his diary on 19 May 1941. Was this the end of the one united international Army? But the General cabled back: 'Deeply saddened but your loyalty during all the years makes me feel that your motive is of the highest.'

The way that Karl Larsson helped to keep the Army alive in Europe and beyond during those trying years is a story in itself. When the war ended, Karl Larsson of course handed the Army in Europe back to the General – and was admitted to the Order of the Founder for what he had accomplished.

Karl Larsson's life-motto was 'Work for the night is coming', based on the words of Jesus: 'I must work the works of him that sent me, while it is day. The night comes when no one can work' (John 9:4, *NIV*). Nobody could miss the motto. He preached frequently on those words of Jesus, and wrote the motto in every guest book, autograph book and corps history book which he was asked to sign.

When Freda and I were appointed territorial leaders for Sweden 50 years later, many took pride in showing us these entries. Karl Larsson had made sure that his grandson too would get the message! And I did. When accepting election to the office of General at the close of the 2002 High Council I referred to my grandfather's motto and committed myself to serve by it.

My grandfather certainly lived his own motto. He was up early every day to prepare messages – whether needed immediately or not. 'I must keep the mind keen,' he would say. Travel was always by night train – 'to save time'. Plans for new projects and purchases of properties poured from his mind. Ever the evangelist, he missed no opportunity to get the message across. Even at holiday times, while the family played happily on the beach, Karl Larsson would sit pasting newspaper cuttings into his scrapbook, only allowing himself the very occasional swim.

His written output was prodigious. On buses and trains and boats, out on his knees would come his portable typewriter and he would pound away. He wrote a weekly column for *The War Cry* for 20 years, translated innumerable songs, articles and books – and wrote as many himself. When he eventually published his autobiography *Under Orders* it ran to three volumes!

But he is most remembered as a prophet. He was a preacher of great force. His radio messages when territorial commander in Sweden made him nationally known, and it was said that simply to announce that Karl Larsson was to preach would fill any church in the land. And he never lost his passion or sense of urgency. It was whilst preaching one Sunday evening at the age of 84 that he collapsed – and a few hours later he went to be with his Lord.

The Benwell heritage

My maternal grandfather, Commissioner Alfred Benwell, was the territorial commander of the North China Territory when I was born. My grandparents were in Peking, now Beijing, for seven years, from 1932 to 1939.

On his deathbed in 1912 William Booth told his son Bramwell that he could not get China out of his mind, and then clasped his hand and said: 'Promise me that you will begin the work in China.' And Bramwell kept that promise. Despite the outbreak of the First World War, a pioneer party of six officers arrived in Beijing on 1 December 1915. Further reinforcements soon followed and, even though the soil was hard, the work grew until the Army became a major force in China. Such was the expansion that in 1936 the China Territory was divided into the North and South China Territories.

But following the communist take-over after the Second World War all overseas personnel had to withdraw and it gradually became impossible for the Army to continue. However, with the parting of the bamboo curtain in the 1980s The Salvation Army was able to return and is now at work in China again, albeit in a more limited way with community and developmental projects. If the Army is like a bird with two wings – evangelistic and social – the Army bird in China is at the moment flying on only one wing!

My grandfather Alfred Benwell came from Shoeburyness in England. His mother, a widow at 29, had been converted in a meeting in London led by George Scott Railton, and Mrs Benwell helped to establish the corps at Shoeburyness. Alfred, the eldest of three children, became a junior soldier and knew something of the persecution that Salvationists in those days suffered. At the age of 15 he began to work in the Architects' Department at International Headquarters in London.

In 1890 when Alfred was 17 he was asked if he would be willing to go to South America to help the four pioneer officers who had started the work in Argentina six months earlier. Alfred knew something of their story. William Booth had received an appeal from the British community to start the work in Argentina. There were 15,000 souls awaiting the Army's ministry, he was told. So he chose four officers, who gathered all the material they needed for ministry in the English language and set sail.

But when they arrived in Buenos Aires it was to discover that an important detail had been omitted in the original appeal. The 15,000 members of the British community were mainly cattle ranchers and their estancias were scattered over an area 10 times the size of Great Britain – hardly an ideal setting for the Army's ministry. But being resourceful, the pioneer officers decided that if they could not preach the gospel in English they would do so in Spanish! So they bought themselves dictionaries, began to learn the language, and within days hired a hall and commenced meetings – in Spanish.

And now Alfred was being asked to go to Buenos Aires to join them. His only hesitation was what his mother's reaction would be. But such was her own commitment that she encouraged him to say yes.

Then nothing happened. He heard no more. But some months later, when in the north of England with the Junior Staff Band, he received a telegram on the Sunday, which said: 'Be ready sail South America Tuesday.' He caught the first train home, spent Monday packing, said goodbye to his mother, and sailed Tuesday. He did not come back to England for 15 years.

Life was tough for the pioneers in Argentina. At times young Alfred used to pick edible scraps from a bin sent round from a hotel. There were rats and floods and earthquakes. When Alfred contracted smallpox, the local hospital had such a bad name that it was deemed better for him to spend six weeks in total isolation in the cook's room on the roof of headquarters.

There was opposition to the Army's ministry. In the corps where Alfred was serving, rubbish and stones were flung through the windows whenever meetings were held. When the iron shutters were closed they were smashed with boulders dug up from the pathway. On one occasion, Alfred asked the ringleader of the gang to leave as the police had been sent for. For reply, the man pulled out his revolver and thrust the muzzle against Alfred's chest, saying: 'Shut your mouth or I'll put a bullet through you.' Suddenly clattering hoofs were heard outside and, despite the jeering of the crowd, mounted police cleared the streets, emptied the hall and promised that in future when meetings were held a policeman would be stationed at the door.

On another occasion Alfred was imprisoned with drunks and cattle thieves for holding an open-air meeting. There were also revolutions. During one such, the rebels took up position just outside the quarters. Had they not surrendered at the last minute everyone in the quarters would have been killed.

Yet Alfred delighted in riding on horseback over the pampas, and singing with his guitar for the gauchos round camp fires, and telling them about Jesus.

After a time Alfred was given officer rank. And then one day a beautiful young lady, Lieutenant Mathilda Byden, arrived from Sweden to reinforce the pioneer team. Mathilda had not set out with the intention of arriving in South America. An appeal had been made for officers to help with the emerging Scandinavian work in the USA. Mathilda was among those who offered, and the group set sail for the USA. They travelled via London, and William Booth received them in his office at International

Headquarters. In the course of wishing them well he told them about the work that had just started in South America, and asked whether any of them would be prepared to head in that direction instead.

'North America or South America, it is all the same to me,' said Mathilda! So that is why she arrived in Buenos Aires instead of New York. And that is why she met the handsome, black-haired and blue-eyed Captain Alfred Benwell, and soon became Mrs Captain Mathilda Benwell. He was appointed editor at territorial headquarters, and she the corps officer of Buenos Aires Central Corps – separate appointments must already have been in vogue. In the next few years three children were born, and the youngest was Flora, my mother.

After 15 years in South America, Alfred Benwell came home to England – with a Swedish wife and a young family. The Benwells held a number of divisional appointments in England before Alfred was appointed as an under secretary at International Headquarters in 1920.

After four years the international journeyings began again. Curiously, though both my maternal grandparents were fluent in Spanish, they were never asked to return to South America. First came an appointment as chief secretary to Denmark, then chief secretary to France. During their time in France Mrs Colonel Mathilda Benwell had a health breakdown and was promoted to Glory. They had been married for over 30 years. My grandfather eventually remarried, and the appointment to China followed.

In 1939 Commissioner and Mrs Benwell were appointed to The Netherlands as territorial leaders. Soon after their arrival the Second World War broke out. The Army's work was proscribed in The Netherlands and my grandparents spent those years under house arrest. As the war was drawing to a close they became part of an exchange of prisoners of war and were taken to the USA. There they settled in retirement, in Pacific Palisades, on the outskirts of Los Angeles, in California.

I met my 'American' grandfather on only one occasion, when he came to stay with us in Sweden for two weeks. Being separated by distance from loved ones is the downside of an international gene.

The parental heritage

My parents, Sture and Flora, have already made their stage appearances in this narrative, and will do so again. Both entered the training college from Penge Corps in London, though in separate sessions. As already noted, they first met when Sture lodged with the Benwells at the time Commissioner and Mrs Karl and Anna Larsson were appointed to South America – and it was no surprise to anyone when they married a few years after being commissioned as officers. They served as corps officers in the South London Division, where my brother David was born. Then in 1937 came the move to Malmö, Sweden.

My story is of course intertwined with theirs until I left home, but to set the scene let me share the full story of my parents' international pilgrimage, a pilgrimage that was to involve them in serving the Lord using seven different languages.

Following service in Sweden, my parents were appointed to Denmark. After that came four appointments as chief secretary and territorial home league secretary, in South America West, South America East, Denmark and France. Following this, Colonel (later Commissioner) and Mrs Sture and Flora Larsson were appointed as territorial leaders to Finland for seven years and then to Norway for three. Their final appointment was to International Headquarters, where my father became the international secretary for Europe. They retired in London in 1974 when my father reached his 68th birthday, which then was the retirement age for commissioners.

Sadly, my father died unexpectedly following heart surgery six months after retirement. My mother lived for a further 26 years – to within a few weeks of her 96th birthday, and was promoted to Glory in the year 2000.

Flora Larsson was a writer, and during her active officership wrote many articles and had a number of books published. But it was in retirement that she really flourished as an author. Starting with *Just a Moment, Lord,* there flowed a series of very popular books of prayer poems. Among her other books was also *My Best Men are Women.* For 18 years she wrote a page entitled 'Along the Way' in *The Deliverer,* a quarterly magazine for women. A collection of her writings, *Just a Year, Lord,* published posthumously, has been in great demand.

With the similarity of names, Freda has frequently been confused with Flora, and on our travels as international leaders people have sometimes thanked her profusely for her writings! At first Freda always used to explain, but it was sometimes difficult to do so without deflating the person who had paid a long tribute. When Freda described the dilemma to my mother, she characteristically suggested that Freda should simply accept the words of thanks! So she did!

No words can adequately convey my sense of gratitude to my parents for the heritage I received from them. Nature or nurture? It was both. From them I inherited a fervour for the adventure of life, for questing and for exploring. They showed me how to love the Lord, and how to serve him – and how to say yes to life. They became my role models in every way.

Both were endowed with creative gifts. They were excellent speakers. They were fine musicians. I admired my father's leadership skills and statesmanship – and I admired my mother's zest and originality of thinking. When my sister Miriam and I were younger we sometimes used to tease our parents by saying that it was a good thing that it was father and not mother who was the territorial commander! I was impressed by their dedication to the task – always hard at it, never complaining about yet another language to be tackled! I will always be grateful to God for the parents that he gave me.

We must now pick up the story from when I was born. My interests in those first days were solely directed to the next feed. But deep in my make-up was the legacy of all the previous generations. And now life lay before me.

Sweden

I have always been proud of my country and still travel on a Swedish passport. But I spent only the first eight years of my life in Sweden. After that there was an interval of 50 years before I returned.

Following Malmö my parents were appointed to Gothenburg and then – still on youth work – to territorial headquarters in Stockholm. By then I was four and my earliest clear memories date from that time.

We lived at headquarters. The four-storeyed corner building, which still houses territorial headquarters today, includes a dozen adjoining flats which are used as officers' quarters. We lived in one, and my grandparents, Karl and Anna Larsson, in another. The Temple Corps was next door. There were two yards – an upper and a lower one. All of this became my world – a world shared with the many other officers' children who lived at headquarters.

It was an idyllic setting for a four-year-old. And the next year – 1943 – should have been a year of unalloyed family joy, for my mother was expecting an addition to the family. But tragedy struck. My elder brother David, aged seven, became ill. As winter turned to spring it was clear that it was very serious. The doctors diagnosed a rare form of leukaemia – a disease even less understood then than it is today. David was taken into hospital just as my mother was reaching the end of her pregnancy. On 15 May 1943 she gave birth to my sister Miriam. But three days later my father had to break the news to her that there was no hope for David.

David was brought home to die. He thought he had come home because he was getting better. He sometimes held Miriam in his arms, but he died after four weeks. That very same night my grandmother Anna, who had not been well for some time, also died. My father lost his mother and his son. My grandfather, the Viking warrior, lost his wife and his grandson.

My grandfather was due to conduct the territorial congress within days and the programme was quickly changed to include a double funeral on the Saturday morning. Three thousand officers and Salvationists gathered in the Immanuel Church for the service. Most of them afterward formed part of the immensely long procession to the cemetery. It poured with rain.

Many years later my mother told me that after breastfeeding Miriam following the service she took a tram to catch up with the funeral cortege. As the tram was held up by the march she heard the passengers comment on the sad scene of the seemingly endless procession headed by two horse-drawn hearses – one with a full-size flag-draped coffin, the other with a small white casket escorted by six cub-scouts. They wondered aloud what it could all mean. Only with the most intense effort of will did she stop herself from crying out: 'That is my son, that is my son in the white coffin.'

My parents had wanted me to remember David as I had always known him, not as a boy who was physically wasting away, so they arranged for me to stay with relatives out in the country during the final weeks. But I came back for the funeral.

David and I had always spoken Swedish together – and also to our parents. They, however, always spoke to us in English. This pattern perpetuated itself when Miriam began to speak. My parents spoke English and we responded in Swedish. When we later moved to Denmark, Miriam and I quickly switched to Danish, and for some time our parents had trouble understanding us.

It was not until we moved to South America – when I was 11 – that we gradually began speaking the same language at home. A knowledge of English then became essential for schooling. Until that point I could understand English perfectly, but I could not speak it, and even less read or write it. My father taught me to read English on the boat out to South America! But I anticipate.

During those early years in Stockholm I attended kindergarten, but as was customary in Sweden, I did not go to school until I was seven. I went to Sunday school at the Temple Corps and became a cub scout. At that time my father was the territorial 'scout chief' so it was all part of a pattern.

As I look back I see that those early years in Stockholm gave me a love for nature – especially wild nature – a love that has sometimes seemed like a burning yearning within. Stockholm is surrounded by breathtakingly beautiful scenery, pine forests and lakes and a rugged coastline. During the long winters we would go out into these forests with our sledges and skis. And during the short but intense summers, with days that seemed endless and nights that were just like the blinking of an eye, we would drink in the sun and whenever possible get out into God's nature.

It was also in Stockholm that I had my first intimations of the life beyond – the life of the Spirit – and they were beautiful, never to be forgotten moments. One spring day my mother took Miriam and me out to some wild nature near where we lived, and as we walked along an indescribable feeling of joy and wellbeing and love suddenly bathed my innermost self.

I now know that it was a moment of intense spiritual experience – though at the time I could not explain it in those terms. I suppose it only lasted for a few seconds, but the impact of the experience was such that I can still recall every detail of the day – the heat of the sun, the freshness of the wind, the beauty of the scene, and the emotion of the moment itself. Even though I was not yet eight I remember hoping and longing that such moments would return to me.

The second glimpse came at the close of one of our cub-scout meetings, held that week in the home of our leader. This time it was music that was the door to God's presence. The leader asked us to stand in a circle and to sing together a classic Swedish evening benediction, '*Bred dina vida vingar*'. It is hauntingly beautiful. It speaks of God surrounding us as with wings of an angel. As we sang the heavens opened for me. The beauty of the music, the beauty of the words, lifted me to a glow of emotional and spiritual experience that I still cannot describe without getting a lump in my throat.

Thank God for youth leaders who make it possible for such doors to open in the hearts of children and young people! Most will never know how they have been used by the Lord. But more than 50 years later when by seeming chance in a quite different part of Sweden I again met my adored Akela, as we termed our cub-scout leader, I was able to tell her about that moment and thank her.

Denmark

In 1946, when I was eight, my parents were appointed in charge of the training college in Copenhagen, Denmark. The international journeyings had begun for me. We lived in an apartment at the training college, and the college in Grundtvigsvej with its large garden became my home. No training sessions had been held during the war years, and the first session was a large one. The cadets became my extended family and my friends.

I went to the school nearest to where we lived. I was put in Mr Jan's class – and soon learned how favoured I had been. Mr Jan had been given permission by the school authorities to experiment with what were then newer forms of teaching. In addition to learning by traditional methods we engaged in all kinds of creative projects, learning by playing and by doing and by exploring. It was great fun. Everything seemed possible. I liked school. I was too young to know how all of this compared with what other classes were doing, but my parents often commented on how fortunate I was, and I had no difficulty in believing them! I recall Mr Jan with great affection. He set alight the creative spark in me.

During the early weeks at school I was sometimes taken to classes which were having lessons in Swedish and asked to read passages for them so that they could hear the 'real thing'. But that did not last long for, as previously mentioned, I soon switched from Swedish to Danish. Children adapt quickly if only for self-protection. I did notice, however, that whereas in my school in Sweden it was the Swedish warriors of old who were the heroes in their frequent battles with the Danes, in my new school it was somehow always the Danes who got the better of the Swedes. Strange.

My parents must have detected some musical potential within me for I was enrolled with Bandmaster Henry Kragh Jensen for piano lessons. The bandmaster was a professional piano teacher. He taught many generations of Salvationists how to play and in fact was admitted to the Order of the Founder for his services to Army music. He instilled in me a lifelong affection for the piano.

Half an hour of daily practice became the order of the day. Despite my appreciation for the piano I was only moderately keen on the hard work of practice. But my parents were insistent – for which I will always be grateful. I often heard the story of how my uncle Wilfred had kicked up such a fuss about practising that his parents had given up, and how he had lived to regret it!

It was in Denmark that I became a reader. A voracious reader. I read widely. I knew the youth section of the local library like the back of my hand. I remember reading my way through all Jules Verne's books. My collection of books at home kept growing, and it was with great sadness that I parted with them when the next move came.

I attended Sunday school at the Temple Corps, and it was there that I took my first outward step in the development of my spiritual life. On one Decision Sunday, when the young people were invited to go forward and kneel at the mercy seat, nearly everyone present did so. I was seated on the front row, and for some reason or other was determined not to go. Various people spoke with me but I only shook my head. Then the young people's sergeant-major, a motherly figure who meant much to me, came and sat with me. As she spoke to me I was soon in tears, and was glad to kneel at the mercy seat. I remember the feeling of relief as she prayed with me.

That was a decisive step in my spiritual questing. But it was not an experience that changed night into day or turned winter into summer. It was another step in a journey – for I already loved Jesus and wanted to be like him. In later years when asked to date my 'conversion' I would usually speak of that moment in the Decision Sunday. But I never did so without wondering whether I was trying to squeeze my experience into some kind of predetermined pattern into which it did not quite fit. And yet, on the other hand, hearing others speak so convincingly of their moment of conversion sometimes made me wonder whether I really had been born again.

It remained a dilemma for me even into my early days of officership. Then William Booth resolved it for me. I came across his book *Training of Children*. In it he asks the question: 'May not children grow up into salvation without knowing the exact moment of conversion?' The answer he gives came to me as a revelation:

Yes, it may be so; and in the future we trust this will be the usual way in which children will be brought into the Kingdom. When the parents are godly, and the children are surrounded by holy influences and examples from their birth, they will doubtless come to know and love and trust their Saviour in the ordinary course of things. The Holy Spirit will take possession of them from the first. Mothers and fathers will, as it were, put them into the Saviour's arms in their swaddling clothes, and he will take them, and bless them, and sanctify them from the very womb, and make them his own, without their knowing the hour or the place when they pass from the kingdom of darkness into the Kingdom of Light.

That mirrored my experience precisely and resolved my problem. And having none other than William Booth as my authority helped me to withstand what I sometimes felt was pressure to make my experience conform to a prescribed pattern.

I was soon enrolled as a junior soldier. It was then decided to form a young people's band – the first after the war years. All boys who were interested – yes, in those days to include girls was simply unthinkable – were invited to come along. Old instruments had been located and cleaned. There were about 15 of us, and we were each given an instrument. Mine was a curious contraption. It was an Eb alto horn, but its bell faced forward and it was played like a large flugel horn laid on its side. Instead of valves it had mechanical keys. Instead of being silver like everyone else's, it was bronze. I tried to love it, but it was a hard thing to love. But I did learn to play it!

Someone then had a bright idea. Before the war there had been a staff band. They had worn bright red high-collar tunics adorned with large white stripes. Real circus stuff. The tunics must be somewhere. Why not make them smaller and dress the boys in them? I believe they were found under the platform. The ladies got to work on them, and on the opening night there we were – the full band in our circus tunics. Everyone said how lovely we looked! And we played a march by Erik Leidzen. We had rehearsed it so often and so well that I can still remember how it goes!

But talk about man's inhumanity to man! As junior band members we were expected to come to Sunday school on Sundays dressed in our bright red high-necked tunics with the white stripes. The thought of anyone from my school seeing me dressed like that appalled me. Cycling from home to the corps and back I used to break all speed records.

But I recall one occasion when my bright red tunic taught me a useful lesson about attitude. It was a congress and I was to accompany an officer on the training staff to a meeting in a public hall. It involved a tram journey. And I had to be in uniform. I kept looking at the sky hoping that it would rain so that I would have to wear my coat. But the clouds were not very obliging. It was a warm summer day with only scattered clouds. But I decided they definitely merited a coat. One never knew! When I came down thus over-dressed the officer expressed surprise, and then with uncanny insight said: 'John, I think you are ashamed of being seen in your uniform.'

He then went on to give me a short pep talk about attitude. 'Don't be ashamed,' he said. 'Look everyone in the face. Be proud of the uniform. Be proud to be a Salvationist.' I decided I would give it a try. I left my coat at home. And as I got onto the tram I pulled my shoulders back and outstared anyone who as much as dared to look in my direction. I think I could have taken on my whole school had they turned up. I can still remember the feeling of achievement it brought me. Being more than conquerors, as Paul put it. I learnt something valuable that afternoon.

After we had been in Denmark for three years I came home from school one day to be greeted by my mother with the news that they had received farewell orders and that we would be moving to another country. I had a large wall map of the world in my room and she suggested I should try and guess where we were going. Sweden? No. I tried other European countries. No. I then went further afield – and as my finger pointed to America she told me it was getting warmer, and South America was warmer still. Eventually I found it. We were going to Chile! To an 11-year-old boy in Denmark, just about as far as one could go.

A chief secretary and territorial home league secretary were needed for the South America West Territory. International Headquarters, knowing of the parental connection with South America on both the Larsson and Benwell sides, reached out to my parents with the classic question traditionally used by International Headquarters on such occasions. It was a question Freda and I were to hear a number of times ourselves as officers, and which later, as Chief of the Staff and then General, it fell to me to ask others: 'Is there any reason why you should not accept these appointments?'

It is a good question. Under the Army's appointment system, the initiative rightly remains with the asker. These are the appointments we have in mind for you. The question does not ask whether one fancies the appointments or not. But it does include an opt-out clause. And if there is some reason why accepting the appointment would be difficult, the position is usually understood and accepted.

For my parents it was a big step, and it is only in later years that I have fully appreciated quite how big it must have been for them. The world has grown smaller since that time. But in those days the terms of service were for seven years, travel was by sea, and communication was by letter. Private phone calls were only for the very rich. My parents' only enquiry was about schooling for Miriam and me. They were assured that schooling in English would be available, and without further ado said yes, and said it gladly.

17

For Miriam and me it was to open a new world that, in retrospect, we would not have missed for anything. Obviously South America was in the blood of our generation as well. In the weeks of preparation our parents encouraged us to look at the prospect as a great adventure – yet another attitude to life that has never left me.

A farewell meeting was held at the Temple. I think I was in tears most of the time – not because I did not want to go to South America, but because I liked Denmark so much and had made so many friends! And when the meeting ended with the song 'God be with you till we meet again' – which I heard for the first time – I thought it the most beautiful song I had ever heard. I cried all the way through!

Chapter Two

SOUTH AMERICAN YOUTH

THERE were no places left on boats sailing through the Panama Canal, so Buenos Aires, Argentina, became our sailing destination with the last stage of the journey to Chile being by train. Our first sight of South America was the entry into Rio de Janeiro. How much the air travellers of today miss! I will never forget that first sight of Rio as early in the morning the ship glided into the spectacular harbour surrounded by towering mountains. High on one of the heights that dominated the city stood the statue of Christ the Redeemer, his arms outstretched in blessing. The scene was magnificent. This was the continent of my forbears. It was love at first sight.

When we arrived in Buenos Aires my mother's past caught up with her. My mother was English by descent and Swedish by marriage, and was travelling on a Swedish passport. As we were about to disembark an alert migration official spotted the fateful words: 'Place of birth: Buenos Aires.' She was Argentinian by birth, they reminded her. Why then was she not travelling as an Argentinian? Why had she not voted in all elections since she was 21? Surely she knew that they were mandatory for all citizens. Serious matter this. The fact that she was in transit was not an acceptable excuse. But a compromise was arrived at. My mother was allowed off the ship on condition that she reported to the police at midday every day during the week we were to spend in Buenos Aires.

After crossing the grassland pampas by rail to Mendoza we changed onto the small mountain train that was to take us over the mountains into Chile. As the train wound its way up the valleys we slowly emerged into a harsh landscape of snow and ice. When the train stopped at the highest point we defied the blizzard and ran to see another famous statue of Jesus, Christ of the Andes, which stands on the border between Chile and Argentina. Our parents had told us the story of the statue.

In 1902 Chile and Argentina were arming for war. At stake was the exact boundary line between the two nations along the Andean mountain range. But many citizens on both sides urged the governments to submit the matter to arbitration. As a result King Edward VII of Great Britain was asked to determine where the boundary line should lie. After much deliberation he carefully drew the exact border line on the map. In 1903 both governments accepted his decision. War was averted.

Then the bishop of San Juan had the inspired idea that the weapons of both countries should be melted down and a statue of Christ erected at the highest border crossing. The statue would symbolise peace between the two nations and would remind them for all time of the words of Christ: 'And I, if I be lifted up from the earth, will draw all men unto me' (John 12:32, *Authorised Version*). Still today, in the icy blasts of 13,000 feet, with Mount Aconcagua as its backdrop rising yet another 13,000 feet towards the skies, stands Christ of the Andes, a permanent pointer to permanent peace.

Chile

In Santiago we quickly settled into our new lifestyle. The first time my mother went shopping with Miriam and me in tow, a large cowboy film-set type of car came whizzing down the road. Men standing on its side-boards were shouting and firing revolvers into the air. My mother told us that we must now get used to that kind of thing and calmly shepherded us on our way. I have sometimes wondered whether the Santiago Tourist Board laid on the event to impress the new arrivals, for in all our years in Chile we never again experienced anything remotely like it.

I lived in Chile from 11 to 14 years of age and look back on those years as a kind of golden age. From my room I could look out on the snow-capped chain of the Andes. In the evenings they would turn into magnificent hues of pink and purple. I spent many hours studying every feature of those mountains – and yearned to be closer to them.

Travel in those days was more difficult, but once on an outing we were taken to a remote location up an Andes valley far above the vegetation line. At one point during the day I wandered off alone from the group. The sense of awe I experienced as I stood on my own in the stillness of the barren yet beautiful desolation of that Andean valley planted within me a hunger and thirst for mountains that has never left me. Throughout my life I have not been able to see a hill or a mountain without feeling a deep yearning within to reach its peak. As I look back, I only wish there had been more opportunities to pursue this passion in my younger years.

I had two very distinct social circles. I had my Army friends and my school friends. My Army friends were the children of other officers and we were a closely knit group. We hung out together, cycled and swam and listened to music together. They were precious times. I always credit one of my friends, David Gruer (later Colonel), with teaching me how to speak Spanish. In the Army social circle Spanish was the *lingua franca*. We later moved into a campus setting at territorial headquarters which for me was paradise – complete with a swimming pool which had once been part of a youth centre but which officer-parents brought back into use by clubbing together every time it had to be refilled.

My school world was a different world. I was privileged to become a pupil of The Grange School, which modelled itself on an English public school. The Grange lay on the rich side of Santiago close to the Andean range, and all the boys who attended the school came from well-to-do families. We lived on the poorer side of Santiago – quite rightly so for that is where the Army was at work. My friends lived in fabulous homes and would be dropped off at school by their parents in the latest model limousines. I travelled across Santiago on the trolley bus. I made many close friends at school, and used to go to their homes, but I never let on where I myself lived. When they pressed me on the point I always managed to be vague. With hindsight there was no need for me to be ashamed of where I lived. I should have remembered to stick my chest out and stare all of them down! But it is easy to be clever after the event.

In the Army way of life, children of officers are often thrown into the deep end of the pool. Most by far, I am glad to say, learn to swim and are the stronger for it. I come in that category and look back on the years in Chile with tremendous affection and nostalgia.

However, coping with the new circumstances and two new languages – spoken and written English and Spanish – did take its toll on self-confidence and must have gnawed away at self-esteem.

For example, a number of our classes at school were in Spanish. Our biology teacher used to spend most of the class dictating material for our notebooks. I did my best to turn what to me were unintelligible sounds into meaningful written words. He seemed to like the phrase *subraya eso*, which of course I faithfully wrote out in full each time. But after some weeks of this I asked the boy next to me what the phrase meant. He looked at my notebook, and then burst out laughing. '*Subraya eso*,' he said, 'means, "underline that".' But there were more painful times as well when in written and oral exams I would not understand a word of the question or know anything about the subject. Yet one survives and, I believe, comes out strengthened in the end.

I became a junior soldier of the Santiago Central Corps, and as there was no young people's band I soon became a member of the senior band. Not to make the band look untidy I wore a senior uniform – high-necked but thankfully navy blue this time. I was not the most enthusiastic of bandsmen – there were just too many other interests in life for that. But Bandmaster Juan Magnenat was very patient with me, and even moved me from horn to cornet as he thought this might encourage me.

I have always thought of Juan as a father figure at a formative time. He disappeared off my radar screen when we left Chile. I heard he had settled in the USA. When I was conducting meetings as General in the USA Western Territory some 50 years later, the band from Seattle Corps was on duty on one occasion and there, right before my eyes, was Retired Bandmaster Juan Magnenat playing in the band. I took the opportunity to thank him publicly during the meeting and went over to where he was seated in the band and gave him a good Chilean hug. When we compared ages after the meeting I discovered to my amazement that he had only been in his early 20s when I was in his band in Santiago!

One of my greatest fears as a youth in Chile was that I might be asked to speak in public – to give my testimony. The thought literally terrified me. I knew no one would call on me in the big Sunday afternoon open-air meetings in the Quinta Normal Park. But the band held an open-air meeting every Sunday morning before the holiness meeting, and in these meetings there was always a testimony time during which the leader would call on two or three bandsmen to speak. Latin-Americans are the most eloquent people in the world, and none of them ever seemed to be the slightest bit put out at being asked.

But for me the prospect of being asked to witness was a weekly torture. So in the end I adopted a pattern whereby I would leave home at the appointed hour and then walk the streets until I was sure the testimony period was over before I arrived at the open-air meeting. I kept this pattern up for many months and never let on. My parents never knew, and Bandmaster Juan was too protective of me to even reproach me for my lack of punctuality!

When Norman Vincent Peale's *The Power of Positive Thinking* was published in 1952 my parents encouraged me to read it. This has since become a best-seller and one of the most influential books ever of its genre, having sold around 20 million copies in 42 languages. But originally the manuscript was rejected by so many publishers that in dejection Norman Vincent Peale dumped it into the waste-paper basket and forbade his wife to remove it. But she was convinced of its potential. So the next day, taking him literally, she presented the manuscript – still inside the waste-paper basket – to yet another publisher, who decided to take it.

For me the book became hugely influential in helping me to gain confidence – and to develop a particular attitude to life. There is an old Chinese saying that when the student is ready the teacher appears. And I was ready for this book.

Norman Vincent Peale's book not only began a process within me to gain more confidence – a process which was to take a number of years and have many ups and downs – but also reinforced within me the value of optimism and a positive attitude to life. I have often commented that, outside Scripture, the most influential couplet in my life has been: 'Two men looked through prison bars, one saw mud, the other stars.'

It seems to me that attitude is everything. It is not that the mud is not there – it is and to ignore it would be wrong. But the stars are also there. And to ignore their existence would be even worse. It is where we decide to place our attention that counts. And it has little to do with our genes. We are not born optimists or pessimists. Though genetic endowment does play a part, we become what we are mainly by the inner attitudes we consciously adopt. An optimistic, questing, adventuresome attitude has always seemed to me to be an intrinsic part of what the life of faith is ideally meant to be. It is by our attitude that we say yes – or no – to life.

Norman Vincent Peale's book was my first introduction to the wide range of inspirational reading in which the realms of the spiritual and the psychological merge – a range of reading I was to explore thoroughly in later years.

Someone also gave me a biography of Winston Churchill which I devoured from cover to cover. As a consequence a life-long interest in biography and history was born in me. Biography and history are still the sections I first head for when visiting a new library.

In those formative years in Chile I met officers who were genuine heroes. They didn't know they were heroes and I myself have only understood it more fully in retrospect. But they influenced me more than I realised at the time. I think of Major Eva Goulding. She was a British officer who ran a social centre not far from where we lived. It was supposed to be a women's hostel but with her warm, caring heart, Major Goulding could not say 'no' to mothers bringing their children, and before long it became home to dozens of children as well. There she lived, right among them, her cheerful spirit lending a radiance to the scene and lifting the hearts of all members of her extended family. In true English fashion the kettle was always on the boil and the door was always open to visitors. In Eva Goulding I saw the ideal of officership.

Piano lessons continued, but it proved difficult to find the right teacher at a price my parents could afford, and my recollection is that the teachers kept changing. But despite that, it was in Chile that I took off musically. I found I could improvise and would spend hour after hour at the piano playing what came into my head and experimenting with sounds and rhythms. The battle cry at home changed from: 'John, do your piano practice' to 'John, play what the piano teacher has given you to play!'

My most memorable spiritual experience of those years in Chile did not take place at the Army but at school. I remember the occasion vividly to this day and can remember exactly where I was sitting at my desk in class. The teacher was reading to us from Pearl Buck's *The Good Earth*. As the writer described the country scene in China, with the farmers going off to till the soil, I could see in my mind the beauty of the countryside and feel the warmth of the sun.

Then suddenly it was as if I had been lifted into God's presence. It was the Stockholm experience all over again. I felt alive, I felt I belonged, I felt that everything was well and would always be well, I felt an intense sense of joy and love and peace. And everything was utterly, utterly real. Nobody around me knew what was happening. As a 13-year-old I had neither the knowledge nor the vocabulary to be able to explain even to myself what had happened. But I knew something had. For some seconds I had experienced the abundant life of the Spirit. Then, as the sound of the teacher's voice continued, the glory faded and the ordinariness of the classroom took over again. But the reality of that moment has never left me.

After three years in Chile, my parents again received farewell orders, this time to Argentina. I didn't want to leave! I had fallen in love with Chile. And the emotional link remains to this day. Santiago has a Mediterranean-type climate with strong and vivid colours in nature. For three years my life had been lived as intensely as the colours around me. There were some darker hues. There had been turbulence. My early teenage years were stormy. I was an expert door slammer at home. Especially when it came to having to go to the corps. But it is the intensity of the bright colours that lingers in the mind. The warmth and the affection that surrounded me and the sheer delight of being alive in a wonderful world – these are the colours that remain.

With Argentina being our destination, my mother knew she had to get her Argentine citizenship sorted out. She went to the consulate and explained the background – and after much to-ing and fro-ing finally got her Argentine passport. This time the crossing of the Andes was to be by air and not by train – but we were warned that oxygen masks would have to be worn by all passengers when the plane reached the higher heights over the mountains.

On the departure day we all went to the airport. Everyone was there to say goodbye. We sailed through immigration. We were headed for the plane on the tarmac when suddenly an official came running. 'That lady there! There's a problem. She came into the country as a Swedish citizen and is now leaving as an Argentine citizen!' Explanations proved fruitless. Surely she should have known that the new passport had to be countersigned by this ministry and double-stamped by the other. Somebody should have told her. The situation had to regularised.

In the end, my father, Miriam and I had to fly on to Buenos Aires, leaving my mother behind. After spending the day scurrying from one ministry to the next to get the right stamps in her passport, she joined us the next day.

Argentina

I was 14, going on 15, when we moved to Argentina. I was a uniformed Salvationist, though technically still a junior soldier, but a reluctant one. With the move to Buenos Aires I saw the possibility of escaping from the Army. In my mind I hatched a plot. I would not join a corps straight away. I would not put on my uniform. I would take my time. I would think about things.

A day or two after we arrived in Argentina, my father's secretary, Captain Edmundo Allemand, asked me if I had decided which corps to join. There were several in Buenos Aires. He recommended Palermo Corps – where he happened to be the bandmaster. Now was the time to put my plot into action. So I explained that I did not want to rush things. I wanted to look round.

'John, I fully understand,' he said. 'You are very wise. But why don't you try Palermo Corps for one Sunday to see whether you like it or not? You don't have to come back if you don't like it.' It was time to be firm, but he went on: 'I could come round for you on Sunday morning.'

Well, I thought, perhaps a 'once only' visit to Palermo would not destroy my plan. So I agreed. 'Sunday morning at nine, then,' he said – and then added as if he could read my mind. 'And you will be in uniform, won't you?' He was gone before there was any time to explain.

Sunday morning dawned, and bitterly regretting that I had not said no, there I stood in uniform when the doorbell rang. We travelled by bus. Captain Allemand was full of fascinating information. He was good fun to be with – that is, until he asked:

26

'What instrument do you play?' I had to confess that I played the cornet. 'Oh,' he exclaimed, 'that is just what we need in our band. We are about a dozen players. Would you play with us – even if just for this one meeting?' Well, what could one say to someone who was being so kind and who was such good company! So I reluctantly agreed. Just for the one meeting and no more.

When we arrived at the hall Captain Allemand introduced me to the young people and especially to the members of the band. He provided me with a cornet and with music and I sat in the band. Then just as the meeting was about to begin he leant over and said: 'I'll introduce you later in the meeting, and it would be nice if you could respond with a few words of testimony.' Words of testimony! Me, who had never spoken in public in all my life! All the old fears came clamouring into my mind. But it was too late. The meeting had started. And when I was introduced, I stood to my feet and spoke my first words ever in public. When it was over, it felt good.

After the meeting the young people gathered round. They liked my Chilean accent! We found we had a lot in common. They were a great crowd. Captain Allemand watched. 'The band meets at Plaza Italia every Sunday afternoon for an open-air meeting at 4 pm,' he said. 'After that we have a meal together here at the hall before the evening meeting.' And without batting an eyelid he added: 'Do you want to take your instrument home with you, or shall I bring it to the open-air meeting for you?'

He read me like a book. I had every intention of going. My inner reluctance had melted in the warmth I had experienced. And I have been going ever since. I have never looked back!

Some years later I came across the *New English Bible* translation of the passage where Paul, following his conversion, tries to join the church at Jerusalem: 'Barnabas ... took him by the hand and introduced him to the apostles' (Acts 9:27). Barnabas took Paul by the hand and brought him right into the fellowship of the church. That is what Captain Edmundo Allemand did for me that Sunday morning, and I will always be grateful to him.

Commissioner Edmundo Allemand retired in the United Kingdom, and many years later I was asked to conduct his funeral. As my personal tribute I told the story of how he had taken me by the hand when I most needed it and had brought me right into the fellowship of Palermo Corps.

I soon settled into the life of the corps, and became active not only in the band but also, after a time, as a Sunday school teacher. Technically I was still a junior soldier. But that was put right one Sunday morning when my father enrolled me as a senior soldier.

I attended St Alban's College, another Anglo-Spanish school. It lay in one of the outer suburbs of Buenos Aires which involved bus and train journeys each way. By a happy circumstance, the college was linked with Cambridge University in England, and for two years we prepared to take School Certificate exams set by that university. At the time, the link with Cambridge meant little to me. England to me was still a closed book. I was Swedish. But those School Certificates were later the keys that would unlock for me the doors to university education in England.

Mr Cohen was our Religious Knowledge teacher. He drilled us – yes, that is the right word – in the early chapters of the Acts of the Apostles for those two years. We explored every possible angle. Those chapters fascinated him, and he succeeded in passing on that fascination to at least one of his pupils.

My parents wanted us to have a good piano teacher this time, and their enquiries led them to a Valentin Zubrisky, a concert pianist. He had a busy schedule and was reluctant to take on more pupils. This was compounded when he heard me play. 'No, no, no,' he said, 'your approach is all wrong. You are playing with your fingers only. You are just tickling the keys. You have to bring the full weight of the whole arm, indeed the weight of the whole body, to bear. Playing a grand piano demands great physical strength. I'm afraid you will have to start right from the beginning again!'

And so for many weeks, which to me felt like an eternity, it was back to the C scale and its equivalents. I had to *feel* the weight of my whole body going through each finger as I played. It was a long time before he was satisfied. Unlearning in order to learn anew was hard work. But it completely transformed my style, and from then on there was no looking back. Once I had got the hang of it, the C scale was replaced by an ever more demanding repertoire.

Musically I launched out at the corps as well. When I was 16 years of age I was asked to form and lead a male voice group in the band. This was new territory to me. But I was soon writing my own arrangements for the group. Then when I was 17 the corps officer asked me to become the bandmaster, Captain Allemand having moved on by then.

As I look back, the story of my life is being asked to undertake tasks that have stretched me. I have a long list of people I could thank for fulfilling that role in my life at just the right point.

I have also discovered that increased demand produces increased supply. And so it was in Palermo Corps. I found that my peers responded to my leadership and that I could meet the musical demands made on me. I had to work fast to master the intricacy of reading band scores and learning how to conduct. And my work in the Sunday school had also increased my confidence for public work.

Musical responsibility opened up a new world for me. The only band music we had was a collection of very ancient 'second series' journals published in England. Most of the tunes used in selections were not known to the congregation. I therefore began experimenting with writing band music to which the congregation could relate. A Christmas selection using Christmas songs sung in Argentina brought the house down at a united occasion. It well and truly launched me as an arranger and composer of brass music. Band music – far more than vocal – was my love. Nothing seemed impossible. When we needed the music for the march 'Star Lake' I transcribed it from the old 78 rpm record – listening to the record again and again until I had every part written out.

After I had taken the Cambridge School Certificate examinations, a year or so remained before my parents' seven-year term was due to end. How was I to spend that year? My plans for the future were vague indeed. I presumed I would be heading wherever in the world my parents would be heading. I was getting used to this idea of a new country every three years!

But in the meantime I went to work – and it turned out to be a year of very varied work experience. I first worked in a travel agency. When that folded, I was the only member of staff taken on by the real estate firm that was to open in the same premises. That firm, too, proved to be short-lived and I then moved to a Swedish company that imported dairy farming equipment. The fact that I spoke English and Spanish and could read the Swedish instructions that came with the equipment was a great help.

Spiritually speaking, one thing was clear to me. I wanted to devote my life to God and his service. I can't remember any real mental conflict about that. For me it was self-evident that it should be so. The only question was how. I had heard mention of 'the call to officership'. I had also heard that it would be fatal to become an officer without such a call. So I kept an open mind. I felt sure that if God wanted me to be an officer I would hear his voice calling me just as he had spoken to Isaiah in the Temple. In the meantime I would simply await developments.

The development came unexpectedly. As chief secretary, my father had to read the proofs of *El Cruzado* – the equivalent of *The War Cry* – every week. I found some proof pages at home one day and sprawled out on the bed to look at them. An article by General Bramwell Booth caught my eye. In the article the General described a house on fire, with smoke and flames ascending into the skies. In the windows were people shouting for help. They were desperately trying to attract the attention of a group of bystanders who stood some distance away seemingly completely unconcerned about the cries for help.

'Help, please help, we're dying!' they shouted. But the group just chatted away. The article described how someone went up to them to remonstrate with them. 'How can you just stand here and do nothing when people are dying within yards of you?' he demanded. 'We too are deeply concerned,' they replied. 'We want to help but, you see, we have not received a call to help people who are dying in burning houses, and therefore, as much as we would like to, there is nothing that we can do!'

Bramwell Booth then went on to press home his point about Christians who hold back from God's service because they are awaiting some great emotional call experience even when the cries for help can be plainly heard. For me it was once again a case of the teacher appearing when the student was ready. When I was ready Bramwell Booth appeared.

I began to see that a call experience like Isaiah's in the Temple might not be God's way for me. Perhaps for me it might simply be a matter of responding to the deep convictions God had planted in my heart about being wholly available to him. But just how that was to be worked out in practice was still not clear to me. On that point my mind remained expectantly open.

In transit

After seven years in South America my parents were appointed back to Denmark, my father as the chief secretary and my mother as the territorial home league secretary. But first my parents had three months of homeland furlough, and our first destination was to be London.

I think the Lord has given me the gift of putting down roots wherever I am. I didn't want to leave Denmark, didn't want to leave Chile, and I now found that I did not want to leave Argentina. I was happy at the corps, happy in my work, happy with my friends. Life was full and satisfying. I even at times toyed with the idea of not returning to Europe with my parents. But I also wanted to be open to all that life might bring and to keep on saying yes to all that lay ahead. So when the ship set sail for Southampton I too was on board. I celebrated my 18th birthday at sea somewhere between Uruguay and Brazil.

Having spent five years in English schools, learning English history and geography and literature and English everything, arriving in the old country seemed just like coming home. So it felt when we booked in at The Salvation Army's missionary hostel in South London. We explored London and met uncles and aunts and cousins who had only been names to me before. The nearest corps was Upper Norwood, and that is where we headed on the very few Sundays when we were not away. My parents had planned that we would spend half the furlough in England and the other half in Sweden before moving on to Denmark.

I was uncertain about my own future. Did I really want to settle back in Denmark? Did I want to settle in England – and if so, where and doing what? And what about the house on fire with people shouting for help? And my own determination that my life would be devoted to God's service? Officership was a door standing wide open before me. Was there any point in exploring other avenues? Here in England was the International Training College. Sessions opened in August – and it was already late April. A decision could not be delayed for long.

One morning when I was out driving the car with my father – I was a learner driver – I made up my mind, and as part of the conversation I almost casually told my father that I had decided to apply to become an officer. It was all so low-key that I think it caught him completely by surprise. But I could sense that he was deeply moved.

There are times in life when one takes steps of faith – steps into the unknown – and then later finds the rightness of the steps confirmed in their outworking. That is how it has been for me. I said yes to God, yes to the sense of vocation within, yes to what seemed the right door before me – and God has confirmed again and again that the step that I took in faith that morning was the step he intended for my life.

Things then moved quickly. Entering training involves processes, processes which become complicated when one is 'in transit' as I was. Unbeknown to me, my parents had anticipated the possibility that I might decide to enter training and had arranged for the necessary backings from the corps officer and other local officers of the Palermo Corps – so that part was covered. My soldiership was transferred in record time to Upper Norwood Corps. I completed the necessary forms. I was interviewed by the divisional young people's secretary at the South London Divisional Headquarters and by the national candidates secretary at National Headquarters – most definitely not shining in my response to the biblical questions – and was given my acceptance star on condition that I completed the candidates lessons before entering training!

So on paper, as *The Salvation Army Year Book* faithfully records each year, I am a product of Upper Norwood Corps, and I have more than once thanked the corps when visiting it. But because we were travelling so much, my links with the corps at that time were very tenuous – I think in fact I attended the corps on only two Sundays and three band practices.

I was later told that during the time I was a cadet a census meeting was held at the corps, and when my name came up someone asked who I was. 'I think we sent him into training,' said the corps officer. 'Should we not check?' asked a local officer. So there and then someone was deputed to phone the training college to ask if there was a Cadet John Larsson in training. A moment later he came back with the reassuring news that there was. So my name stayed on the roll.

But to return to the main narrative, with my newly acquired status of candidate I accompanied my parents and Miriam to Sweden and travelled with them to Denmark. I helped the family settle into their new quarters. But within a few weeks I was off to London to enter training. I did not know it then, but with my father's death in 1974, the four of us would never live in the same country again, and it was to be 32 years before my mother, Miriam and I were to find ourselves in the same country.

During all of those years, whenever Miriam or I or both of us were in a different country, my mother wrote an individual letter to us every week, and we wrote home every week as regularly as clockwork. When in later life Freda and I served in Chile one of the weekly joys was to go each Saturday morning to the Santiago central post office to collect my mother's letter from the box. My mother kept all of those letters – hers and ours – and when she was in her 90s handed them back to us. So we each have a complete record of our lives. When we were in the same country a daily phone call home became the pattern, so those years are less well documented.

Chapter Three

AT THE BATTLE SCHOOL

ARRIVING from the Harwich ferry at Liverpool Street Station in London one August day in 1956, I caught the bus to Denmark Hill. I remember pausing for a moment as I went up the steps of the International Training College and saying to myself wistfully: 'The moment I walk through those doors I will never belong to myself again.' And so it has turned out to be. But I overdid the wistful bit. Life has been a great adventure.

We were 184 cadets in the Faithful Session. Because of the International Corps Cadet Congress held in London in the summer of that year, there were more overseas cadets than usual.

The name Faithful was not the most exciting of sessional names. Our training principal, Lieut-Commissioner Frederick Coutts, probably sensed this, for in the opening meeting he began his welcome address by saying that when a comrade in a corps dies, and no one can think of anything noteworthy to include in his obituary, the invariable tribute is that 'he was faithful'! But the commissioner then moved on to show us in an unforgettable way how rich the word faithful is in its full biblical meaning. By the time he had finished we thought we had the sessional name to end all sessional names!

If ever there was a sponge just waiting to absorb everything around it, it was this 18-year-old Swede from South America via Upper Norwood. Training in those days was for nine months, and we lived at an intense pace, with each day packed with activities, classes and meetings. The timetable that appeared at the beginning of each week accounted for every minute of the day from 6.30 am until 8 pm. Thirty minutes every morning was reserved for 'quiet time' and this introduced me for the first time to the challenge of an extended period of personal devotions.

Wednesday and Saturday afternoons and every other Sunday were field days. An 'outline' had to be prepared and handed in for checking for every speaking assignment or other form of participation – and what with open-air meetings, joy hours for children, weeknight and Sunday meetings this was a major industry. Curiously the timetable made little or no provision for this kind of preparation. That had to be tucked in as best one could. Excellent training for the life ahead of us, we were told. But the reason for it was no doubt the tug-of-war between 'education' and 'field' – the creative tension between academic and practical training when time is limited – a tension which every training college experiences to this day, and which can never be fully resolved.

Having since spent many of my officer years on training work, I still stand in awe at the training programme as I experienced it, fine-tuned and honed for years by the Army's most intense spirits and best brains. Like every training college before or since, it was a battle school designed to turn out what the regulations still call 'blood and fire' officers. 'We begin with the heart,' Catherine Booth had once written about the early-day training of cadets, 'then we try to train the head, and then we train in practical skills.' It was training of the heart and the head and the hands, and this was exactly what the training programme at the ITC was designed to do.

The college had an immense record of success. This was to a great extent due to the fact that the training staff made great demands on us, and expected and got the best out of all who were prepared to throw themselves wholeheartedly into the training programme. One couldn't get away with anything slipshod or second-class.

What stands out in my mind is that the officers took the trouble to follow through on every detail – whether to do with the heart, the head or the hands. They bothered when they did not have to – they were determined to draw out every ounce of potential. And as I gave myself without reserve to life at the training college I found that I thrived on this structured and action-packed approach to life.

The college buildings were so constructed that we lived in brigades, with a sergeant in charge of each floor. Each brigade had its own training corps. But all cadets in turn had the opportunity of being withdrawn from their corps brigades for about six weeks in order to become part of a special service brigade. This was a commando-style brigade that was at the front line of ministry in the very heart of London. And, as it happened, I landed in that brigade straight away. It was a baptism of fire!

Almost before I had time to unpack, there we were in Soho, in London's West End, conducting late-night open-air meetings. These drew great crowds and we were expected to hold their attention through our speaking and also to contact bystanders personally and urge them to accept Christ. This was all new to me. But I was determined to conquer any lingering fears I had about speaking in public and also to conquer the new fear – of speaking to people personally about their spiritual state.

I used to look round at the crowd, select a person who looked responsive, then glance at my watch and determine that when the second-hand came up to 12 I would go and speak to that person! Sometimes, to my relief, the person had moved away by the appointed hour, but if he had not, I went. I will never forget the first time that a man responded to my invitation to kneel in the open-air ring. That was at Hyde Park Corner. He was the first person I led to Christ.

The classes at the college were a revelation to me. I drank in new knowledge by the bucketful. I found myself in the top class. We covered the Bible in nine months – Matthew to Revelation between August and Christmas, and Genesis to Malachi between Christmas and commissioning in May. It may have been fast, but it was effective.

Colonel Gordon Mitchell, the education officer, was my doctrine teacher. He had a marvellous way of illustrating abstract truth with pin-men drawings on the blackboard. I copied them all into my *Handbook of Doctrine*, and have never parted with that book even though it has been overtaken by newer editions. Colonel Mitchell opened my eyes to what for me was a new subject and gave me a lifelong interest in theology.

The study of orders and regulations sounded forbidding – the subject has since been re-named 'Salvation Army Principles and Procedures' – but, with real-life illustrations based on first-hand experience, it gave me a vision that has never left me of what the Army is called to be. And so it was with every subject. The student was more than ready, and the teachers were there.

Personalities

But training is not only or even mainly about the acquisition of abstract knowledge. Its chief ingredient is the impact of personalities, and the convictions and attitudes and the 'spirit' which they convey to the cadets. Jesus called his disciples 'to be with him'. And it was the 'being with him' that was the key to their preparation for the future, even more than his teaching. A very large responsibility therefore rests on the members of staff of a training college. It is what they personally are that will shape the officers of tomorrow.

In this, we of the Faithful Session could not have been more fortunate. I could write about all of the members of staff, for my indebtedness extends to them all, but that is not a practical possibility in these pages.

The officer closest to me was my sectional officer. Where a training college is organised on a sectional pattern, the sectional officers are like mini-training principals for their sections. They are responsible for the welfare of their cadets, for overseeing their overall development, and have special responsibility for their spiritual development and their practical field work. They are concerned with the head and the heart and the hands. It is a big responsibility and sectional officers are hugely influential. On the first day I discovered that my sectional officer was to be Captain Harry Read.

No other officer has been more influential in my life than Harry Read. As I sat in his office in House 5 on the opening day, little did I know how our lives would be intertwined. As a cadet he became my father-in-God and my role model. When I became a sergeant the next year he again was my sectional officer. When after a year as a corps officer I returned to the International Training College as a house officer, Harry Read was my sectional officer yet again. During those years we became creative partners in a 'words and music' partnership, but that story belongs to a later chapter.

As we conversed together on that first day I did not know that Harry and Win Read were to become not only my leaders but also my mentors and close friends, and that they would be praying for me by name every day of their lives to this day. Even less could I have foreseen that when six years later Harry Read farewelled from the training college I would move into his chair and be his successor as the sectional officer in House 5. It would also have needed an impossible leap of the imagination for me to foresee that when 'British Commissioner' and Mrs Harry and Win Read retired from the leadership of the British Territory in 1990, Freda and I would succeed them as territorial leaders of the United Kingdom Territory.

The traditional pattern for training colleges in those days was to have a men's side and a women's side – with a great gulf fixed between them. Presiding over the men (and the married cadets) as chief side officer was Lieut-Colonel Albert Mingay, who later was also to become the British Commissioner. We venerated this saint of God. The field training officer was Major Albert Drury. He too was to be influential in my life, not least in my public speaking.

Within a few weeks of the opening of the session, the special service brigade was to visit an eventide home one afternoon before proceeding into the West End of London for the evening open-air meetings. I was down to give a three-minute talk to the residents. We were taught that the optimum format for such three-minute talks was: a) an illustration, b) some comments, c) a verse of Scripture. This was a new art form for me and I enjoyed the challenge of preparing a talk that must not on any account exceed 180 seconds. I prepared an outline, submitted it, and got it back without comment. I kept polishing my little gem and rehearsed it carefully in my room.

On the day, just as I was called on to speak in the eventide home, in walked the field training officer, Major Albert Drury. His face was inscrutable as I delivered my piece to the residents seated in their armchairs.

The next day I was summoned into his presence. This was not unusual. We knew that cadets who had been observed in action by a member of the training staff would get feedback. I sat in his office and awaited the verdict. He caught me by surprise. 'You will never give a better three-minute talk,' he said. 'It had everything.' Part of my surprise was that my report card had not taken the standard line of 'Good – but can do better'. I felt as if I had peaked too soon! But Major Drury was known for being direct of speech, and obviously believed in giving praise where he felt that praise was due. I glowed for days. But the story has a sequel.

Some weeks later the whole of the men's side was going to campaign in Bristol, and on the Sunday evening I had to give my testimony in the salvation meeting. It was going to be a big event, with the training principal himself presiding. The trouble was that my testimony wasn't all that exciting. It lacked the life-transforming drama of Saul on the Damascus Road. I felt that a gala occasion demanded a gala testimony. So I set to work. I ransacked my life for anything that would entitle me to join the ranks of great sinners, added plentiful splashes of colour, and in the end had a story that even Saul might have envied. On the night I poured out this tale, and also thanked God for the way that he had transformed my life.

'Please see the field training officer,' said the note the next day. I was happy with the way things had gone and went to see Major Drury with a sense of anticipation. The major lived up to his reputation for directness. 'Never ever do that again,' he began. 'Your attempt to convince us that you were once a dyed-in-the-wool sinner was nothing but an embarrassment. Even the commissioner was embarrassed.' That hurt.

'What on earth were you trying to do?' he continued. 'One of the greatest blessings God has given you is that you have been brought up in a loving Christian family and have been protected from evil. Think of what that means for the health of your body and mind and spirit. The fact that you were nurtured in a sheltered environment is one of the most precious gifts you have. You should have been thanking and praising God for that gift, not rubbishing it for effect as you did last night. Never ever do it again!' I knew he was right. Deep down faint alarm bells had been ringing in my own mind but I had chosen to ignore them. I thanked him warmly. And I have never ever done it again.

Major Stan Golbourn, the second side officer, was also greatly influential in my development. Major Golbourn, a widower, combined gentleness of character with a shrewd mind. He had the kind of gracious personality that made it easy for us to relate to him, and he seemed the very embodiment of wisdom. In fact, he was the men's side trouble-shooter, as I was to find out from personal experience. It all had to do with our 'record books'.

One of the less inspired training ideas was that cadets should keep a personal log of how they had spent each moment of each day. This might well have dated back to the days when all corps officers were required to keep a log of their daily activities, a log which the divisional commander would inspect on his visits – but this had long since been discontinued. At the training college they were known as 'record books' and we each received an A5 size hardback book, with printed columns showing each week, each day, and each hour in the day.

We were meant to update the record books daily. We had to take them to the personal interviews we regularly had with members of the staff, and they were sometimes also called in for checking. Because of the highly structured days that we lived it really was just a matter of copying the timetable into our books. Perhaps it was for that purpose that each new timetable was pinned on top of the previous ones in the entrance hall. That meant that when the record books were called for, we all queued up to copy the timetables of any weeks that we had missed. It all seemed a bit pointless. And when it came to the 'private study' periods one never knew whether to let on or not that these had mostly been spent preparing the outlines for public work that so dominated our lives.

Just before the Christmas recess all record books were suddenly called in for checking. I was many weeks behind and had a lot of catching up to do in the short time available. I dashed down to check the old timetables on the board – and found that they had disappeared! The illogicality of the record book system had been simmering within, and now it boiled over. After taking a deep breath, I wrote in large letters across each of the blank pages: 'I spent the time as I thought most appropriate at the time.' And for good measure I drew a bold box around this statement on every page.

I then handed in the book to the sergeant. The men's side had a minor rebellion on its hands. I was sure that retribution would flow – but also recall my unconcern about that prospect. I would take the opportunity to point out how ridiculous the system was. I would tell them a thing or two. I quite relished the thought.

I spent the 10-day Christmas recess in Denmark with my family. A couple of days after my return, I found a small slip of paper summoning me for an interview – it was to be with the second side officer, Major Stan Golbourn. I had a pretty good idea what the subject would be, and mentally armed myself for the confrontation.

When I entered his office, sure enough the record book was lying on the desk. The major greeted me warmly, and then asked me about the Christmas break. How were my parents? What had I been reading? I had been reading Henry Drummond's *Natural Law in the Spiritual World*, which I had come across in the college library, and we had a fascinating discussion about this 19th-century classic.

The major was warmth personified and as we ranged over a number of subjects related to the development of my 'heart, head and hands' I found myself relaxing and opening up – yet all the time wondering when the subject of the record book would come up. It never did in the interview. As was customary, we knelt for prayer at the end. We shook hands. Then just as I was turning to leave the office, he pointed to the record book and said with a kind voice: 'Oh, this.' He paused. Then with a smile added: 'Silly, wasn't it?'

At this point my carefully loaded guns aimed at the record book system were supposed to fire. But the fight had long since gone out of me. Killed by kindness. I had to admit that perhaps, yes, it had been a bit silly. I wondered what I should do. 'Why don't you call next door and apologise to the field training officer.' Major Albert Drury was responsible for administering the record book system. So I knocked on his door. He was absolutely gracious about it all. And that was the end of the matter.

But that morning Stan Golbourn taught me how potentially explosive situations can be defused by sensitive handling. I have many times smiled at the memory of the skill he showed that day.

Later on we were all delighted when we saw Major Stan Golbourn and Captain Win Putterill becoming friendly. They were even seen walking hand in hand! But in those days the age differential for officers contemplating marriage had restrictions. The permitted differential at the time was 17 years, and sadly Stan and Win were five weeks over that limit and therefore had to resign in order to marry. It was a great loss for the Army.

Stan and Win became local officers at a London corps, and for the rest of Stan's life he engaged in a ministry of encouragement to those who had been 'his boys' at the college. Whenever I participated in large central meetings in London as Chief of the

Staff and later as General, Stan was always there to cheer me on. And after the meetings I used to go over to him to thank him for what he meant to me. He was 97 when he went Home to be with his Lord.

We admired and loved our training principal. As a session, we considered ourselves supremely fortunate to have Lieut-Commissioner Frederick Coutts at the helm. We used to look forward to his lectures which were a regular feature of the training programme. Since those days, education theory has moved against the lecture method in favour of smaller, inter-active groups for teaching and learning. The training principals of today therefore do not have the same opportunity to influence cadets. But I shall always be grateful that I experienced the impact of the mind and personality of Frederick Coutts in the lecture setting. Many of his key sayings – which he would repeat often so that we would remember them – are written as banners across my mind and heart.

On Thursday evenings we marched down Denmark Hill to Camberwell for the weekly holiness meetings, and his addresses there during our session later became the heart of his book *The Call to Holiness*. Spiritual days were another highlight for us. We admired everything about him.

One of the college traditions was that at the Christmas social selected cadets would mimic members of the staff. That was always fun for the cadets – perhaps less so for the victims. Some weeks before the event the organisers entrusted me with the task of imitating none other than the training principal. I had to give a five-minute speech as if I was Frederick Coutts.

From that moment on Frederick Coutts became the most closely observed person on the campus. I studied his voice, the way he spoke, his choice of words, and I watched the way he stood and how he sometimes seemed to wrap himself around the reading desk. I carefully noted his arm gestures. And I practised them in my room!

I found that when he was trying to explain something difficult he would often use a gesture with both his hands whereby he seemed to be trying to open a jar of jam. 'Cadets, cadets,' he would say as he twisted the jar lid in vain. Then, with a mighty twist the jar lid would open as he said: 'It's like this!' I made sure I had every inflection and movement right for that one.

43

On the occasion I appeared in commissioner's uniform, and gave my carefully rehearsed speech. Everyone was soon laughing – including, I noted with relief, the commissioner himself – and the laughter reached its climax as I ended with the jar sequence. I walked off to a great round of applause.

But I now had a problem. Having spent weeks being Frederick Coutts I found I couldn't stop being him! Every time I stood up to speak, his gestures, his voice, everything about him had become mine! I had to start an intensive campaign of de-Couttsification! After some weeks I decided I had succeeded and could relax again.

But some things are hard to unlearn. And on one occasion in my first corps when I was trying to explain a difficult point in a message, I found myself trying to open the jar with my hands and saying: 'Comrades, comrades … it's like this!' But there and then I decided: never again!

Other aspects

Training days were full of fun. We were young and energetic – and we were cooped up. We could leave the college only at designated times, and always in full uniform. Apart from free time on Friday afternoons, we could only go out Monday evenings and Tuesday evenings for 30 minutes – women cadets from 8 to 8.30 pm and men cadets from 8.30 to 9 pm!

The surplus energies from this state of affairs had to be spent on campus. And somehow I ended up heading a special events team. We decided that at least once a month proceedings needed to be livened up by some prank or other. We used to spend considerable time planning these – it was yet another thing to be fitted into the schedule. Fortunately space prohibits me describing our special events programme in detail, but I think I can claim that we kept the session entertained – and had the staff worried.

At one point the principal asked those responsible for a particular bit of fun to see him in his office afterwards. I think it was after one of his lectures on Army music when the grand piano in the lecture hall had been turned into a honky-tonk instrument by judicious placing of teaspoons on the piano strings. As this was the second time that the same group made its appearance before him, he ended his words with: 'Lads, lay off.' So we did. Cadets today are more mature, most of them are married with families, and the doors of the colleges are wide open. There is not the same need to let off steam. That is why the cadets of today are more sensible. But we had plenty of fun.

In November we were divided into groups for the traditional 10-day campaign and I headed for Folkestone Corps. The campaign party was under the leadership of Captain John Elsworth – another officer for whom I have great affection. Towards the end of the week, the captain wondered if I had ever asked a congregation to suggest two choruses that I could improvise on and weave together in an impromptu piano item. I said that I hadn't and, suspecting what he had in mind, added that I really didn't want to try either. 'It's very easy,' said the captain with his characteristic chuckle, 'Eric Ball does it all the time.'

With that not very reassuring thought he launched me into the deep end of the pool that evening. And it worked! I have used the approach in some form or other many times since. Perhaps the largest occasion was in the Massey Hall in Toronto attended by several thousand young people gathered for the North American Youth Congress in 1975. Thank you, Lieut-Colonel John Elsworth.

Colonel Gordon Mitchell always referred to the 'second half' – the training period from Christmas to commissioning in May – as a hop, skip and a jump, and so it turned out to be.

As commissioning approached we knew that the fellowship of the session would soon be broken up. I had made many friends – with some I am still in touch all these years later. We sometimes wondered where our first appointments might be. I could not add much to those discussions. There were nearly a thousand corps in Britain. I knew only those I had visited as a cadet. The rest were a closed book to me.

At that point I was asked to see the international secretary for the Americas, Commissioner Charles Durman. He came straight to the point: my application to serve in South America – which he was very pleased about. That caught me by surprise. There must have been some misunderstanding for no one had ever raised the subject with me. I said to the commissioner that of course I was ready to go wherever the Army sent me, but that the matter of returning to South America had never been mentioned.

The commissioner handled the situation superbly. He dropped the subject and then proceeded for the next hour to give me a 'one to one' seminar on leadership. It was absolutely fascinating. Many years later I had occasion to see my own personal file from training days, and I found a reference to this interview and the question of whether I should return immediately to South America. I read that the training principal had taken the decision that 'this gifted lad' should be allowed to remain in the UK for some time before a return to South America was to be considered. That period of 'some time' turned out to be 23 years.

Commissioning

The solemnity of Covenant Day in the assembly hall and the splendour and excitement of commissioning in the Royal Albert Hall made a deep impression. Signing my covenant at the mercy seat was no problem at all for me. I was glad to do so. My commitment to God and the Army had been made long ago – when I told my father in the car that I would apply for training. It was therefore with some surprise that I noted that a few of my colleague cadets seemed to struggle for a long time before signing their covenant – some even seeking the aid of an officer.

When attending other Covenant Days since then, I have sometimes noticed the same pattern. To me that has always seemed as if the groom at a wedding service has to enter into a long agonising struggle of indecision requiring the help of a counsellor before he is able to respond: 'I will.' To my mind the 'I will' of Covenant Day is like the glad 'I will' at a wedding service – a confirmation of promises already made, a culmination of everything that has gone before.

On commissioning day I was appointed a sergeant, and thus with others became a very junior member of the training staff for the next session. I was pleased. I delighted in college life, looked forward to the responsibility and was glad to have a further opportunity for personal development before taking up a corps appointment. Sergeants, in addition to their leadership responsibilities, had their own programme of classes. But before the next session opened came the opportunity to understudy a corps officer for three weeks during the summer.

The time spent with Major and Mrs Rhys and Gladys Dumbleton at Sheffield Citadel was like a super-charged training session all of its own. Sheffield Citadel was one of the colossus corps that then adorned the British Territory. Each Sunday evening when the corps officer headed the march from the open-air meeting, with all music sections and all uniformed soldiers taking part, the march stretched for blocks.

For three weeks I was part of that life. Wherever Rhys went I went, whatever he did I did, and after each new activity he would share with me from his accumulated experience of corps officership. In those days corps officers did not usually have a car, but Rhys had a very old one, and we used to sit in it after each event discussing corps officer ministry in all its forms.

Back at the college I had to write a report on the experience of those weeks. I hang my head when I remember that I wrote that those three weeks had taught me more than all of the previous nine months added together. But that is how I felt at the time.

We were sorry to say goodbye to our training principal when Commissioner and Mrs Coutts were appointed territorial leaders of the Australia Eastern Territory. But we were glad to welcome Lieut-Commissioner Kaare Westergaard as the new principal. With his wife Mona they were a sparkling couple, and I count it as one of the further blessings of my life that I was able to work under their leadership.

I had revelled in the freedom of training days. As a cadet I had been spontaneous and uninhibited in my reactions, and had literally been carefree. In a world divided between 'us' and 'them' I had been a fully paid up member of the 'us' club. That changed when I became a sergeant. I became one of 'them'. I now had the weight of leadership and pastoral care responsibilities. And I have had them ever since. Perhaps that is why I look back on those nine months as such a halcyon time of my life.

With the arrival of the Courageous Session, the training programme swung back into action. A surprising amount of responsibility for the practical field training of the cadets rested on our shoulders as sergeants. But we were veterans by now! The days, weeks and months whizzed by – and soon it was commissioning time all over again.

Yet again I stood on the platform of the Royal Albert Hall, and when my name was called stepped up smartly to the training principal and saluted. 'Sergeant John Larsson,' said Commissioner Westergaard, 'you are appointed in charge of the Sunderland Southwick and Washington Corps with the rank of lieutenant.' I was fully launched as an officer!

Chapter Four

EARLY OFFICER YEARS

SUNDERLAND and Washington lie in the far north-east corner of England. On the day of departure there were so many newly commissioned officers heading north that the training college had booked a whole carriage on the train for us. It was a wise thing to have done, for with our high spirits and laughter and chorus-singing anyone else in the same carriage would have felt out of place.

But gradually the ranks began to thin. As the train stopped at the various stations it would be someone's turn to say goodbye and leave for his or her appointment. There were some tearful moments. The morning turned to afternoon and then into evening, and in the end there were only two of us left in the carriage – Lieutenant Ken Stubley, who had been appointed as my 'second', and me. It was difficult to keep up the chorus-singing with only the two of us. Bit by bit the fellowship had broken up. And as the darkness fell I felt my spirits sinking.

Thank God for sessional names! I had no trouble being 'faithful' – that was mainly just a matter of keeping going. It was being 'courageous' that was proving difficult. But for the last nine months in the Courageous Session I had been hearing messages based on every reference to courage in the Bible. Some of those words now flooded back in my mind: 'Only be thou strong and very courageous … As I was with Moses, so I will be with thee; I will not fail thee, nor forsake thee' (Joshua 1:7 and 5, *AV*). Those words were to strengthen me from within many times during the days ahead.

As the train pulled into Newcastle Central Station, there stood Corps Sergeant-Major Doris Griffiths to welcome us. Doris, a former officer, was in her early 50s and was to become our indispensable guide and support. The Army in Britain has a tradition of local officership unrivalled by any other territory in the world. When necessary, some corps can manage for years without a corps officer, such is the strength and ability of the group of local officers. Doris was the first of many such outstanding local officers that I was to encounter during my service in the UK. With my South American background, corps life in Britain was a new world to me, and I could not have had a better teacher than Doris.

Sunderland Southwick and Washington Corps

On the bus Doris explained that the quarters were in Washington and told us something about the locality and the corps. Washington, the place from which George Washington's forbears hailed, was then a mining community built around three coal mines. It has since become a thriving new-town. Doris told us that the corps in Washington had once been a large concern with a band of some 25 players, but was now only a shadow of its former self.

Sunderland was an industrial city about three miles from Washington. The Army was very strong there, with three large corps in addition to the smaller corps at Sunderland Southwick on the outskirts of the city. Doris was the corps sergeant-major at Sunderland Southwick and had been instrumental in bringing about the building of a new hall. The corps was doing well and my corps officer duties would include being the singing company leader and pianist. The two corps of Sunderland Southwick and Washington had shared corps officers for some years.

Ken and I soon settled into the new routine of corps and home life. Our quarters were the upstairs of a terraced house, with the toilet outside at the bottom of the yard. We soon got things arranged. I made a prayer corner for myself in my bedroom. We looked at the halls, became familiar with the books, got to know the layout of the district, and began to visit our people. It is to me an ever-recurring miracle how Salvation Army officers arrive at new appointments, quickly take stock of what is often a totally new scene, and within days are fully engaged in ministry and in giving leadership to the local team. It is simply amazing how one copes.

Every day there seemed to be something new. But Doris was always there with sage guidance and advice. There were the first meetings. The first round of activities, like the first singing company practice. There was the first 'pub round' to sell *The War Cry*. The first making-up of the books – counting the cartridge money and the money in the pub tins with Doris, and in the end parcelling out the coins for whatever portion of my £3.50 weekly allowance there was money for, once all bills had been paid.

There was rarely enough for our full allowances. But I knew that with the autumn Harvest Festival collecting, the Christmas carolling collecting and the February Self-Denial Appeal collecting, a certain proportion of the income would come to the corps, and this would give opportunity for us to recoup most of what was owing to us. So I looked on the lack of a regular full allowance as a useful form of saving!

Then came the first funeral. Every officer remembers his or her first funeral. But it so happened that at the corps in Southwick we had the retired divisional bandmaster. When he was promoted to Glory, all of the members of the divisional staff plus many corps officers from the division announced that they would be attending the funeral. The divisional commander insisted that it was the corps officer's place to take the service. So my first funeral was to be conducted in the full glare of publicity. Before the event I worked through every detail with Doris, and all went well on the day.

And so it was with every 'first' – the first dedication, the first sale of work, the first door-to-door collecting, the first Christmas, first Easter – we would pick Doris's brain, prepare as carefully as we could, and then launch out. And Doris was always there, right behind us – literally so, for I say to her everlasting credit that she never sought to usurp the position of her young corps officers.

Wednesdays soon became a highlight each week. We did not have a bath at our quarters, so every Wednesday afternoon I would catch the bus to Seaham Harbour for my weekly bath at the quarters of a colleague lieutenant. We would then have tea together before we journeyed to Sunderland Citadel for the divisional holiness meeting. In those days every division had its weekly holiness meeting, and because of the distances between the corps the Northern Division had two – Wednesdays in Sunderland and Thursdays in Newcastle. This Wednesday outing became a focal point of the week – with cleansing of the body combined with cleansing of the soul. What more could one ask for?

The divisional commander, Lieut-Colonel Edmund Taylor, presided over these holiness meetings. He had once been a fisherman, and with his short stature it was not surprising that he was known as 'the little fisherman'. But what a great figure he was! His warmth and cheerfulness in personal contact and his uplifting approach to the meetings were enough to renew courage in any needy soul – young officers included. The Taylors were such an inspiration to me that, for better or worse, all of my subsequent divisional commanders were to be measured against that exacting yardstick.

For many and varied reasons weekly holiness meetings are now rarely a regular feature of divisional life. The loss is double. Not only is there a loss of focus on holiness teaching, but there is also a loss of supportive fellowship for officers and comrades. For me the weekly divisional holiness meeting was a lifeline. But I also recognise that times change.

Washington in those days was a small and closely knit community of some 3,000 people. We tried a number of new initiatives to renew life in the corps, some more successful than others. There were enough former Salvationists living in the area to make a very substantial corps. We planned a 'reunion Sunday' with the aim of encouraging them to renew links with the corps. We tracked them all down and visited them personally. Many committed themselves to attending. But on the day very few came. It was an idea that did not work as well as we had hoped.

At that time over-60 clubs were just becoming part of corps life in Britain and were not only providing a service but also opening doors to wider outreach for corps. I asked the corps officer of one of the large Sunderland corps to show me how to establish one. He advised me to contact the leaders of all existing clubs for the elderly in Washington and to ask for an opportunity to speak to their members about the new club being planned. He offered to come and speak himself.

I was surprised. The method he was suggesting seemed like sheep-stealing. 'Not at all,' he reassured me. 'You will find that leaders are only too pleased for their members to have additional interests in their lives.' And so it proved to be. I did the contacting and the speaking myself, and invariably got a friendly and warm reception.

What with these visits and helpful publicity in the local press, so much interest had been shown in the great opening day of the new over-60 club that we prepared to provide refreshments for a whole invasion of senior citizens. But to our complete surprise only a handful turned up. I was genuinely nonplussed. So many had said that they would definitely be coming.

I remember clearly that I was not discouraged. I felt it in my bones that there must be some factor we had not reckoned with. And so it turned out to be. On that very day, three of the existing clubs had had outings. How that fact had never emerged in all our talking about the day I will never know. But sure enough, the next week the hall was full, and from then on the new over-60 club went from strength to strength.

The Sunday school in Washington Corps attracted only a few children. I decided to test out what they had taught us at the training college. So one afternoon I waited at the school gate, and as the children emerged I used a puppet to draw their attention and then announced that there would be a 'joy hour' at the Army at 6 pm. I went down to the hall early. Ken must have been away for I recall turning the corner and finding the street awash with children and that I was the only adult. They had taught us a thing or two at the college, so I made them file into the hall in strict order. There were about 100 of them.

I then started up the programme – taught them choruses, told them stories, used visual aids, engaged in simple games, and tried to get the message across. But it is amazing how quickly one can run out of material! After 30 minutes they were still with me, but the material was running low, and I knew that if I lost their attention a revolt could break out. So I urged them to attend Sunday school the next Sunday and then had them file out in the same orderly fashion, after which I sighed with relief! But it worked. On the Sunday about 30 of them returned and they became the core of our new-look Sunday school.

Among features which were becoming increasingly part of Army life in those days were community carol services at Christmas time. We decided to have a go even though we did not have many resources to draw on. We hired a public hall, chose a Sunday date and a late time when church services would be over, asked a neighbouring corps to lend us their young people's band, and began to advertise in the press, by word of mouth and through ecumenical contacts. It was a venture in faith, and when the divisional commander announced that he wanted to come and be part of it all, I wasn't at all sure it was a good idea. But, nothing ventured nothing gained, and on the occasion several hundred people filled the hall and a new tradition was born in Washington.

We led very active lives and would often go for many weeks without any time off – not to be recommended. The Lake District was only a few hours away by bus, but there never was time to go and see it. Considering that for Freda and me the Lake District would in time become one of our favourite spots on earth, I can only shake my head in disbelief that I did not devote a single free day to it when I worked next door. But I somehow found time during that year to read the six volumes of Winston Churchill's *The Second World War*.

I grew close to the group of people for whom I was pastor. When I had been appointed to the north-east at commissioning, some colleagues had said to me that I would find the Salvationists in the north-east to be fiery. They told me not to be surprised if from time to time there were stand-up fights in the hall after the Sunday night meeting! I didn't know whether to believe them or not. I suspected they were kidding – and they were. I found the people to be most warm and friendly. I grew not only to love them but also to admire them. What exceptional followers of the Lord we have in the ranks of the people of God called Salvationists! Salt of the earth!

On the move

When it came near to the general change in May, the divisional commander told me he was sure the training college would ask for me back. I had not given the future much thought and didn't know how such things worked. Some weeks later he said to me that there had been no request from the college and that he had a good corps in mind for me. When he next was in touch it was to confide, with a hint of 'I told you so' in his voice, that the college had indeed asked for me. He also informed me that the corps he had had in mind for me was Hexam. This was the first 'what might have been' in my officer service and more were to follow. Hexham was a fine corps, with many soldiers and with well-established music and other sections, and it would have been a great honour to be its corps officer.

But instead, in May 1959, shortly after I celebrated my 21st birthday, I was appointed back to the International Training College, this time as a house officer. I was to remain there for the next seven years.

Ken Stubley too moved on to another appointment. He later married, and after some years of service he and his wife June left officership and have been pillars of a London corps ever since.

Ken's name and mine have been linked in a curious way. I discovered after some time that on my service record my first appointment was listed as: 'Sunderland Southwick and Washington with Stubley' – as if Stubley was an outpost. It was an amusing and unimportant error, but as service records moved from being handwritten to being typed to being computerised the error seemed to get perpetuated. So I drew the attention of the personnel section at International Headquarters to the matter and they said they would attend to it. But each time I had reason to see my service record, 'with Stubley' still figured.

Many years later, knowing that the details of the service record were about to be published in connection with an international conference of leaders, I asked my sister Miriam who worked on International Headquarters if she would see that the entry was corrected. She responded that with her own eyes she had seen the words removed. But to the surprise of us both, when my service details appeared in printed form at the conference, the phrase 'with Stubley' was still there! Was there to be no escape? Would the words appear in the 'bio' printed in the programme at my funeral?

Apparently the commissioner ultimately responsible for such things had spotted the omission of 'with Stubley' and, thinking that it was an oversight on someone's part, had personally inserted the words again into the service record! But the phrase has definitely now gone and it will be no use looking for it at my funeral service.

Training Officer

As a house officer at the training college I lived on the job – in the ground floor flat of House 5. We were five house officers in all. Everyone else, including the sectional officers, lived off campus. It was a good life. We thought we owned the place, and in summer when there were no cadets in residence, we did!

During the session, with having a group of cadets to look after and help train, it was like being a corps officer. But instead of the corps officer changing every year, it was the corps that changed. I can still recall the sense of excitement with which I anticipated the arrival of the new 'corps' each year. I had always memorised the names of the cadets who would be living in my house and had begun praying for them, and it was now a matter of fitting names to faces. I lived for those cadets.

Each house formed a section, and I was house officer in Captain Harry Read's section, becoming a captain myself after a year. My task was to assist him in the overall development of the cadets – heart, head and hands – with special attention to the practical training on the field. I also had increasing opportunities to teach in the education programme. Though our lives were very busy, Harry and I always seemed to have time for conversation, and many were the hours that I spent in his office as we ranged over every subject in the world. Those conversations were part of the mentoring process.

Creative projects

The year I arrived back, Harry Read was given an assignment by the training principal, Commissioner Kaare Westergaard, that was to change my life. He was asked to take responsibility for the pageant at the next commissioning.

Commissionings were held in the Royal Albert Hall and it had become traditional that the evening session would end with an hour-long feature involving the cadets in large-scale drama and pageantry. Pageants usually included incidental music – the women cadets' singing brigade would often sing while the next scene was being prepared – but music was not an integral part of the production as in a musical. Harry decided to turn the pageants into musicals. He would create the pageantry and write the script and the lyrics for the songs, and he asked me to write the music.

I was flattered and I was pleased. When I entered training as a cadet, music was one of the things I had placed on the altar – to be burned. It was one of those things that I had given up. I was now

56

going to be an officer. I kept playing the piano, of course, and would sometimes spend hours in the assembly hall playing in the evening darkness. The music would flow from my fingers. I would play whatever came into my head, and I would find myself creating themes and melodies and harmonies and rhythms, developing them in a hundred different ways before they were lost as I closed the lid of the piano.

Once or twice I had sought to capture some of this inspiration on paper in the form of songs. But I saw music as a luxury not to be over-indulged – officer-life had far more pressing concerns. And now here was Harry asking me to make music part of my officer service! A new dimension to my ministry was about to open, and I looked forward to it.

The first of the musical pageants featured a number of songs for women's voices – songs that actually carried the drama forward. On the basis of these simple compositions, the training principal took a big step of faith: he asked me to write the music for the next sessional song, for which his wife had written the words.

Sessional songs in those days were virtually oratorios, to be sung by 200-voice choirs accompanied at commissioning by the full International Staff Band. The commissioner was taking a big risk. I had never written anything remotely as complex as that. Once again I was being trusted with what seemed beyond me. But once again I found that demand created supply. Mrs Commissioner Mona Westergaard had written stirring words. Inspiration flowed, and the sessional song 'Soldiers of Christ' was born.

Harry Read wrote and produced three pageants and in each of them the musical content became more prominent. The final one, the pageant of the Soldiers of Christ session in 1962, was a full-blown musical. Our song 'God's soldier marches as to war' (Song 801 in *The Song Book of The Salvation Army*) dates from this pageant – and was in fact my first published vocal item for mixed voices.

Helping with the creation of these pageants and writing the music for them was to prepare me for the later partnership with John Gowans. I picked up useful tips which became cardinal rules for me. One of these rules was never to set 'evil' words to music! They can become too memorable.

In one of Harry's pageants, he featured two Greek-style choruses – one the good chorus clad in white, and the other the evil chorus clad in black. So far so good. But the evil chorus were given some songs to sing. And human nature being what it is, these turned out to be some of the best songs and the most popular with the cadets! But it was distinctly disconcerting to walk through the college grounds in the weeks leading up to commissioning and hear cadets singing with loud voice: 'Sin will win is our marching song'.

Looking further ahead for a moment, when Harry farewelled from the college, the pageant writing team became a threesome, with Major Fred Hill, Major Leo Ward and myself. When in 1965 I needed to concentrate on my studies, Captain Joy Webb, also a member of the college staff, wrote the music for the pageant. The next year, my final year on the college, I headed the team that created and produced yet another musical. But now back to the main story.

Classroom training in young people's work – in addition to practical training – was part of the curriculum at the training college, and at one point I presented proposals for a completely new look to this aspect of training. As a result I was given the task of designing, introducing and supervising the new programme.

In this connection I conceived the idea of producing a *YP Manual* – a book of ideas to help young officers with their work among children and young people. I began collecting material, and for many months my 'spare' time early and late was dominated by writing and editing and typing the duplicating stencils for what turned out to be a volume of 220 foolscap pages. The pages were professionally bound into book form, and the *YP Manual* became a useful tool for the cadets of successive sessions. For me it was also a valuable initiation into the world of writing, editing and publishing – and into the world of lengthy creative projects. I often glanced with a wry smile at the couplet I had placed on my desk: 'Tasks in hours of insight willed must be in hours of gloom fulfilled'.

Two-year training

The 1960s were historic times to be at the International Training College, for with the entry of the Soldiers of Christ Session in 1960 two-year training was about to begin. As Commissioner Westergaard often reminded us, quoting General Bramwell Booth, we were building the ship as we sailed in it. And so it proved. Part of the new thinking was not to throw people into the deep end of the pool. We now had to teach them to swim first. To that end the first year was to be mainly academic – to teach them to swim – with the summer training period and the second year being mainly field oriented, thus providing them with plenty of opportunity to try out the swimming strokes learnt.

As with many such changes, the pendulum swung too far at first. We were all doing our best to put into practice a new theory of training. But it soon became evident that one cannot take a group of enthusiasts for God and confine them to barracks for a year and expect them to have retained their fire by the time they are released for action. However right it might have seemed on paper, the theory was faulty, and two-year training has rightly settled into a pattern in which emphasis on the academic and the practical run parallel throughout the course.

The supreme test came in the autumn of 1961 when for the first time there would be two sessions in residence. How would that work? The cadets of the Servants of Christ Session arrived in August and took up residence just as all previous sessions had done. But six weeks later the Soldiers of Christ returned from their summer term appointments. None of us had quite anticipated what happened.

The Servants of Christ went out of their way to welcome back the returning second-year cadets, but one could sense that even they felt put out by the fact that the college was no longer exclusively theirs. The Soldiers of Christ on their part reacted unhappily at finding usurpers residing in a college which previously had been theirs alone. It took some time before the two sessions settled into a pattern of happy co-existence. Fortunately it proved to be a one-off problem. Future sessions were only to know the two-session pattern and accepted it as a matter of course. Training staff also prepared the cadets better for what was to occur when the second-year session returned.

A new appointment

In May 1962, after three years as a house officer, I received farewell orders. It was an internal move, and I was appointed as assistant to the field training officer. Harry Read was leaving the college and it was sad to say goodbye to him. And however much I appreciated the field training officer, Major Fred Hill, I was not pleased with the appointment. As a house officer I had been right among the cadets – I had literally lived with them. Now I was being moved to what seemed the sidelines and would no longer be in their midst. But I knew what I had to do – get used to the idea. And whilst attending the Brengle Institute held at Sunbury Court that summer I made my peace with God and the Army. I was going to make the very best of the new challenge.

In that spirit I returned to the college – only to find that farewell orders had come yet again. It was to be an Abraham and Isaac situation – it was the willingness that was being tested, the actual sacrifice was not required! The session due to enter in August had turned out to be larger than expected. Another sectional officer was needed – and I was to be the one. My appointment as assistant to the field training officer had lasted all of six weeks! It was the shortest appointment I ever held.

I learnt some years later that at this time the Norway Territory had asked for me to be their territorial music secretary. The response from the training principal had been that there were other plans for me. I record this further 'might have been' for had I been asked to go I would undoubtedly have seen it as a tremendous adventure and would have gone with a happy heart.

But how different my life would have been. I would almost certainly never have met Freda, and, though it seems inconceivable as I look back, I would probably have married someone else. I would probably not have met John Gowans either and there would have been no Gowans/Larsson musicals. 'My times are in your hands,' writes the psalmist (Psalm 31:15, *NIV*) and I can only say with the songwriter from my heart: 'My God, I wish them there'. Thank you, Commissioner Kaare Westergaard, for being God's agent at that moment.

Instead I moved into the sectional officer chair that Harry Read had occupied. It was a great honour. I was 24. And because I was single I was to live in the ground floor flat and be the house officer as well. Within weeks I found myself responsible for 36 single men cadets in House 5. Again, a larger responsibility than I had anticipated. But again, demand created supply. I found that I was able to meet the requirements of the task. Those cadets became the very centre of my life – I literally yearned for each to do well. I was to remain sectional officer and house officer for the next four years.

A questing mind
Intellectually the seven years on the college staff were important formative years for me. The interaction with the other members of staff was an education in itself. No idea was ever left unexplored. And the cadets' thirst for knowledge had an immensely stimulating effect. In this field as well, the demand was great and there had to be supply.

I found that the Cambridge School Certificates I had taken in Buenos Aires opened the way for me to take further Advanced Level exams and then to enrol as an external student with London University in order to study for a Bachelor of Divinity degree. As an overspill from these studies came a series of articles I wrote for the Army's youth magazine *Vanguard*, which were later published in book form under the title *Doctrine Without Tears*.

In those days, there was an 'all or nothing' approach to the sitting of exams for university degrees. After five years of study everything depended on how one did in 10 three-hour papers. There were no credits gained in course work to be taken into account. My exam time was to be in the summer of the year 1965.

I had studied fairly regularly during the preceding years, but I knew that the intensity had to be much increased for the last year. I was still holding down the two appointments of sectional officer and house officer, and I was determined that the cadets in my section were not going to be short-changed in any way.

So I went into a high alert mode. I resolved that I would study five hours every day – early mornings and late evenings – and I then organised my life down to the smallest detail around that immovable fact. Even writing music for the commissioning musical had to go. I still look back on that year as one of the best of my life. The cadets in my section received my absolute full attention, perhaps more than ever before, and I protected my study hours as fiercely as a lioness protects her cubs. I was firing on all cylinders. I had endless energy.

I then undertook the marathon of exams – and awaited the result. I can remember some weeks later going up to the notice board at London University on which the registration numbers of successful candidates were to be displayed at a certain time. My parents were on holiday in London and we were going to see the film *The Sound of Music* which had just come out. I searched the board. After five years, was it to be 'all' or was it to be 'nothing'? It turned out to be 'all'. My number was there! I now had a London University Bachelor of Divinity degree.

As I sat in the cinema watching the film the thought kept coming back to me: 'It's in the bag – it's in the bag – nothing can now take it away.' What a relief! The Chief of the Staff, Commissioner Erik Wickberg, later sent me a congratulatory note, enclosing a cheque for £5. It was the only financial help I received towards the studies. But that is how we did it in those days. And the feeling of achievement was very real.

My period of intense study coincided with the peak of the 'God is dead' movement. There was a wide gulf between the world of ideas at the university and the world of ideas I was part of at the college. When Bishop John Robinson published his book *Honest to God* in 1963 I felt I almost needed to smuggle it into the college to read it.

At the university just about everything about the Christian faith and the Scriptures was being questioned. It was immensely bracing – almost too much so at times. But through my studies I was introduced to the greatest intellects of the past and of the present. I met Christians who had faced the most difficult of questions and had discovered answers that did not compromise their intellectual honesty. It was good company to be in. At times I really did have to cling to the sage advice to 'hold to Christ and for the rest be uncommitted'. But having had to face and overcome the intellectual onslaught on my faith gave me an inner confidence of mind that has remained over the years.

As so often happens with currents of thinking, just as the winds of the 'God is dead' movement were sweeping over the Christian scene, the first gentle breezes of a totally different air current began to be felt. These were the winds of the Holy Spirit renewal movement, winds that were later to reach storm force. They were to be very influential in my own spiritual development.

A questing heart

As a cadet I had been introduced in our doctrine classes to the full scope of the Army's teaching on sanctification and the work of the Holy Spirit. I have to confess that the teaching about entire sanctification came as something of a surprise. Had I been asleep in all of the holiness meetings I had attended?

I knew that to live a holy life was to live a Christlike life, and that our aim must be to be more and more like Jesus. And I rejoiced in the boldness of faith whereby, in article 10 of our doctrines, Paul's prayer for the believers in Thessalonica is turned into an affirmation: 'We believe that it is the privilege of all believers to be wholly sanctified, and that their whole spirit and soul and body may be preserved blameless unto the coming of our Lord Jesus Christ.'

Those words became even more precious to me later when the *New English Bible* translation appeared in 1961 – a translation which became my meat and drink for many years, until the appearance of the *New International Version*. Can there be a more beautiful prayer than this? 'May God himself, the God of peace, make you holy in every part, and keep you sound in spirit, soul and body, without fault when our Lord Jesus Christ comes. He who calls you is to be trusted; he will do it' (1 Thessalonians 5:23-24, *NEB*). These words were so meaningful to me that I later set them to music.

But I was troubled by the footnote to article 10, which at that time was still part of the article of faith. This spoke of 'roots of bitterness' that remained in the heart after conversion, but which could be removed, seemingly in an instant, leaving the heart entirely sanctified, after which we could be kept unblameable and unreprovable before God. The exposition in the *Handbook of Doctrine* (1955 edition) was even clearer on the point: an *unregenerated* person is *under* sin, a *regenerated* person is *over* sin, and a *sanctified* person is *without* sin. There was even mention of Christian perfection. All of this was new to me.

I was troubled intellectually. Was sin really an 'it', something that could be removed as one removes a decayed tooth? Could sin as a removable 'it' be squared with the complexity of the human personality that increased understanding of human psychology was revealing? Was it really possible here and now to be 'without sin' and to be so 'perfect' that one could here and now stand unblameable and unreprovable before God?

I was also troubled spiritually. For all of this was far removed from my own experience of life. Yet if this was the promise to all believers, then I wanted to enter fully into my heritage. So the questions in my head were paralleled by a questing in my heart to enter into this further dimension of experience. I began to long for 'something more'.

In my studies as a cadet I had been introduced to the writings of Commissioner Samuel Brengle, and in the intervening time I must have read virtually all of his books. They warmed my heart and increased my inner longing. I noted his repeated emphasis on the two-sidedness of the 'something more' experience – yes, it was a cleansing, but even more, it was an infilling. He often spoke of it as the baptism of the Holy Spirit. But I observed that with the passage of time, holiness teaching in the Army had come to major on the cleansing side. Holiness meetings would begin with 'Tell me what to do to be pure, in the light of his all-seeing eyes'. The accent was more on the negative than on the positive.

But what I noted most was Samuel Brengle's personal story, how as a 25-year-old student at the Boston Theological Seminary he had yearned to be sanctified, and how, after weeks of searching the Scriptures and ransacking his heart, he had entered into the new dimension one Saturday morning. A sense of peace filled his soul – and he testified to the change the next day when it was his turn to give the Bible message to his fellow students. But most of all I read and re-read many times how the fire burst into flame three days later on the Tuesday morning. It is a passage of classic beauty, and I quote it in full because of the significance it has held for me personally:

> I awoke that morning hungering and thirsting just to live this life of fellowship with God, never again to sin in thought or word or deed against him, with an unmeasurable desire to be a holy man, acceptable unto God.
>
> Getting out of bed about six o'clock with that desire, I opened my Bible and, while reading some of the words of Jesus, he gave me such a blessing as I never dreamt a man could have this side

of Heaven. It was an unutterable revelation. It was a heaven of love that came into my heart. My soul melted like wax before fire. I sobbed and sobbed. I loathed myself that I had ever sinned against him or doubted him or lived for myself and not for his glory. Every ambition for self was now gone. The pure flame of love burned it like a blazing fire would burn a moth.

I walked out over Boston Common before breakfast, weeping for joy and praising God. Oh, how I loved! In that hour I knew Jesus, and I loved him till it seemed my heart would break with love. I was filled with love for all his creatures. I heard the little sparrows chattering: I loved them. I saw a little worm wriggling across my path: I stepped over it; I didn't want to hurt any living thing. I loved the dogs, I loved the horses, I loved the little urchins on the street, I loved the strangers who hurried past me, I loved the heathen – I loved the whole world.

I read that passage so often that it was engraved on my heart and mind. I not only longed and yearned for such an experience of God. I knew that I had already touched the fringes of it. I had been there. It would be a coming home. Something of what Samuel Brengle described I had fleetingly touched that moment when as a child in Stockholm the heavens had opened for me as I walked in the spring sunlight. What he described I had experienced for a second that moment when as a teenager at school in Chile God's glory had filled my soul.

I longed for it to happen again, and for it not to be a fleeting experience. I understood that such mountain-top experiences cannot last forever. Samuel Brengle himself had noted that. 'In time,' he wrote, 'God withdrew something of the tremendous emotional feelings. He taught me I had to live by my faith and not by my emotions.' But I longed to live always in the dimension of the Spirit.

And here, with the winds of the Holy Spirit renewal beginning to blow, came the teaching that it was God's will that all believers should be baptised in the Spirit, and that this experience would lift the soul permanently into a higher dimension of experience, bring a new immediacy into the believer's relationship with God, and open the way to undreamt effectiveness in his service.

I read all I could lay my hands on about the charismatic renewal and attended some of the large inter-denominational meetings that began to be held in London at that time. There was a literally incredible sense of divine electricity in those meetings. The testimonies of Christians whose lives had been changed were so powerful they made the sparks fly. It was impossible to argue against what they had experienced. The words of personal testimony had the absolute ring of truth. There was no doubt that God the Holy Spirit was at work in a new way.

It was incredible because for years the Holy Spirit had been the forgotten person of the Godhead. With the emphasis that there has been on the Holy Spirit in the past 40 years, it will be hard for younger generations to believe that, before the time of the Holy Spirit renewal, Bible messages on the Spirit would be greeted with yawns and glazed-over eyes. But the Spirit had now come alive! And it was almost beyond belief.

The personal testimonies I was reading and hearing had all the characteristics of what Samuel Brengle had experienced in his baptism of the Spirit. Here was the Brengle experience happening before my very eyes. The experience was the same. I knew that intuitively. There is after all only one God whom we can encounter experientially. But the scriptural basis adduced for the baptism in the Spirit was very different from the Wesleyan framework that I was familiar with.

And there was a snag. A major snag. In the early days of the charismatic movement it was axiomatic that the absolutely necessary sign of having received this baptism in the Spirit was that you could pray in tongues. If you could not pray in tongues you had not received the fullness of the Holy Spirit – full stop.

Understandably, believers who had found their lives transformed by the Spirit reached out for ways of explaining what had happened to them. Unfortunately they simply took over unquestioningly the narrowest teaching from within the Pentecostal movement – teaching that was already being questioned by sizeable segments within that movement. And with the enthusiasm of the new convert they gave the teaching not only a new currency but also a new rigidity.

In time the charismatic renewal movement was to recognise that the linkage between fullness of the Spirit and the gift of tongues does not have scriptural support. It became accepted that the Scriptures teach that the gift of tongues is a gift of the Spirit just like any other spiritual gift – given to some and not to others – and that *any* spiritual gift is evidence of the presence of the Spirit in our lives. It became accepted that all of God's gifts are to be valued, and that it is perfectly possible to be filled with the Spirit without receiving the gift of tongues. And once tongues were no longer seen as the indispensable evidence of the fullness of the Spirit, most of the heat which that subject had generated simply vanished.

But, sadly, by the time the charismatic renewal movement modified its teaching much damage had already been done. Instead of believers everywhere rising up to welcome a new movement of the Spirit in their generation, many seekers after 'something more' found the emphasis on the gift of tongues an insurmountable obstacle. And those who had entered into this new spiritual dimension were not always wise in how they urged the experience on others as mandatory for all believers. Serious rifts emerged in some congregations. The mistaken teaching about the necessity of tongue speaking as evidence of the Spirit's presence in fact provoked a backlash against the Holy Spirit renewal in a number of denominations, not least in the Army.

As I look back, how I wish that we as an Army had been more positive in our response to the Holy Spirit renewal. Had we had prophets who taught us to welcome this movement of the Spirit whilst rejecting the wrong teaching that accompanied it, the story could have been so different. But instead of hoisting our sails and setting them to catch the full force of this gale of the Spirit, we as a Movement lowered them. Instead of fanning the fire of the Spirit we sometimes quenched it. And all because the explanation of an experience that was so right was so wrong. It is of course easy to have 20/20 vision with hindsight, and none of this was clear at the time.

It also has to be said that despite our hesitations as a Movement, the Holy Spirit renewal succeeded in bringing about climate change in the Army – in a positive sense. The temperature in our worship has risen markedly since those days, and we are still rejoicing in the new warmth. It seems that enough Salvationists have been open channels to his Spirit for it to make a difference to the whole. For that one can only praise God. But it is what might have been that will always tantalise.

My own longing for a personal spiritual breakthrough remained intense during these years on the college staff. Like young Samuel Brengle I sometimes agonised spiritually for days and even weeks and would then go into the assembly hall at the college in the evenings and spend long times at the mercy seat praying that something might happen. I knew off by heart every step recommended by spiritual counsellors. I followed each one carefully. I laid everything on the altar again and again and then again. I was entirely open as to what spiritual gifts the Spirit wanted to grant me. That was for him to decide. I took steps of faith. Not once. Many times. And I waited for the fire. But the fire did not come. I did not experience what Brengle had experienced. However, I did not give up. My personal quest continued.

Time for a new challenge
As I entered my seventh year as a member of the training staff I knew that I was ready for a new challenge. Life at the college was demanding and it was stimulating, but perhaps it was too good. I felt a call to the frontlines.

Lieut-Commissioner Clarence Wiseman had by this time become our training principal. His dynamic and clear-cut character and his virile evangelical preaching had been a further strong influence on me. I went to see him one day. My request was a simple one: that when it became time for me to have a change of appointment I would return to a corps appointment. It is the only time I have taken the initiative in speaking to my leaders about the future. Perhaps it was not even necessary then, for the commissioner reassured me by saying that this was exactly as he himself saw things, and that it was likely to happen at the next general change.

And so in May 1966 I was appointed to Hillingdon Corps in the West London Division, with Lieutenant Gunnar Granholm as my colleague. Gunnar was a fellow Swede who had spent his second year of training at the International Training College.

Chapter Five

CORPS, MUSICALS AND MARRIAGE

IF you drove west out of London along the Uxbridge Road at around 6 pm Sunday evening in those days you would, in the space of a few miles, come across a succession of open-air meetings. They were the 'open-airs' held by the Shepherds Bush, Acton, Ealing, Hanwell, Southall, Hayes, Hillingdon and Uxbridge Corps. It was to the seventh in this line of corps in the outer suburbs of London that I was appointed.

Hillingdon Corps

Hillingdon Corps was temporarily meeting in a school, but within a few weeks we would be marching to our brand new hall built on the site of the former one on the Uxbridge Road. The new premises symbolised the development that the corps had seen over a number of years. The trend was for Salvationists to move to the suburbs of London, and Hillingdon was changing from a country corps into a modern suburban corps. We even had a telephone installed at the quarters! That saved a lot of queuing at the public coin-box telephone.

With the new hall came a fine group of local officers and soldiers. Gifted musical leaders were soon to make the music sections – especially the songsters – nationally known in the Army world. Hillingdon became the place to be. Salvationists moving into the area from other parts of the country would choose to soldier there. The corps was on the crest of a wave. It was a case of 'to them that have it shall be given' for new local people also began attending, found the Lord and became part of the corps. It may not have been anything spectacular. But it was a good time to be the corps officer there.

The mayor of the London Borough of Hillingdon was the special guest at the opening. Some weeks before the event, his secretary phoned to say that the mayor would like me to write his speech for him. That also was a first for me. What on earth do mayors say on such occasions? I began drafting what I thought might be suitable expressions. I wondered whether the mayor would want to thank the Army for its work. Perhaps mayors did that kind of a thing. It seemed a bit of a cheek to be putting such words into his mouth, but I did include some modest words of appreciation.

When the mayor unfolded his script on the occasion I could see that it was the very paper I had typed. And when he reached the paragraph of appreciation he read it out with all appropriate feeling. But having read it he put the paper down – and started ad-libbing. In words far more eloquent and effusive than I had dared to give him, he thanked the Army in generous phrase after generous phrase for its magnificent work. 'I sometimes wonder,' he climaxed, 'how we would ever cope with our work for the needy in the London Borough of Hillingdon without the help of The Salvation Army.' He then returned to the prepared script.

Those words were to haunt me in the coming months – and were to determine my approach to corps ministry from then on. I knew that however well meant, those words were not true of Hillingdon Corps. Community service by corps was far less developed in those days than it is today. And I knew that however rich and meaningful the fellowship of the corps was, the impact of Hillingdon Corps on the community around it was virtually nil. The mayor had in fact been generous to a fault, for not even the Army's social services had any centres in the London Borough of Hillingdon. He had been thanking us for the Army's well-deserved national reputation to care for the poor, feed the hungry and comfort the lonely. But we weren't doing any of that.

It began to weigh heavily on me. So I gathered the soldiers together, and shared my convictions with them. Putting it dramatically, I reminded them of what the mayor had added to the prepared speech, and then said: 'The truth is that if by some misfortune Hillingdon Corps were to disappear off the face of the earth overnight, no one but ourselves – the Salvationists – would notice.' We determined together that we must expand the dimensions of our ministry. And that began to happen. The influence of the mental connections made during the mayor's extempore contribution were to be long-term for me as well, for they have shaped my thinking about corps life ever since.

Musical *Take-over Bid*

Soon after I arrived in Hillingdon a letter landed on the doormat. It was to be another life-changing moment. The letter was from Brigadier Denis Hunter, the recently appointed national youth secretary. He was thinking ahead. It was now June 1966 and 1968 was going to be Youth Year, and Denis had been toying with the idea of young people throughout the territory taking part in a kind of 'Oberammergau passion play' musical event. Knowing of my long connections with the musical pageants at the Royal Albert Hall, Denis wanted to get my reaction.

I saw the possibilities immediately. The idea of young people taking part in a musical happening was inspired. But in my reply I did wonder whether a musical based on the passion of Jesus would not be somewhat sombre for a youth year. Would something more sparkling offer wider opportunities?

Denis did not waste any time. In August 1966 I received an invitation to be part of a group of about a dozen people who were to meet at the West London divisional headquarters to discuss the idea further. In the group was a Captain John Gowans, stationed with his wife Gisèle at the Kingston-upon-Thames Corps, also in the West London Division. We hardly knew each other. In the discussion about possible approaches we perhaps did more speaking than any of the others, or perhaps Denis had planned it all along, for when the discussion moved on to who might tackle the writing of such a sparkling musical he handed out his marching orders. As John Gowans describes it in his memoirs *There's a Boy Here*:

At this point the eagle eye of Brigadier Hunter scanned his circle of collaborators. 'Captain Larsson,' he said, 'you write music, do you not?' John diffidently admitted that this was the case. The travelling eye fell on me: 'Captain Gowans,' he said, 'you write verses?' It sounded more like an accusation than an enquiry! I must have paled, I think, as I confessed that I had written a few. 'There we are, then,' said Denis, adding his most beatific smile.

'Captain Gowans will write the words and Captain Larsson the music. We have everything we need!'

John and I remain eternally grateful to Denis Hunter for thus bringing us together and giving us this commission. Denis was to become another mentor in my life. Even when I became General, retired Commissioner Denis Hunter phoned me with a list of helpful points. The last of these was the surprising 'enjoy it', which, seeing none other than Denis himself had suggested it, I determined to do.

Colonel Brindley Boon, in the official history of Salvation Army vocal music, *Sing the Happy Song,* writes that 'in 1966 two brilliant young officers came together to form the Army's own Rodgers and Hammerstein team'. The new Gowans and Larsson team now had to learn to work together in partnership. Kingston lies about 12 miles from Hillingdon and my Lambretta scooter soon knew the way there and back as if on autopilot. As John and I worked together we found that we had much in common. We soon gained a healthy respect for each other's gifts. We soon became friends. Our assignment was to write and produce a musical that could be test-performed in the autumn of 1967 in readiness for presentations by youth groups throughout the territory in the autumn of 1968.

We set ourselves certain specifications for the musical. It had to be lively, colourful and joyful. It had to say something important to both non-Salvationists and Salvationists. It had to be capable of production under the most varied circumstances – by large groups, small groups, on stages, on platforms, anywhere – and it had to fit into a time limit of about two hours. It also had to say something related to Youth Year and yet at the same time be of permanent interest.

We also set ourselves certain personal specifications, the chief being that our responsibilities as corps officers would be paramount, and that writing a musical would be an 'extra' that neither of us would allow to distract us from our main appointment. I mention that for two reasons. Firstly, because we both scrupulously held to that throughout the 23 years during which we were to write musicals together. Secondly, because the amount of space given to the musicals in this book might make it seem as if they dominated our lives far more than they ever did. I tell the story of the musicals in some detail because it is a unique story and seems to be of interest. But the musicals were never our vocation. They were our avocation.

The baby nearly died at birth. Establishing the specifications was the easy bit. Finding a theme that would fire our imagination proved much harder than we had anticipated. We thrashed around in our minds. We tried idea after idea. But nothing was right. The paper remained blank. We were both under great time pressure with our corps work – John even more so because he was taking a course of studies at the time. The next meeting of the planning group was soon due, and we had nothing, absolutely nothing to show. In the end – and I find this hard to believe as I look back – we decided to ask to be relieved of the task.

When the group met we told them that, regrettably, they had backed the wrong team and that we had come to the conclusion that we must admit defeat and let someone else have a go. We meant it. But to his everlasting credit, Dennis Hunter simply refused to consider that option. He told us that he and the group were convinced that we had it in us to write the musical – and would we now, please, go back and try yet again. We did. And the rest, as they say, is history. But John and I have a double indebtedness to Denis. Not only did he create the Gowans/Larsson musical partnership, he refused to un-create it!

The inspiration for *Take-over Bid* eventually came. The concept was simple. The young people of a corps think the answer to the lack of life in the corps lies in them taking over the running of the corps. But they discover a deeper truth. The answer lies in them themselves being taken over by God the Holy Spirit.

We got to work. John wrote the lyrics. I wrote the music. And as with nearly all our musicals, the script we did together. For most of the songs, John wrote the lyrics first and I set them to music. Occasionally the music came first, and the challenge was then how to communicate the tune from my head to John's. We arrived at a system of nonsense words. We would together devise a set of meaningless lyrics whose only merit was that they matched the musical notes perfectly – and John would then turn nonsense into inspired poetry.

Sometimes songs were written from only a phrase. For example, we decided that *Take-over Bid* needed a song on the theme of 'someone cares'. I remember going to the piano in the hall at Hillingdon and feeling my way musically around that phrase until the melody of a chorus, and then a verse, formed in my mind. Apart from the words 'someone cares' everything else was 'la, la, la' until John brought his skill to bear. John and I have written around 250 songs together, but 'Someone Cares' is still our favourite.

At first I often composed the music for a song and then said to myself: 'I can do better than that' – and the next day would write another melody. I would repeat the process until in the end I had a number of melodies – all for the same set of words. Then came the problem that only one of the tunes could survive. I would try combining the best bits of some to make a 'golden' tune, but that did not work. So a choice had to be made. But selecting the tune that would live and condemning the others to death proved painful. All of those tunes were my children! So I began working to a general pattern of whatever came first was 'it'. That certainly speeded things up and caused far less mental pain.

I have always wanted my songs to be singable – even by a congregation – and a further personal rule that I developed was that the congregation is always right! Congregations have an instinct for these things. And if, as sometimes happened, I later found that the congregation intuitively wanted to go one way in a melody line when I had charted another path. I would philosophically accept that I had probably got that sequence of notes wrong. If there was still time before publication, I would amend the music.

Presentation of the musical

To stage the musical we gathered a cast of young people drawn from corps in the West London Division and began rehearsing. Those young people were the guinea pigs not only for *Take-over Bid* but, because of all that we learnt from working with them, for all of the musicals that were yet to come.

It was a hand-to-mouth existence. Script and songs were written to meet the needs of the next rehearsal. And no sooner was one rehearsal over before the next one loomed. But eventually the full musical took shape. As was to become the pattern for our later musicals as well, John was the producer – director in American terminology – and I was the co-producer, musical director and pianist. I controlled the show from the piano which was placed front-stage in the orchestra pit. In *Take-over Bid* John also took the role of Harry, premiering the song 'A Dif-ferent Man'.

As good entrepreneurs we have made sure that most of our musicals have had more than one premiere. Why waste such occasions by having them only once? In the case of *Take-over Bid* the first performance was to be a private one for the 1,600 corps officers of the British Territory who would be gathered in councils at the Butlins holiday camp in Clacton-on-Sea. The public premiere was to be held two weeks later in the Reading Town Hall on Saturday 14 October 1967, with a second performance in the Acton Town Hall the next week.

Take-over Bid was conceived on a grand scale and had an option for the overture, arranged by Major Ray Steadman-Allen, to be played by a full brass band, with a large massed chorus of several hundred voices augmenting some of the songs during the performance of the musical, accompanied by the band. We used this option for the performances in Reading and Acton. But the option was rarely taken up when the musical was later performed around the territory, and we decided not to make this provision in subsequent musicals.

The dress rehearsal prior to the first performance before the audience of officers was a classic. We had hired a school hall for the occasion. Brigadier Denis Hunter came to see his dream come true. But instead it turned into a nightmare. Everything went wrong. The cast forgot their lines. They forgot to speak into the mikes and could not be heard. They sang out of tune. They had never done that before! Cues were missed and props failed to appear. At the end Denis came on stage and thanked everyone. Based more on faith than works, he assured us all that it would be wonderful on the night! To compound my misery, my scooter broke down on the way home and I had to push it for a couple of miles in pouring rain. It was a night best forgotten.

But Denis had been right. When the curtain opened that Sunday in the campus theatre, the cast rose to the occasion as if they were seasoned professionals. They sang like angels, remembered their lines, and everything worked like a marvel. The officers attending had not been given much information about what was to happen.

We wondered what their reaction would be. But we need not have been concerned, for at the end of the performance the officers rose to their feet in a standing ovation that never seemed to want to stop. That applause spoke volumes. The era of the musicals had begun. 'It's a winner,' declared *The Musician*. And we dared to believe it was.

Publication of the musical

With his gift for marketing, Denis had arranged for potential production teams from all of the divisions to be at the performances in Reading and Acton. It was October 1967, and everyone wanted copies of the music and script immediately so that divisional groups could start rehearsing in readiness for Youth Year 1968! But creating and staging a musical is very different from publishing one. And there was an immense amount of work that needed to be done.

There were due processes to be observed. The International Music Board had to approve all new music. The National Drama Council had to approve all new drama. But to which of these bodies should the musical be submitted? The Music Editorial Department, which belonged to International Headquarters, prepared all music for printing – but scripts were not their line. Salvationist Publishing and Supplies Ltd, which also was part of International Headquarters, printed and published all music. But SP&S did not consider that there was a market for a musical.

The road ahead seemed unclear – until Commissioner William Cooper, then British Commissioner, flexed his administrative muscles. He decided to cut through all the red tape and informed us that as a territorial commander he was going to exercise the right of every territorial commander in the world to publish music and drama without reference to any international body. He then announced that the Youth Department at National Headquarters was going to publish *Take-over Bid,* informed us that everything was now approved and would we please get on with it.

That was good news. But at a stroke I found myself a one-person music editorial and drama editing department. My task was to produce the script and music in 'camera-ready' form – so that each page could be photographed for printing – and the Youth Department would take the publishing process from there.

76

We decided that two separate volumes would be best and I first set to work on the script. Every word sung and every word spoken lay before me on the typed sheets we had used. What had to be added were directions about staging, choreography, props, costumes, lighting, amplification – everything that would enable someone who had not seen the show to stage it. It was a matter of capturing a two-hour visual and aural experience on paper. John and I went through the script and sought to record and describe everything that had happened minute by minute. Through separate production notes we also shared everything we had learnt in the course of producing the musical.

With corps commitments, the process of typing the script with these notes took me many weeks. The 18 hours of visitation expected of me weekly as a corps officer could not simply be abandoned. But I got to the electric typewriter whenever I could, and in the end 116 camera-ready pages lay before me. When we later saw presentations of *Take-over Bid* and our other musicals around the world, we noted how carefully producers had followed our notes, and were often amazed to find that the reproduction of the original choreography was identical down to the last detail.

But becoming a one-person music editorial department was an even greater challenge and took me into waters in which I had not swum before. For one thing, the music had to be written down first! The only music I had committed to paper were the vocal lines. There had been no point in writing out the accompaniments – the time-consuming part of composition – for I played the piano myself. It also meant that if we changed or even abandoned a song as we rehearsed the musical for its premiere, time and effort had not been wasted. But now the task had to be faced. And each page of music – vocal lines with lyrics and the full accompaniment – had to be written out with pen and ink in camera-ready form and the words typed in. The day of computer-generated music lay far in the future.

The clamour for the printed version of the musical was building up. But I was equally determined not to neglect my corps duties. Denis must have withstood a lot of pressure at that time, but he never showed impatience with me. In the end, however, he arranged for me to go to one of the Army's holiday homes on the coast in order to be able to concentrate on the task.

With large blank sheets of paper, a music pen – a special five-pointed pen with which to draw the music lines (for each page needed a different layout) – my typewriter with which to insert the lyrics, and a piano nearby to test the music as I wrote, I settled down to the task.

It was a fairly daunting prospect. I was going to be composer, editor and engraver. And apart from the piano lessons I had had, I was self-taught when it came to music. I had learnt composition mainly by analysing works of classic and Army 'masters', but as a teenager I had found on the bookshelf at home an old copy of Ebenezer Prout's classic *Harmony* dating from the 19th century and had absorbed that. I was therefore very conscious of the rules of harmony and part-writing, and was anxious not to commit some blunder that would expose my lack of a formal music education.

I was later to discover that in modern music practice much of the rigorous discipline represented by classic harmony teaching has been discarded. Nowadays, whatever sounds OK seems to be OK! But I didn't know that at the time. Perhaps that was all to the good, for I took immense pains to ensure that my musical 'grammar' was of a standard that would be acceptable to the International Music Editorial Department.

The task took me about two weeks. But at the end of that time, 47 camera-ready pages of music and lyrics lay on the table. I guarded them as if they were gold. The music did not have quite the quality-look of engraved music – but even I was surprised how much like the 'real thing' it turned out to be. The pages were soon on their way to the printer.

I have been blessed – or is it cursed? – with a strong perfectionist streak in my make-up. To this day I am not sure whether it is a bane or a boon. That streak dominated my life during those days as I sought to capture *Take-over Bid* on paper. I know that the musical was the better because of it – just as all my other creative projects have benefited from it. I always sleep on any writing – music or prose – for my subconscious mind will often provide me with a string of improvements when I wake.

But the streak can be a nuisance. I have sometimes felt like the writer who spent the morning putting in a comma and the afternoon taking it out again. I remember once taking the music of a new composition to the mailbox only to return home before posting it because I had thought of one note out of many thousands that could be improved. But however much a nuisance the perfectionist streak might be, deep down I don't think that I would be without it.

As Youth Year 1968 got under way, the script, the music, the parts I had scored for the pit orchestra and the lighting plot became available – and soon became best-sellers not only in Britain but around the Army world too. For interest I added together the amount of time I personally had invested in *Take-over Bid* to that point. Counting everything – writing, rehearsals, performances, travelling and everything else – it came to a thousand hours.

At one point I did wonder whether music should really be so dominant in my life. Was that not something I had put on the altar when I entered training? And music was taking me into the limelight. Was that right? Should I not be giving myself absolutely 100 per cent to being a good corps officer and shun everything that might detract from that?

I decided to consult Major Fred Brown, an officer all we young officers looked up to, who now was the corps officer at the Regent Hall Corps. I shared my dilemma with him in the officer's room at the Regent Hall. Was it not time I gave up music and devoted myself to the really important things in life? He listened attentively, and then gently said: 'John, if the Lord has given you a gift it is because he wants you to use it.'

Insights are often embarrassingly simple. I suppose a child could have spoken those words. But in my muddled state I had not been able to see the obvious. Those few words came to me as a revelation from God, and determined my course.

I am now more than ever sure that those 1,000 hours spent on *Take-over Bid* were hours well invested. *Take-over Bid* is still being performed in various parts of the world all these many years later. And I don't think that Hillingdon Corps suffered. If anything they seemed to be proud of their corps officer. Best of all, *Take-over Bid* was to bring Freda and me together – but that is a story yet to be told. And as I look back it seems to me that what was true for Hillingdon and musicals has been true for all my appointments since. For me the ten-thousands of hours I have given to the ministry of music have all been part of saying yes to life.

The inner life

Life is always lived in many dimensions, and while I was engaged with the corps ministry at Hillingdon and the writing of the musical, things were happening on other fronts as well.

Spiritually the yearning for 'something more' was as intense as ever. I set aside time on a regular basis to work my way through the New Testament in the *New English Bible* translation. I underlined in red every phrase which I felt demanded something from me, and I underlined in green every promise I met regarding fullness of life in the Spirit. I saw promises that somehow I never seemed to have seen before. I knew they were meant for me, and they intensified even more the sense of inner longing. These yearnings were further deepened through prayer partnerships.

Something else happened to me at Hillingdon. As a counterpoint and in utter contrast to my spiritual yearnings, the lights suddenly went out. Totally without warning and for no reason that I could discern, I found myself in the depth of depression.

I had never experienced anything like it. On some days it almost immobilised me. It was frightening. I was in a dark tunnel and no light at the end of it was to be seen. But by the grace of God I came through that experience. I consulted the doctor. I sought help from wise spiritual counsellors. And I kept going. I was determined that no one in the corps should know how desperate I felt. And despite the utter emptiness I sometimes felt when leading worship on Sundays, they never did. But Gunnar did and I will always be grateful to him for his understanding and discretion. Then after some months the clouds gradually started to scatter. I began to glimpse the sun again. And one day, as surprisingly as when it had all begun, the sun shone fully once more from a blue sky.

I have never again been through anything similar, even when I have been under the greatest of pressures. I still do not understand what happened. Perhaps it was a necessary experience. It has given me a deep empathy with all who are called to go through a desert experience. I can agonise with them. I do know that God used the experience to strengthen my faith. I learnt to live by faith and not by feelings.

I often took comfort from a scene C. S. Lewis paints in *The Screwtape Letters.* Screwtape, the chief devil, is writing to the junior devil, Wormwood – and in the upside-down world of devilry he refers to God as 'our Enemy':

> Do not be deceived, Wormwood. Our cause is never more in danger than when a human, no longer desiring, but still intending, to do our Enemy's will, looks round upon a universe from which every trace of him seems to have vanished, and asks why he has been forsaken, and still obeys.

It was by the grace of God, for I cannot take any credit for it, that I still obeyed. I simply went on. And I came through. What adds to the wonderment for me as I look back is that much of the music for *Take-over Bid* was written during those months. It is by far the most sparkling of all our musicals. When Eric Ball heard the music of *Take-over Bid* he thanked me publicly for putting the joy back into Salvation Army music. How does one explain the miracle of joyous music born in pain?

Ealing Corps

In May 1968, after two years at Hillingdon, I moved down the Uxbridge Road to corps number three along that road – Ealing Corps. Gunnar Granholm had returned to Sweden after a year. Lieutenant John Howarth had been with me for some months of the second year. But now I was heading for my next appointment, where Cadet David Botting would be joining me for his summer-term appointment. It was good to work with both John and David. Ealing was a well-established corps with a long tradition, but lying closer to the heart of London it had suffered over the years from the migration of Salvationists towards the suburbs. Through the inspired ministry of Major and Mrs Robert and Bronwyn Menary the corps had experienced a resurgence and was in fine form as I took over. There I met another splendid group of local officers and Salvationists determined to reach out to the community around the hall. I look back with joy on the two years spent at Ealing.

But when David went back to the college, I was only alone for the remainder of the first year. For Freda joined me for the second!

81

Marriage

My spiritual questing had not been my only quest over the years. I had been asking the Lord for a long time to help me find my life companion. I hadn't left it all to him either. During the years at the college I had had opportunity to get to know many attractive women cadets. But the 'aha' moment had not yet come.

I had noticed, more than noticed, a certain Cadet Freda Turner who entered training in 1963. But any contact was because a cadet in my section had started going out with her! Such extracurricular activities by cadets were still officially frowned on, but I had been giving my tacit support – and in the process had discovered that part of me envied my cadet colleague.

Now as the corps officer in Ealing I knew that Captain Freda Turner had become the youth officer for Cornwall, in the south-west of England. I also knew that the other friendship had come to an end. So when Freda in her youth officer capacity wrote to me about the possibility of the West London cast of *Take-Over Bid* visiting Cornwall, I decided that this could do with some personal follow-up. I suggested we should meet at the October officers' councils, which once again were to be united councils for the whole territory at Clacton-on-Sea, to chat about it.

We met over supper one evening. And we met the next evening. And the next. Arranging visits for musical casts are complex matters! I knew immediately that this was 'it'. We were meant for each other. We both knew it. Following councils I drove down overnight to Cornwall a number of times – I had a car by then – to spend a day with Freda, but within weeks we decided to get married.

Getting to know Freda's parents was a delight. Brigadier and Mrs Thomas and Winifred Turner were outstanding corps officers, who were to give nearly 40 years in corps ministry before moving into public relations work, and were to lead some of the most significant corps in the British Territory. Dad Turner was an exceptional preacher, but most of all he had a gift of caring for people, often in very practical ways, when they most needed it. The Turners are still spoken of with affection bordering on awe in the corps where they were stationed. I could not have wished for better parents-in-law.

In those days orders and regulations required a letter to be written to the divisional commander requesting permission to start courting. Later this had to be followed by a letter requesting permission to get engaged. And following engagement of at least six months, a third letter was required in due course for permission to get married.

We were both mature people. I was by then 30 and Freda was 29. There was no point in hanging about. So I sat down and wrote three separate letters to the divisional commander. I dated them each with one day's difference so as not to confuse the filing system at divisional headquarters. I asked for permission to court, become engaged to, and marry Freda. I put the letters in the mail. Within a few days I had three letters back granting the three requests!

So on 5 July 1969, Freda and I were married at the Kingston-upon-Thames Corps – the corps from which Freda had entered training. At our request, Freda's father conducted the actual wedding ceremony and my father led the opening part of the service. Freda was welcomed with open arms by the comrades at Ealing Corps and we quickly settled into a pattern of shared ministry.

Musical *Hosea*

During the Ealing years, John and I began work on a second musical. But meanwhile in Youth Year the original West London cast of *Take-over Bid* was much sought after for performances of the musical. John and Gisèle Gowans had moved to Bromley Corps in the South London Division, and at the request of that division had produced the musical there also with a cast of young people from South London. When *Take-over Bid* was presented in the Royal Albert Hall that year during national youth councils, the two casts worked together. West London handled the stage-work and South London formed a backing chorus.

John Gowans took the part of 'Harry' in both the West and the South London casts! He was therefore in great demand. And no more so than when both casts were asked to perform the musical simultaneously one Sunday afternoon at the Butlins Holiday Fellowship at Clacton-on-Sea. The fellowship used to draw crowds of 5,000 and two of the cavernous theatres on the campus had to be used for the presentation. 'Harry' is not on stage throughout, but makes appearances from time to time, especially to sing 'A Dif-ferent Man'. We discovered that if we timed the South London presentation to start 30 minutes after the West London one, John would be able to dash back and forth between the theatres for the several times required. We knew it was going to be tight. And so it proved on the day. At one point I had to stretch the *allargando* almost to breaking point – but he then appeared!

The suggestion for a second musical came from Commissioner William Cooper, and it was he who came up with the idea that it should be based on the Old Testament prophet Hosea. We got to work. The story speaks of God's unconditional love for us. If Hosea could love his wife Gomer even though she left him, how much more will God love us even though we have let him down. For the title we hovered between *For Better for Worse* and *Hosea*, but finally settled for the latter.

As we had done with *Take-over Bid*, a cast was gathered and rehearsals began while the musical was still being written. This time it was South London that was the chosen guinea pig division. We got off to a false start with our writing. The original setting for *Hosea* was in a secondary school, with Bill – the Hosea of the story – as a teacher. But that setting proved too limiting, and we therefore switched the setting to a youth club, with Bill as the youth club leader. Bill and Betty get married in the musical, and the song featured in the stage wedding – 'What shall I ask for you?' – was first sung at our own wedding. After much writing, re-writing and rehearsing, the musical was eventually ready to be presented to the world. There would of course be two premieres!

The first presentation of *Hosea* was at the territorial officers' councils in October 1969 and was followed some weeks later by the public premiere in Lewisham Town Hall on 12 November 1969. The united territorial officers' councils were held in Bognor Regis that year. We had not been given the best time slot – starting 9 pm on arrival day, with many officers having made long journeys. We wondered whether they would be in a mood to watch a musical.

I grew quite concerned at one point during the presentation. As the musical director in the orchestra pit I had my back to the audience. But I could hear that the audience had become restless.

There were all kinds of noises that I could not identify. We were at a very tender point in the drama on stage. Were members of the audience beginning to walk out? I turned round to look. I need not have worried. The noise I was hearing was of 1,600 officers blowing their noses into their handkerchiefs – so moved were they by what they were seeing. We had rehearsed these scenes so often we had forgotten that they were meant to produce just that kind of effect.

After the public premiere came the matter of publishing the musical. With the success of *Take-over Bid,* SP&S Ltd offered to undertake publication. But Commissioner William Cooper was not having that. *Hosea* was again to be published by the Youth Department.

The musical had over-run the two-hour limit for which we had aimed, and John and I therefore met for a couple of pruning sessions. They were painful! But I have to admit that a bit more pain would have been even better. For though the published version of *Hosea* can be performed in the space of two hours, it requires immensely slick movements from one scene to the next with no time being lost for changes of scenery.

We were to discover in the future that few production teams managed to perform the musical within the two-hour slot. That to us was a disappointment. And I have always regretted we did not prune more thoroughly while we had the chance! But when it came to the publication process, I am glad to say that this time help had been drafted in. The script and music still had to be prepared – to the last word and the last note. But the preparation of the pages to camera-ready standard was outsourced.

After a special presentation of *Hosea* in London's West End, John Lambert, the drama critic of the *London Evening News* wrote: 'Hallelujah! The Sally Army's got a hit! Given a break this musical could become a smash hit, playing in the ordinary theatre ... That's the place it should and deserves to be.'

John Gowans and I have sometimes wondered whether there should have been a third person in the partnership, someone with the time and skills and connections to market the musicals professionally. Perhaps the break into the world of theatre would then have come. But we ourselves were too busy with our main appointments to devote much time and energy to such considerations. We were glad that the musicals were serving a useful missional purpose within the Army, and were pleased when they later were taken up by other churches.

Bromley Temple Corps

In May 1970 Freda and I were appointed to Bromley Temple in the South London Division. I was 32 and Freda 30 at the time. We were to follow none other than the Gowanses, who had moved there from Kingston three years before. Seeing that by then 'Gowans and Larsson' was a phrase that tripped from the tongue, we never quite knew whether the move to Bromley was simply the result of an automatic reflex reaction on the part of the powers that be – after Gowans, who? – or was a brilliant idea on their part. But whatever the thinking behind the move, it turned out to be inspired – and for us it was another indication that our times were in God's hands.

Bromley was a remarkable corps. There were 380 soldiers on the roll, of whom 120 were active or retired officers. This included 30 commissioners. Bromley also had a large young people's corps. For youth councils we could muster a contingent of 100 in the 15-30 age group. Every section of the corps was alive and well. The corps engaged in many forms of community service. There were 300 chairs in the hall, and if you wanted to be sure to get one of them on Sunday morning you had to get there early. Often additional seating had to be brought in.

Within six weeks of our arrival I was due to leave for a two-month session at the International College for Officers. We therefore decided to try to visit as many of the soldiers as possible before then – working our way through the roll from number one up – and put everything else to one side. That got us off to a good start. Freda was in charge in my absence.

We were to be in Bromley for nearly four years, and for us they were memorable and very precious years. Both our children were born there. Karl on 17 December 1971 and Kevin on 15 May 1973. With Bromley Corps usually having had very senior officers in charge, the corps had not in living memory had children born to its officers. So Karl and Kevin were considered to be very special.

86

God also blessed our ministry there in a singular way. Ours was the privilege of experiencing something akin to what happened in the Early Church, as described in the Book of Acts: 'Day by day the Lord added to their number those whom he was saving' (2:47, *NEB)*. New people came – sometimes directly through our activities but as often as not quite spontaneously – and found the Lord. At one point we noticed to our surprise that we had been enrolling on average a new soldier from outside the corps every month.

We turned the evening meeting on every first Sunday of the month into a 'Festival of Gospel Song', and the hall was always full for these occasions, with new people attending. For these events I specialised in seven-minute messages and aimed to make them presentations with a punch. My messages in the Sunday morning meetings were also often brief. The meetings always had to finish exactly after one hour because of other activities which followed. I therefore found myself acquiring a reputation for short speaking. But when people commented I used to kid them that the messages only *seemed* short! Those three-minute talks I had given at the college were good preparation!

The team of local leaders was an inspiration. But as often happens with suburban corps in London, there was a continual inflow and outflow of transferring Salvationists as work either brought them to Bromley or took them away. This meant that there was also a continual turnover in the ranks of the local officers. It was quite a task to make sure that all the positions in the corps were covered. There was much latent leadership potential in the corps, and at one time we decided to engage in a major campaign of consultation and visitation to seek to discover and release that potential. The aim was to fill every possible leadership vacancy in the senior and junior corps, and it involved us in many hours of work. But there was a heart-warming response, and the campaign culminated one Sunday morning when at a special commissioning service we commissioned 35 new local officers.

Musical *Jesus Folk*

With the success of *Take-over Bid* and *Hosea* the musicals were now on a roll. John and I were asked to write and produce a short musical for presentation as a finale to the British Congress being planned for July 1972 – to be held in the Wembley Arena. It was suggested that this might be performed by young people who would be gathering the previous week at Sunbury Court for a 'vocational house party'. The concept of vocational weeks for young people who wanted to think about their future was the inspired brainwave of the newly appointed national candidates secretary, Major Hubert Boardman. We did not know it then, but musicals and the annual vocational house party were to be associated for many years ahead. They dovetailed beautifully!

John and I met to discuss what the musical might be about. We had some material available. At the invitation of a Christian group in Australia, we had previously written some songs about personalities mentioned in the gospels who had met with Jesus. They were very simple songs for it was a musical for children. We wondered whether this material could be expanded.

Ideas flowed and the embryo of what was to become the musical *Jesus Folk* began to take shape in our minds. The children's songs could be woven into new material – and a 45-minute musical could be written. The musical would not only tell the stories of people whose lives had been transformed by Jesus, it would tell the story of his death and resurrection as well. The result exceeded our expectations. The new material focusing on the crucifixion and resurrection of the Lord proved to be very powerful, whilst the original songs gave lightness to the earlier part of the musical. This short version of *Jesus Folk* was performed on Sunday 10 July 1972 in the Wembley Arena.

There were immediate requests for the music and script to be published. But by this time we had become convinced that the concept of *Jesus Folk* had even greater potential. We therefore incorporated still more material into the musical, especially in the early scenes, in order to expand it into a two-hour production.

John by then had moved to Hull as the divisional youth secretary, and the honour of presenting the first performance of *Jesus Folk* in its final full-length version fell to the young people of Bromley Corps, with me as producer and music director. The premiere of *Jesus Folk* in its full-length form was on 25 January 1973 at the Fairfield Halls, Croydon. And this time it was to be published by SP&S Ltd!

Top: With my parents and sister Miriam when we returned from South America in 1956

Top right: In Denmark with my 'hard-to-love' instrument

Above left: Grandfather Karl Larsson

Above right: Grandfather Alfred Benwell

Right: As a junior member of the senior band in Chile

Clockwise from left: Cadet of the Faithful Session; in action; holding the flag with the sergeants of the Courageous Session. Seated on the front row, left to right: Major Stan Golbourn, Lieut-Commissioner Frederick Coutts, Lieut-Colonel Albert Mingay and Major Albert Drury. Captain Harry Read stands behind Lieut-Colonel Mingay and Major Drury.

Left: Cadet Freda Turner

Below: The looks say it all!

Bottom: Next to Freda are Captain John Gowans (my best man) and Freda's parents, Brigadier and Mrs Thomas and Winifred Turner. Next to me are Brenda (Freda's sister and bridesmaid) and my parents, Commissioner and Mrs Sture and Flora Larsson.

Top: Arriving in Santiago, Chile, in 1980, I speak my first words in Spanish after 24 years. Freda stands with our sons Karl and Kevin.

Above left: Speaking at the opening of the new training college in Chile

Above right: A large parcel causes Christmas excitement for our sons

Left: Pausing on the way to the Trail of the Incas

Above: General Eva Burrows inaugurates the new United Kingdom Territory

Left: Divisional congress in Newquay, United Kingdom Territory

Below: Finding refreshment in God's nature

Top: The Gowans/Larsson team in action on a visit to the USA

Above left: Musical *Son of Man* in Chile

Above right: Working together at Sunbury

Left: Writing a new song at the vocational house party

Right: Commissioner Denis Hunter, who brought John and me together, prays the final prayer in our retirement service at International Headquarters

Take-Over Bid (The Salvation Army, British Territory, 1968)

Hosea (The Salvation Army, British Territory, 1970)

Jesus Folk (SP&S Ltd, 1973)

Spirit! (SP&S Ltd, 1975)

Glory! (SP&S Ltd, 1977)

White Rose (SP&S Ltd, 1978)

The Blood of the Lamb (SP&S Ltd, 1979)

Son of Man! (The Salvation Army, USA Western Territory, 1984)

Man – Mark II (The Salvation Army, USA Western Territory, 1985)

The Meeting (SP&S Ltd, 1990)

Above: With Karl and Kevin just before we leave for New Zealand in 1993

Left: In snowy Sweden

Below: At dedication of a new fishing boat in Tonga, donated by The Netherlands Territory

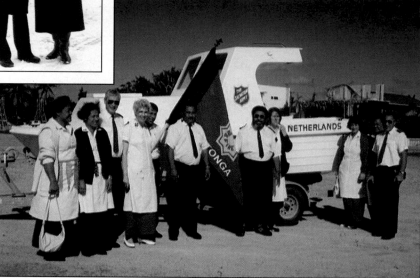

That Bromley Corps could handle the logistics of an extensive series of presentations of *Jesus Folk* was largely due to Ernest Adnams. Ernie was the corps organising secretary. I think the position had been created especially for him, for he was an organisational genius. His application to his duties was so phenomenal as to often give us a bad conscience. He would ring up at around 10.30 pm when Freda and I were enjoying our evening cup of cocoa to say that he was just about to begin organising the Self-Denial Appeal door-to-door collecting for the next year and could I let him have this or that detail?

When it came to the performances of *Jesus Folk* by the Bromley cast – and many of those were held in various centres – Ernie organised them down to the smallest detail and made sure that every ticket was sold. When he suggested we should hire the Westminster Central Hall – a 2,500-seater hall in the centre of London – I thought he was being over-ambitious. 'Don't you worry, Captain,' he said. 'If you are prepared to produce the musical there, I'll make sure that the hall is full.' And on the night, so it was.

Musical *Spirit!*

The musical *Spirit!* also belongs in part to our time in Bromley. But the birth of the musical took place one inspired, sunlit Monday morning in the divisional commander's quarters in Cleveland, Ohio, in the USA. John Gowans and I had visited the division for youth councils which included a presentation of *Jesus Folk*. Major Hubert Boardman had asked for another musical for the 1973 vocational house party. As we sat in the front room of the quarters we looked at possibilities.

There are times when ideas just flow, and that morning was one of them. With *Jesus Folk* telling the story of the life, death, and resurrection of Jesus, a sequel that would continue the story seemed the natural 'next'. And *Spirit!* – with an exclamation mark to emphasise vitality – seemed the obvious title.

As we talked, ideas and concepts tumbled out, and before the morning was over the shape of the musical lay ready. It was to be in two parts. The first part would deal with the coming of the Holy Spirit and the impact of the Spirit on the Early Church, ending with the martyrdom of Stephen and the conversion of Saul. The second part would deal with Paul's missionary journeys, climaxing with

Paul's martyrdom in Rome. We planned to write part one in time for the 1973 vocational house party and present it then. Part two we would write in time for the 1974 vocational house party, and we would then premiere the full musical that year.

Without us realising the full significance at the time, a procedural pattern was becoming established. If Denis Hunter impelled us to write the first two musicals, it was the vocational house parties that over a period of years prompted us to write the next four – *Jesus Folk, Spirit!, Glory!* and *The Blood of the Lamb.*

The yearly pattern ran something as follows. Around January the candidates secretary would phone to ask what the title would be for that year's musical in July as he needed to book the hall and print and sell tickets. That would prompt John and me to get that absolutely crucial point settled. We had to know what the musical was going to be about! In May he would phone again to remind us that he needed to get the script and music stencils run off – had we anything to show yet? That would prompt us into a flurry of creative activity. I am pleased to say that the material was always ready by the due date in July – but sometimes only just.

Sunbury Court could accommodate 100 young people in those days, so our musicals were always written for a cast of 100. The delegates would meet on a Saturday, and that evening John would introduce the musical and I would play the music and begin teaching the songs. So tight were our time-lines that John himself would often be hearing some of the songs for the first time. British young people are incredibly good at sight-reading and learn fast, so by the end of the evening great strides would have been made.

Late evening, John and I would interview each of the hundred delegates for about a minute each to ask about their gifts and previous dramatic experience. The two of us would then continue into the night and draw up the cast list. By Sunday morning the cast list would be published.

The musical was to be presented to the public the next weekend. There was no time to lose. A creation that as yet existed only on paper had to be made to come to life. There were spoken lines and songs and choreography to be mastered, costumes to be sewn, staging and stage props to be prepared, amplification and lighting to be sorted out. A constant spur was the knowledge that every seat in the hall was already sold – and the halls booked seemed to get larger each year! But apart from the final day or two, rehearsals through the week would be mornings only, for the candidates secretary quite rightly did not want the musical to dominate the week to the exclusion of everything else.

Somehow it never failed to work. As with the passing of the years the demands of the musicals grew greater we sometimes took the precaution of ensuring that one or two key young persons who might take the lead roles would be present for the week. But for the most, we simply took what came! And considering that the young people came together for their vocational, not musical, interests it was all something of an annual miracle. They were simply wonderful and never let us down. But I think John and I must also have had nerves of steel in those days.

When on the opening evening of the 1973 vocational house party we introduced part one of the musical *Spirit!*, I think we all felt that we were about to experience something very special, and so it turned out to be. As planned, part one of the musical was presented at the conclusion of the week – at the Regent Hall, London. The atmosphere that evening sparkled with the electricity of the Spirit. The impact of that performance remains vividly with me. There is more to tell about the musical *Spirit!* – by far the most influential of our musicals – but as its writing straddled two appointments I will leave the remainder of the story to the next chapter.

To pastures new
We became majors during our time in Bromley. When farewell orders came in January 1974 we were very sorry to sever the links with Bromley Temple Corps. The corps people had become very precious to us in those years. What we did not know was that the link with the corps would be renewed many times in future years. We were to be soldiers of the corps during the years when I was training principal, assistant to the Chief of the Staff, territorial commander, Chief of the Staff, and General – and Bromley is our corps in retirement. Karl and Kevin were to spend their teenage years in the corps.

Bromley Corps is home to us. During the years of territorial and international leadership it was good to be part of a family where we could slip in and just be John and Freda. And Bromley continues to be a remarkable corps. It combines all the virtues of a traditional corps with those of a contemporary one. The young people's work still flourishes and attracts a steady stream of new children and young people. The Lord is still adding to the Bromley Corps those whom he is saving.

Our new appointments were as territorial youth secretary and territorial guide organiser for the Scotland Territory. By 1974 the British Commissioner was Commissioner Kaare Westergaard, my former principal when I had been on the training staff – and who, as mentioned, had not acceded to the request from Norway that I should be music secretary there. I later learnt that there had been another 'might have been' with our move to Scotland. The commissioner shared with us that he had planned to make us divisional leaders, but had drawn back at the last moment because our children were so young. I never became a divisional commander, one of the Army's key appointments.

Out of curiosity I checked while writing this book which Generals since the era of William and Bramwell Booth had not been divisional commanders. I found I was in good company: George Carpenter, Frederick Coutts, Arnold Brown and Eva Burrows. I sometimes wished that the DC dimension could somehow have been part of my experience. But I would not for anything have wanted to miss Scotland or miss the national youth secretary appointment in the British Territory that followed. So it really boils down to the fact that you can't do everything in life!

Chapter Six

YOUTH, MUSICALS AND MORE

JANUARY was not the best month in which to arrive in Glasgow. Our quarters had not been occupied for some weeks, and we sometimes wondered whether our one means of heating – an open fire in the front room – would ever heat the whole house. But it eventually did. And the warmth of the Salvationists was immediately evident. We look back on our years in Scotland with special affection. Karl was just over two and Kevin eight months when we arrived. They were precious years when we watched them grow and develop. In time they acquired rich Scottish accents!

We enjoyed the country and the people, and we enjoyed working with the Salvationists of Scotland. The Scotland Territory was then a separate territorial unit. The territorial leaders were Colonel and Mrs Ernest Anderson, and we could not have wanted better leaders to initiate us into the world of territorial leadership. The Scotland Territory was comprised of about 100 corps, so getting to know the young people's workers and the young people themselves was a manageable proposition. I was not only territorial youth secretary but also territorial candidates secretary, and those who were preparing to become officers soon became members of our extended family.

As the territorial guide organiser, Freda quickly found herself immersed in the world of scouting. She also found time to be the home league fellowship secretary at Springburn Corps, where we were soldiers.

Most of the corps were within easy reach by car from Glasgow, and visits to the more distant locations – including the remote Orkney and Shetland Islands – added a sense of adventure. The Sunday 'specialling' challenge was how to cope with a huge Scottish Sunday dinner followed three hours later by an equally large Scottish tea-meal – often cooked complete with chips. 'Balvonie', then the Army's conference centre, soon became our second home because of the many residential weekends held there for candidates, young people's workers and young people.

After we had got over the initial shock of finding that our official day ended by 4 pm – so different from the life we had known in corps and at the training college – we discovered that there was extra time for channelling energies in new directions. What with exploring new initiatives in the fields of youth ministry and candidates, and developing further my interests in writing and composing, the years in Scotland were to prove some of my most creative.

Within a couple of weeks of arrival in Scotland I travelled back to London for the retirement meeting for my parents at International Headquarters. Sadly I had to return just six months later when my father was unexpectedly promoted to Glory. The news reached us the day we began our first territorial music camp. I left the camp in the capable hands of Freda and the assistant territorial youth secretary and his wife, Major and Mrs Ron and Barbara Johnson, and drove down to London that night to see my mother through the trying days ahead.

My regard for the young people's local officers with whom we were called to serve in Scotland, and later in England, Wales and Ireland, was and remains unbounded. Young people's work in the United Kingdom has traditionally been very strong, and rests on the willing service of thousands of young people's workers who week in and week out give of themselves to their tasks. This ministry to children and youth is becoming increasingly difficult. And the tide of secularism that flows today was already being felt in the 1970s.

A continual challenge was how to attract new children to Sunday school – the company meeting – with little or no support from parents. Sunday school attendances had been in decline in all churches for many years. In the Army, the greatest and very sudden declines in the United Kingdom had occurred in the 1930s, and it was proving difficult to reverse a negative trend.

For one conference of young people's local officers at Balvonie I invited the head of the National Association for Sunday Schools in Scotland to come and speak to us. When he arrived I discovered he was well into his 70s. But he charmed us and disarmed us all by telling us that he personally was a walking illustration of the challenges that the Sunday school movement as a whole was facing. From heading for many years a large and bustling office of Sunday school experts, only he was now left – and as a volunteer.

'I sometimes wonder,' he said, 'if historians of the future, when looking back on the story of the Christian Church through the centuries, will record that for a period of about 250 years the Church used a concept that it called "Sunday schools" to attract and evangelise children – but that with time this concept lost its effectiveness and was replaced by different methods.' At the time it sounded akin to heresy to me. But the more recent emphasis on families worshipping together on a Sunday – with children going into classes for a time according to ages – and the increased use of weekdays for communicating the truths of the gospel to children, point to the prophetic nature of the comments made.

Spiritual Breakthrough

The inner spiritual quest for 'something more' had not abated and became more intense as we settled in Scotland. At one point we invited friends of ours, a young officer couple stationed in England who had both been baptised in the Spirit, to travel north and stay with us for the express purpose that we might explore the subject further and that they might pray with me. I desperately wanted to experience what they had experienced. The occasion of their coming remains a warm and vivid memory. I treasure the intimate conversations we had – and their prayers for us, and especially for me. But despite their long and intense pounding of the doors of Heaven on my behalf, and my taking hold of every ounce of faith of which I was capable, the breakthrough I yearned for did not come.

My quest was partly spiritual and partly intellectual. With my heart I wanted to experience the fullness of all that I believed God had in store for me. With my mind I wanted to understand *how* God grants such experiences to his children. Always before me was the picture of what Samuel Brengle had experienced on that Tuesday morning long ago when a heaven of love filled his soul and he walked out over Boston common weeping for joy. How did one account for such moments of spiritual breakthrough?

For a number of years I had been collecting written testimonies about such experiences. They were drawn from biographical sources both historical and contemporary. I often used to warm my heart by reading these accounts. And the idea of writing a major thesis exploring such experiences began to form itself in my mind.

The outline of the thesis soon began to take shape. I would call it *The Brengle Experience*, and in the first part would examine the nature and content of such moments of intense spiritual experience, using the biographical material I had gathered, and would then move on to explore how such moments are best accounted for. Are they best explained in terms of entire sanctification, or baptism of the Spirit, or moments of spiritual illumination, or are there other terms? And are there factors that are common to all such doctrinal explanations?

I discovered a research library near territorial headquarters that had an amazing collection of Christian books and documents bearing on the theme I was going to explore. For many months I spent time there early in the mornings before territorial headquarters opened, and occasionally in the lunch hours and in the evenings as well. I was excited by this creative task, and the manuscript grew apace.

My mother, with her literary interests, followed the treatise's progress with avid interest, and one day in the course of conversation mentioned its existence to a friend of hers, Commissioner Kathleen Kendrick, who happened to be the literary secretary at International Headquarters.

Commissioner Kendrick asked if she might see a copy, and this led in time to me having an interview with Mr Edward England, the religious editor of Hodder and Stoughton, in which he expressed interest in publishing some of my material. We both recognised that for publication the material would have to be shortened and reshaped. Mr England suggested that a new biography of Samuel Brengle might be a suitable vessel for this purpose and offered me the task.

After reflection I felt that to try to fit my material into a biography would be too limiting and would divert me from completing the thesis. Apart from anything else, a great deal of my material would have to be omitted as being too specific to the Army. But the idea survived and Colonel William Clark was in due course given the task and wrote the fine biography of Samuel Brengle that Hodder and Stoughton published in 1980.

Having closed that door for use of the material, I then began to condense and reshape what I had written in order to offer it for internal publication by the Army. The basic structure remained the same. The manuscript of *The Brengle Experience* examined what had happened to young Sam at the age of 25, instanced parallels in the lives of other Christians, and explored how such experiences could best be accounted for.

The writing of the book was a labour of love that spanned both our time in Scotland and my subsequent appointment to the Youth Department in London. By the time the manuscript was nearing completion Lieut-Colonel Walter Hull had become the literary secretary at International Headquarters. The colonel informed me that there were misgivings about the title *The Brengle Experience*. It was felt this linked the subject too strongly with the experience of one person. I took this on board, and after thought changed the title to *Spiritual Breakthrough* and added the subtitle 'The Holy Spirit and Ourselves'. I then further reshaped the material whilst still retaining Samuel Brengle's testimony as the starting point.

The manuscript was in due course accepted for publication and was typeset, and proof copies were printed. But it fell at the final hurdle. General Arnold Brown apparently still felt a measure of discomfort about the basic concept and with some of the nuances in the book. The literary secretary told me that the book was lying in the General's bottom drawer – and that it was likely to remain there.

I did not give the matter much further thought. My life was too busy with other activities and other projects. Writing the book had helped me to sort out my thinking, and if it was not to see the light of day, it was just one of those things. You can't win them all. The book moved out of my field of consciousness. And in time we moved on to our next appointment, which was to Chile.

Some years later while we were serving in Chile I received a letter out of the blue from the literary secretary at International Headquarters, who by this time was Lieut-Colonel Lyndon Taylor. The colonel said that whilst exploring the files of the department he had come across the proofs of *Spiritual Breakthrough*. He felt that the book had something important to say, and that the points at issue were not insurmountable and could probably be taken care of with some rewriting. Would I be prepared to revive the project?

I was of course pleased with this development and grateful to Lieut-Colonel Taylor. I understood why the General had had reservations, and as I re-read the proofs I could see ways of taking these into account by reshaping some of the sections. Adding to the fascination of the rewrite was the fact that I had to seek to retain as much as possible of the material that had already been typeset in order to save costs. I spent long hours in recasting the material, and so that the book should speak more clearly to the heart as well as to the mind, I also added two pastoral chapters at the end.

The conclusions I reach in *Spiritual Breakthrough* are that these moments of intense inpouring of the Spirit are best accounted for as completing experientially what was always potentially ours in the experience of new birth. Scripturally, theologically and in experience the 'something more' is not something different. It is more, much more, of the same. We are like people who have received an inheritance, who then discover that the inheritance is far larger than we realised.

In this connection the old term 'full salvation' is rich in meaning – a theme which I develop in the book. 'Full Salvation' is now the title of the chapter on sanctification in the 1998 edition of the handbook of doctrine, *Salvation Story*. We are not called to 'half salvation'. We are called to the fullness of what God wants to give us through his Spirit. And, as I write in *Spiritual Breakthrough*, 'If for *any* reason we have failed to be filled at the heavenly banquet, we must come again – and if needs be, again and again.'

John of the Cross, the great Spanish religious leader of the 16th century, speaks of 'touches' of God on the soul. 'Such touches,' he writes, 'enrich it marvellously. A single one of them may be sufficient to abolish at a stroke imperfections of which the soul during its whole life has vainly tried to rid itself, and to leave it adorned with virtues and loaded with supernatural gifts.'

Such experiences of the Spirit can fill us and cleanse us to an unimaginable degree. We fortunately no longer make exaggerated ethical claims about being 'without sin' and being 'unblameable and unreprovable before God'. The footnote to article 10 of our doctrines, which had troubled me when I was a cadet, was never an intrinsic part of the doctrine and has since been removed. But neither is it for us to set any limits whatever to what God might accomplish in us through the fullness of the power of the Spirit in our lives.

The prayer of Paul for the Thessalonians already quoted must be our own constant prayer – for ourselves: 'May God himself, the God of peace, make you holy in every part, and keep you sound in spirit, soul and body, without fault when our Lord Jesus comes.' And we have the great assurance: 'He who calls you is to be trusted; he will do it' (1 Thessalonians 5:23-24, *NEB)*.

But I have also had to conclude that not all believers will experience such breakthroughs of the Spirit as vividly as Samuel Brengle did that Tuesday morning. The wonder and glory of never-to-be-forgotten *felt* inpourings of the Spirit are not given to all of God's children. Some are called to experience the presence and power of the Spirit in less intense ways. Those ways may not be as spectacular, but they are just as real and just as valid. For it is the same Spirit that is at work within – enriching, removing imperfections and adorning us with virtues.

In accepting that truth, I myself have found rest from the yearnings within. It is a deep, abiding and satisfying rest. I can truly say that it is well with my soul. It is not a resigned rest. It is an expectant rest, for I want always to be ready for any new touch that God might have in store for me. And best of all, I know what it will be like to be with him in Heaven one day. For as a child in Stockholm and a youth in Santiago and in hallowed moments since, I have for a few seconds already been there.

General Jarl Wahlström approved the revised version of *Spiritual Breakthrough* and after a process that had lasted nine years, involving three literary secretaries and two Generals, the book was published in 1983. It remains my major work to date and I am pleased to say that it seems to have proved very influential and personally helpful to many. People still refer to its impact in conversations or letters. The book is now out of print but it is good that in this age of modern technology it has been made permanently available on the webpage of the United Kingdom Territory.

Musical *Spirit!* – the full version

But we must now retrace our steps to Scotland and the year 1974. A major creative project awaiting my attention when we arrived in

Glasgow was to complete, together with John Gowans, the writing of the musical *Spirit!* and plan its premiere performance. Major Hubert Boardman had been succeeded by Major Arthur Thompson as national candidates secretary, and Arthur responded favourably to the idea of the vocational house party in 1974 being held in Scotland – at the University of Stirling – with the full version of *Spirit!* being presented at the territorial congress in Glasgow.

When John and I began to work on part two of the musical – Paul's missionary journeys culminating in Paul's martyrdom in Rome – we found that we had both gone cold on the original plan. The martyrdom of Stephen, with which part one ended, had made such a dramatic impact that it seemed inconceivable to stage a second martyrdom in the same musical. Saul's conversion and the song 'What does the Spirit say to the churches?' had concluded part one on a high note. There was a real danger that the ending to part two would not reach a comparable climax. We therefore decided to abandon the idea of a second part. Instead we added new scenes and songs to the earlier stages of part one and left Stephen's death and the conversion of Saul as the ending of the full musical.

The premiere of the full version of *Spirit!* took place in the Kelvin Hall, Glasgow, on 2 September 1974. The electricity of the Spirit felt in the Regent Hall the previous year had not diminished. If anything, the voltage had increased! It was an inspired production. The Spirit moved in our midst that evening, and we felt in our bones that the musical would have a powerful ministry in the future.

Our *modus operandi* of launching a musical after just a few days of rehearsal was not without risks. I recall that with the initial full presentation of *Spirit!* we came near the edge. In the musical, Gamaliel, the wise counsellor in the Book of Acts, has a speak-song in which he speaks to the rhythm of the underlying music. 'Be careful what you do, and be careful what you say, my friends,' he warns. At the beginning of the week we had selected a young man to play this part. But as the week progressed we noticed that he frequently forgot the lines of his speak-song.

Should we make a change or not? We decided to persevere. But just before the performance in the Kelvin Hall we took him aside and said to him: 'Remember, the important thing is to keep going.

Even if you forget your lines, keep talking, say something – if necessary, give your testimony!'

When we reached that part of the musical, Gamaliel began confidently, but from my vantage point as conductor-pianist I soon noticed his eyes glazing over – the usual signal in rehearsals of trouble ahead. But Gamaliel never faltered. When he forgot his words – he simply kept going. He proceeded to give us his testimony. He shared with us what the Lord had done in his life. As if he were a seasoned trouper he kept this up until the music reached its end. The rest of the cast did not bat an eye – and, believe it or not, no one from the audience ever commented about it afterwards! Various territories interested in producing the musical had asked for the performance to be audio-recorded – and none of them ever commented either. The power of just keeping going! I record my unbounded admiration for the young man who played Gamaliel.

Our various musicals were translated into many languages and were performed on the Salvation Army circuit around the world. But *Spirit!*, more than any other of our musicals, crossed over to the ecumenical world and was presented by other churches. I remember driving past a giant motorway-style billboard at the Elephant and Castle intersection in London which announced '*Spirit!* – a musical'. For a moment I thought someone else had hit on the same idea. But when I looked closer I saw that it was advertising a performance of our own musical at Spurgeon's Tabernacle.

Some churches found it a challenge to get brass players to play the instrumental parts, something we in the Army handle as a matter of course. I heard of one church which found itself short of someone to play the demanding solo cornet part for *Spirit!* 'There's a Salvation Army corps in the next town,' said some. 'Let's borrow a corner player from them.' 'No, let's keep it local,' said others. 'Why don't we ask the trumpet player who plays in the pub – the tavern – in the high street?' 'He isn't a Christian,' commented others.

But after discussion it was decided to invite the pub player. He was pleased to accept and became a valued member of the team. In the rehearsals he was always first to arrive and last to leave. And what joy there was in the church when following one of the early performances of the musical, the trumpet player came on to the stage in response to the invitation to accept Christ as Saviour.

He immediately started attending the church services. After a week or two he asked whether he could bring his trumpet and play it when the organ was playing. This presented the elders with a dilemma. It was explained to him that music in the actual church services – unlike in the musical – was strictly organ only. He accepted what was said. But some weeks later he returned to the subject. 'I believe God has given me a gift – and I can't use it. What should I do?' he asked.

The elders conferred – and had to agree that the trumpet player had a point. They came up with a possible solution. 'There's a Salvation Army corps in the next town,' they said to him. 'We hate the idea of losing you, but we fully understand that you want to use your gift for the Lord, and we are sure the Salvationists would be delighted to receive you into their band.' And so introductions were made, and a happy corps officer and bandmaster welcomed a new arrival at band practice. The former pub trumpet player became a staunch Salvationist.

Musical *Glory!*

With the success of *Spirit!* as the climax to the territorial congress in Scotland in 1974 the idea of having a Gowans/Larsson musical as part of congresses began to catch on. The British Territory was planning a major British congress in London for 1976. Could we provide a musical? We saw the possibility of creating something for the vocational house party in 1975 which could be staged privately that year and then premiered publicly the next year at the congress.

John and I had often spoken of the dramatic potential contained in Edward Joy's book *The Old Corps*. The book is an account of the Army's early days in Folkestone, and the stories about personalities in the corps have become classics. Each chapter is devoted to one of these characters. In our working relationship it fell to me to explore whether these individual stories could be woven together so as to form an evolving plot, with the characters interacting with each other and the various stories resolving as the musical climaxed. It proved a delightful intellectual exercise. At the end of it we had before us a detailed working document describing the various scenes and possible song situations. We decided to call the musical *Glory!*

John and I have rarely been stationed near each other. The musicals have had to be written when separated by distance, much of the content being worked out by correspondence or by telephone. At one point it looked as if the Army's leadership had at last got its act together in this regard. The Gowans and the Larssons were appointed to America – and both to the west coast of America at that. Excellent! But the Gowans were appointed to the west coast of North America and we were appointed to the west coast of South America. Yet that did not stop us from writing a musical at that time – and it was North America that paid the telephone bills! Fortunately the great regard that John and I have for each other's gifts and the almost intuitive feel we share for what is required have enabled us to avoid pitfalls. But not always.

When John sent me the words for the theme song of *Glory!* – 'When the glory gets into your soul, my brother' – I quickly set it to music in my mind. I was pleased with the result. The tune had energy and pulsated to a quick rhythm. In my mind's ear I could hear it being sung by the full stage chorus. Then the phone rang. It was John from London. He was particularly interested in how the theme song was going. When I told him that I thought we had a 'hit' he asked me to whistle or sing it down the line. I did.

But that was a mistake. I will always maintain that if Beethoven had been asked to whistle his 9th symphony down a telephone line it would never have seen the light of day. For when I finished singing there was a long pause before John spoke. 'That's *very* nice,' he said in a tone that simply cried out to be followed by the word 'but'. 'But,' he said, 'it is not quite how I had pictured it.' He then described how in his mind he had gone back a couple of centuries and had pictured the black slaves of Alabama sitting around the camp fire. With the whites of their eyes gleaming, and the palms of their hands making slow circular movements, they had sung with plaintive yet joyful voices: 'When the glory gets into your soul, my brother.' As he quoted the line John lengthened the word 'soul' to give it the typical southern emphasis.

I saw the picture immediately – and went straight back to the drawing board. Within minutes the music of the song, as it eventually appeared in the musical, had formed itself in my mind.

In the way that it blends drama and music together, *Glory!* is probably the best crafted of our musicals. At the end of the vocational house party at Sunbury Court in July 1975 the musical was given a private performance for invited guests at the Mermaid Theatre. The following year the vocational house party cast premiered *Glory!* in the Royal Festival Hall on 23 July 1976 as part of the British Congress. It met with great acclaim.

On the way out of the Festival Hall to catch the night train back to Scotland, a Salvationist thanked me for the musical and then added an intriguing comment: 'It doesn't contain as many well known songs as the other musicals,' he said. I smiled, but inwardly wondered what he meant. After all, this was the premiere!

Perhaps it was a backhanded compliment – that the music for *Glory!* seemed to him more original and did not remind him of songs written by others! Creating something new and different, but not too way-out, from just the 12 notes available to composers is a constant challenge. But it is more likely that he missed hearing songs that he already knew. Producers of professional musicals know that feeling and for that reason issue singles of the key songs before the premiere of a new musical.

But whether known or unknown at the first performance, five of the songs from *Glory!* subsequently made it into the 1986 edition of *The Song Book of The Salvation Army*, the highest number drawn from any one of our musicals.

National Youth Secretary

In the autumn of 1976 came farewell orders. We were appointed to the Youth Department at National Headquarters in London. After some preparatory months as Assistant National Youth Secretary I was appointed the National Youth Secretary, and for the next three years had the joy of heading the youth service of the British Territory. With its 21 divisions and more than 800 corps this was quite some task, but I looked forward to the challenge of it. The British Commissioner was Commissioner Geoffrey Dalziel – an outstanding Army leader by any reckoning.

Travelling the length and breadth of the territory for visits to divisions and corps for reviews, youth councils, other youth events and meetings confirmed my admiration for the officers, local officers and young people of Britain. What a force and example the British Territory has been in the world – and remains under its new name of the United Kingdom Territory.

The Youth Department hummed with activity. Among the initiatives was the production of a series of 'how to' booklets written by William Metcalf giving practical guidance to leaders of most aspects of work among children and young people.

We also felt the need to provide an Army-based outreach group for boys that would parallel scouting, and therefore created and launched 'SABAC' – The Salvation Army Boys' Adventure Corps.

The International Congress to be held in 1978 at Wembley was to have a fully-fledged youth programme throughout its 10 days, and much creative energy flowed in the preparation for that event.

A surge in corps cadetship took place in those years. It became the 'in' thing to be a corps cadet. An annual national corps cadet rally had for many years been held in London. The traditional venue was the Regent Hall, into which one could just about squeeze 1,000 young people at that time. With the surge in corps cadetship we moved the annual rally to the Westminster Central Hall with seating for 2,500. Such was the response that in the end we moved it to the Royal Albert Hall which seats 5,000.

On the personal creative front I ventured into brass composition. My first interest in Army music had been brass. As a teenager in Buenos Aires all my original compositions were for band. But when I began writing vocal music at the training college my interests switched in that direction. Over the years I wrote extensively for songster brigades and singing companies – often with words by my mother. I also still wrote for brass, but mainly in the form of accompaniments for full band or for small ensembles as in the musicals. Some of these arrangements were eventually published. But for some reason I developed a mental block with regard to writing original music for brass band.

During that time in the Youth Department I made a new year's resolution to break that 'composer's block'. I would write a march! Perhaps that would dissolve the mental block for all time, and perhaps a flow of compositions for band might follow. I literally had to force myself to sit down with score paper. But I did. The result was the march 'It's New'. It broke the mental block, but did not turn out to be the first of many further brass compositions. In fact it remains my only original composition for band. It is therefore little wonder that we heard it often as we visited territories around the world during my term as General. Enterprising bandmasters who wished to impress the General did not have much choice!

For Freda and me those London years were very satisfying. In those days when appointments for married women officers were not automatically given, Freda at first offered her services to the local divisional headquarters in South London which lay near our quarters. Then when Karl and Kevin became older Freda joined me as an assistant in the Youth Department. We soldiered at Catford Corps and Freda became the home league fellowship secretary there.

Musical *White Rose*

The Home League was approaching its 70th anniversary, and the enterprising national home league secretary of the day asked John and me to write a musical that could be part of the great anniversary celebrations being planned. *White Rose* was the result, and its first performance was in the Royal Albert Hall on 27 June 1977.

The action of the musical is set in Paris and tells the true story of how the gift of a white rose transformed a woman's life. The emblem of a white rose has for many years been cherished by the home leagues in France. *White Rose* is the shortest of our musicals – perhaps a contributory reason for its widespread and continuing use throughout the Army world.

Musical *The Blood of the Lamb*

The pattern of having a new musical for congresses was not lost on the Army's international leaders, and soon we were asked to provide a musical for the 1978 International Congress. By then we had got into a good routine of linking such requests with the annual vocational house party. We suggested that the congress musical should be written and produced a year ahead, with a private performance in 1977, and that it should then be polished up in time for its public premiere at the 1978 congress. I imagine that the thought of having everything ready a year ahead of time must have been music to the ears of the congress organisers!

With 1978 marking the centenary of The Christian Mission becoming The Salvation Army the musical needed to be centred on the Army. But having just explored that theme through *Glory!* the challenge was to come up with something different. Vachel Lindsay's epic poem 'William Booth Enters Into Heaven' provided the key. We had both been captivated by the poem, and it had made an especially profound impression on John Gowans during his term of military service in Germany. John devised the brilliantly simple plot whereby, through a series of flashbacks, the audience is introduced to the stories of some of those who are waiting to march into Heaven with William Booth.

The classic song from this musical is 'They shall come from the east, they shall come from the west, and sit down in the Kingdom of God'. When I received the words of this song from John, I immediately recognised their beauty and power. As is my custom I put the words up before me at the piano. Before beginning to play I said to myself that all I was looking for was the 'feel' of the words – their rhythm. I wasn't looking for a melody. That would come later. All I wanted for the moment was to sense the pulse of the lines.

I began to play. As I read the words, my fingers moved with ease over the keyboard. The music I was making was not a series of meaningless chords. On the contrary, I found myself playing a fully formed composition. I almost blush to record that when the music drew to its close I said to myself: 'OK, I have the "feel" of the words and their rhythm. All I now need is a melody.' For as I reflected I realised that the full song had already come – melody, harmony and rhythm. In those moments I had played the song exactly as it was later to appear in the musical. I never changed a single note or chord. The composition had come as a gift from Heaven.

When the International Youth Congress was held in Macomb, Illinois, USA, some years later, 5,000 of us gathered one evening in the open-air stadium. The sun was beginning to set and we looked down on an Army brass band playing in the middle of the field. At one point the band began to play 'They shall come from the east, they shall come from the west, and sit down in the Kingdom of God'. As the band played, I heard the young people around me begin to sing. They knew the words, they knew the music. As I looked and listened, I heard these young people who had come from the east and the west and the north and the south spontaneously singing the words in their own language – French, Spanish, Japanese, Indonesian, Shona, seemingly every language under the sun.

As I heard those thousands of young people singing the song that evening, and remembered how the music had come as a gift from Heaven, I felt myself choking up. And I lifted my heart to God to thank him yet again for the marvel of having been a channel for his creativity.

Sometimes songs have to be created on the spot when a new musical is being prepared for presentation. As we rehearsed with the members of the vocational house party at Sunbury Court for the initial private performance of *The Blood of the Lamb* we noticed that the musical seemed to sag at one point. It needed a rousing number. But we were only three days away from the performance.

Over a late supper that evening with Gisèle and Freda at a local restaurant, John and I wrote the chorus of the song 'There's only one flag for me', noting it down on the paper napkin. 'I'll stay up late and write the words of the verses,' said John. 'I'll get up early and set them to music,' said I. To John's question as to what kind of metre I would like I carelessly replied that anything would do – but the metre of 'Mine eyes have seen the glory of the coming of the Lord' would be perfect.

In the morning I found that John had pushed the words of the verses under the door – written to the metre of 'Mine eyes have seen the glory'. But when I got down to composition, I discovered that, however much I experimented, the metre I had suggested simply would not match the chorus we had written. I therefore composed the melody of the verse on a 'la, la' basis, and when John awoke confessed my error to him and asked him if he would mind starting all over again and write a new set of words.

John took it well and settled down to the task in the library. In rehearsal that morning I taught the cast the words and music of the chorus, and I then taught them the melody of the verse – without words. Every time John completed a couplet, the words were brought through from the library and chalked on to a board. Very soon the 'la, las' were replaced by words, and a new song was born.

Fortunately it provided exactly the 'lift' for the musical that we had hoped for.

The private performance of *The Blood of the Lamb* before invited guests took place in the Mermaid Theatre in July 1977. Just before it began General Arnold Brown arrived unexpectedly to watch it. He was checking up on the musical that would be presented at the congress over which he would be presiding the next year! He seemed pleased with it. The public premiere took place on 7 July 1978 in the Wembley Auditorium, the first of three performances during the congress.

In 1980 the musical was featured at the congress celebrating the Army's centenary in the USA, and for this production John and I wrote an additional American segment. This features two songs 'You've got to demonstrate' and 'The hoodlum and the hooker and the hobo' – two of our better songs – which are not included in the published version of the musical.

The international gene again

One morning in January 1980 the Chief of the Staff, Commissioner Stanley Cottrill, called for me. Were we to be on the move? We wondered. Some months earlier, John Gowans had unexpectedly found himself on a train with the territorial commander for the USA Eastern Territory. In his forthright way John had asked the commissioner what was happening in his part of the world. To his surprise he was rewarded with the nugget of information that the territory had asked IHQ for the Larssons to become the divisional leaders of the Puerto Rico Division – a Spanish-speaking division – but had been told that there were other plans. Another 'what might have been'. Were these other plans about to be revealed?

The Chief of the Staff informed me that the General wished to appoint us to the South America West Territory – me as chief secretary and Freda as territorial home league secretary – with promotion to lieut-colonel. Enquiries had already been made regarding schooling for Karl and Kevin in Santiago, Chile, and a positive response had been received. Then came the classic question that had also been asked of my parents. Was there any reason why we should not accept these appointments? We shared the question with our parents that evening. There was no hesitation on their part

– not even by my widowed mother. Our parents were used to Army ways. The next morning I saw the Chief again to say that we would be honoured to accept.

I left South America when I was 18. I was now 42. Not having used Spanish in the intervening years I wasn't sure whether I still spoke it. We had been given unusually long advance warning, and during those months I rearranged my daily programme to include three hours of language study per day. It was an investment that would yield a good return. For Freda and the boys, Spanish and life in South America would be a new adventure.

Chapter Seven

RETURN TO CHILE AND DENMARK HILL

AS we flew over the Andes mountains and looked down on the central valley of Chile, eight-year-old Karl exclaimed: 'That's our new country!' The remark summed up our spirit as a family, and made a useful addition to the brief mental notes I had prepared for any response to words of welcome that might be needed at the airport. I still wasn't sure that the Spanish would flow when needed. On landing we found a large contingent of officers, cadets and soldiers awaiting us.

Colonel and Mrs Ruben Nuesch, the territorial leaders, had been my corps officers at Palermo in Buenos Aires, so I knew them well. 'Do you want a translator for your response?' the colonel asked me. This was the moment when I either stepped out of the boat and tested the water or played for safety. I decided to step out of the boat. 'I'll be all right,' I responded. And at the appropriate moment I opened my mouth, and to my relief – and to the evident delight of the group of Salvationists – I found that I had complete freedom in Spanish. The language had returned.

The South America West Territory was at that time comprised of Chile, Peru and Bolivia. During the four years we were there, Ecuador was added to the territory, the ministry pioneered by Erik Theinhardt, an Argentinian Salvationist working for an international agency.

It is a remarkable Salvation Army in South America. Since the early beginnings, which I described previously, the Army has spread and grown. This process has continued since our own time in South America, and the Army is now at work in all the countries of Central and South America. As seems to be the pattern in countries with a Roman Catholic background, the Army is influential far beyond its numerical strength.

My own world widened suddenly. From dealing with corps, training and youth work I now had to add territorial finance, property, social services, public relations, editorial and the myriad of other matters which form part of territorial life, as well as being the 'assistant shepherd' to the officers and soldiers of the territory. With Colonel and Mrs Nuesh shortly leaving for homeland furlough, I had to be a quick learner. Chief secretaries are appointed to be trouble-shooters. One of the first tasks I faced was to resolve a situation where an officer who had resigned was refusing to leave his quarters.

As I was soon to learn, the problems to be resolved were at times related to the rapid growth that the territory was seeing. Some years there were more cadets about to be commissioned than there were appointments available. A delightful challenge. Very different from what I had known in the UK. It was not unusual for cadets to be sent straight from the training college to open new work in some carefully selected location. When we returned many years later as the international leaders, it was reassuring to see how these new plants had taken root and are now strong expressions of work.

The regard I had felt as a teenager in Chile for the Salvationists working at the cutting edge of human need and despair grew even more in its intensity in my new role. Some of the officers were coping with seemingly impossible demands and with very few resources. All the slogans about 'Where there is a need, there is The Salvation Army' and 'With heart to God and hand to man' were being lived out before my eyes. It was a privilege to be able to minister alongside such colleagues.

We were soldiers of the Santiago Central Corps – where I had been as a boy. With the Latin gift for extemporaneous speaking, testimony time in meetings could be exhilarating. Understandably they assumed that everyone else had the same gift. I spoke the language so could handle the unexpected. But Freda was in the process of learning it. This did not stop whoever was leading the testimony or prayer period from suddenly calling on her to speak or pray. Freda made sure she had appropriate words in Spanish written at the back of her song book to be able to cope with any request!

Most visits to corps in Chile we were able to do together, but we visited Bolivia and Peru separately so that one of us could be at home with the boys. This enabled Freda to give oversight to the home leagues also in these more-distant parts of the territory.

The visits to Bolivia and Peru were always significant events on our calendars. La Paz, the capital of Boliva, lies at 11,000 feet, and its airport a thousand feet higher. These heights are well above the tree-line, and landing at La Paz airport is like landing on the edge of a lunar crater, with the houses of the capital dotted on the steep sides of the cavity. La Paz can be icy cold and with its thin air and sharp gradients is not a city for the weak. Bandsmen who can march up these hills whilst playing their instruments double forte must be specially endowed!

Cochabamba, where we also have strong work, lies at a lower altitude and its climate is more temperate. Santa Cruz lies right down in the Amazonian basin and its climate is tropical. I will never forget a day spent trudging the streets of that city in burning tropical sun looking for a suitable property in which to commence our work.

That redoubtable Bolivian officer, Lieut-Colonel Jorge Nery, was the divisional commander when we arrived. What a man! He ruled his people like a chieftain. But he loved them, and they loved him back. No wonder he was admitted to the Order of the Founder. The Army's work in Bolivia has seen even more remarkable growth in recent years, and is now the strongest part of the territory.

On the personal front

When we arrived in Chile we had wanted the transition to be as smooth as possible for Karl and Kevin. The very next day we had visited the English-speaking school which had been recommended, and with which we had been in correspondence. The following day we bought school uniforms, and on the third day after arrival the boys started at their new school. They settled well and the process of picking up Spanish began.

But we soon discovered that the English-language aspect of the school was weak. It was more a place for Spanish-speaking children to learn English. This had a happy spin-off for Karl and Kevin. Invitations from parents for them to spend time with their children poured in! But we began to be concerned when after just a few weeks Kevin in particular seemed to be losing his English. However, the die had been cast and we began to plan remedial measures.

About a month after they had started in their new school, a pamphlet arrived at territorial headquarters advertising the Santiago

Christian Academy – a school for the children of missionaries (as they were still called in those days). The school was sponsored by the Southern Baptist Church of the USA and the teaching was almost wholly in English and was linked to the educational system of the USA.

What a pity we had not known before, Freda and I thought. But we had bought school uniforms for their present school. International Headquarters had kindly agreed a grant towards the school fees. The new fees would be higher and it would mean reopening that subject. The boys also seemed settled in their new environment. So we tried to put the thought of a change out of our mind.

However, the very next week it was the Army's turn to host a meeting of the fellowship of 'ex-pat' missionaries serving in Santiago. This was an informal fellowship that met quarterly. At supper we found ourselves at a table for four with a young American couple. We soon discovered that they too had two young sons, that their boys attended the Santiago Christian Academy, and that they considered the Academy to be an absolutely first-rate school that they could warmly commend. We took that as a sign from the Lord and it was not long before Karl and Kevin were at their new school.

The Santiago Christian Academy gave the boys four years of superb education in a warm Christian setting. We could not have asked for a better start in life for them. In addition to their general education, they learnt American geography, history and literature – and in their speaking even adopted the drawl of the American south. It was not surprising that their great dream became to visit the USA one day.

Quite unexpectedly the way opened three years later for that dream to be fulfilled. As it was near Christmas when it became clear that we would be able to make a family visit to the USA, Freda and I decided we would make the visit a special Christmas present for the boys that year.

We wrote on a card: 'A special gift – a visit to the USA next summer', put it in a small box, and covered the box with Christmas paper. We then put that box inside a bigger box, padding out the space with crunched newspaper, then covered that box too with Christmas paper. We repeated the procedure with an even bigger box, and then again and again and again – until the final box was bigger than the boys themselves. We put the giant box by the Christmas tree some days before Christmas. It was clearly labelled 'To Karl and Kevin'. And the process of guessing its contents began.

We saw them lifting up the box, checking its weight, wondering what it could possibly contain, making wild guesses. Huge parcels create huge expectations – and we could see it happening before our eyes.

And then Christmas arrived. Ignoring all the other unopened gifts, at the appointed hour the boys headed straight for the monster box and began tearing off the Christmas paper. They were a bit surprised to find that inside the box was a smaller one that also needed opening – and another and another. But they soon got the idea. Their excitement and expectation kept growing – but as the boxes got smaller and smaller I began to detect a note of anxiety in their reactions. Perhaps the gift wasn't so special after all. I even wondered for a moment whether we had overdone the drama.

But then they reached the small final box. They opened it, took out the card, read it, looked at us – and then went wild! They let out whoops of joy! They jumped up and down! And as we told them of the places we would visit in the USA their joy and excitement knew no bounds. They wanted to share the news with their friends as soon as possible. Never in their wildest imagination had they thought that the box would contain such a gift. And the family holiday when it eventually came remains a memory that the four of us will always treasure.

With the love of the USA born in those years in Chile, it was no surprise to us when later in life both Karl with his wife Sarita, and Kevin with his wife Jacqui, chose to settle in Los Angeles. And that is why we now have American grandchildren.

But on what small decisions the big things of life sometimes hinge. As I think back to that missionary fellowship evening, had we not sat at that particular table for supper and met that particular couple, would we have moved the boys from one school to another? I somehow doubt it. And life would have been very different for them. We have thanked God for that encounter many times since.

And I record this story as a way of praising him yet one more time for his detailed care for his children.

A new training college?

One of our territorial concerns was the need for a new college building for the training of cadets. The existing building was simply a terraced residential house that had been adapted as best possible, and was wholly inadequate. As a territory we regularly prayed that the necessary resources might become available. We kept wondering when the answer would come.

When dealing with the mail one morning at territorial headquarters I came across a small, crumpled and insignificant-looking envelope addressed in handwriting. The postage stamp showed me it was from England. As I opened it, I had no idea that in that envelope, after the many ups and downs and twists and turns that were about to unfold, was the answer to our prayers. God had a strategic plan in place.

The handwritten letter was from a Mr Walter Vis, who together with his wife lived near Maidenhead, in south-east England. It was brief and matter-of-fact. He was writing to say that he had some oil shares in the national petroleum company of Chile and that these were deposited in a bank in Valparaiso, Chile. He wished to donate the shares to The Salvation Army in Chile. And that was that.

There was no indication of how many shares or their possible value, and when we made enquiries with the bank we had no great expectations. So we were taken aback when the bank informed us that at their present value they were worth around half a million US dollars – a vast sum at that time! We were looking at the possibility of the territory receiving the largest single cash donation in its history. If the shares yielded their current value there would be enough money to build a new training college.

It all seemed a bit unbelievable. Who was Mr Walter Vis? How did he come to have shares deposited in a Chilean bank? What had prompted him to make the donation? Did he realise how valuable the shares were? We telexed the Army's public relations department in England and they rose to the occasion magnificently. They arranged for an officer to visit Mr and Mrs Walter Vis in their home, and then shared with us their story.

116

The Vises were an elderly couple living in retirement near Maidenhead. Walter was Dutch by nationality and in his younger years had been a seaman. His ship often sailed down the west coast of South America. On one such visit to Chile it was suggested to him that he should buy some shares in the national oil company as an investment. They were going cheap, for at that time no oil had yet been discovered! He purchased some shares, deposited them in the bank in Valparaiso, and then from time to time added to them as his ship returned to the port.

That was many years ago, and they now wanted to settle their affairs. When they had enquired about getting the shares transferred to England there had seemed to be much red tape involved. They knew that with the discovery of oil the value of the shares had greatly appreciated and were aware of their estimated market price. But they had decided to give them to a worthy cause. Which cause would it be?

As Walter and his wife talked about it one day, he recalled that when he was a boy in Amsterdam his family was so poor that one Christmas it looked as if there would be no Christmas dinner for them. His mother was in despair. Just then there was a knock on the door. On opening it they found a large hamper filled with every kind of Christmas food – and disappearing down the stairs of the block of flats was the retreating figure of a woman clad in navy blue. She was wearing a very large bonnet. In his mind Walter could still recall the picture of this angel making her way downstairs. 'That's the lady from The Salvation Army,' his mother whispered to him. And he had never forgotten.

Giving the shares to The Salvation Army in Chile would be a way of saying thank you. But was there a Salvation Army in Chile? The Vises had no connection with the Army in England. But they thought that some day in the future it would be interesting to find out if there was an Army in Chile.

Lo and behold, the next Sunday morning a 25-strong Salvation Army band formed up outside their house to conduct an open-air meeting. That had never happened before. It was the band from Maidenhead Corps. For some time the members of the band had been concerned that their open-air outreach followed a very predictable pattern – always the same set of streets. Following discussion and prayer it had been decided to adopt a new approach and to make forays to more outlying parts. That Sunday morning was the first time that they had ventured so far.

And here they were – right outside the house of Mr and Mrs Walter Vis. Walter looked at his wife. She smiled affirmingly. So Walter went out, was introduced to the corps officer, and asked the question they wanted to ask: was there a Salvation Army in Chile? The corps officer promised to look up the *Year Book* and a few days later was in touch with the address. Walter's letter to us was the result.

But God's strategic plan was to be put to the test. Following receipt of the necessary authorisation from Mr Vis, the manager of the bank in Valparaiso refused point-blank to hand over the shares to us. 'Anyone who wants to give shares of that value to The Salvation Army must be out of his mind!' he said. 'Before I can comply with the request, Mr Vis will need to visit the Chilean consulate in London so that the consul can issue a document certifying that Mr Vis is of a sound mind and that he is not being forced against his will to make this donation.'

My heart sank, and more so when our lawyer confirmed that the bank manager was within his rights. Would the Vises, now an elderly couple who disliked red tape, be prepared to devote a whole day to journeying into London and going through the process at the Chilean consulate? Was it 'goodbye, training college'?

But no, it was not. The Vises agreed to travel into London and, accompanied by a public relations officer, made their way to the Chilean consulate. However, the staff there were not having a good day. Today was not convenient. The Vises would have to come back some other day. Yes, a great pity about the long journey. But it could not be helped. And so the Vises left empty-handed.

That could have been 'goodbye, training college'. But the Vises, to their everlasting credit, agreed to make the journey again. And this time they came away with the vital certificate signed by the consul.

In the meantime our lawyer had suggested that we should ask the bank to transfer the shares to the bank's head office in Santiago so that we would be dealing with the absolute top people of the bank. I think the Valparaiso branch manager was only too pleased to see the shares go. All now seemed set for us to receive them. But, no.

Our lawyer phoned some days later to say that the bank's head office had been in touch. On receipt of the authorisation certificate from Mr Vis they had routinely referred it to the bank's legal advisers. A major snag had been discovered. The legal advisers pointed out that under Chilean law, anyone making a donation of that size to a charity would need to present himself before a Chilean court to prove that in making the donation he was not disinheriting some member of his family. Mr Vis would need to travel to Chile and make a full declaration of all his assets before a court. Our own lawyer confirmed that it was so, and that there was no way round this requirement.

This time my heart really did sink. I knew that Mr Vis would never agree to that. This time it definitely was 'goodbye, training college'!

But the next day our lawyer was on the phone again. 'Get yourself a new attorney,' he began. 'I am a terrible lawyer.' I listened in surprise. He then described how he had told his colleagues in his legal practice about the situation that had arisen. 'But the law about disinheriting a relative was repealed when the last government came in,' said one. 'Don't you remember? It was part of that large group of laws that were simply abolished.'

They all dived for their law books. The colleague was right. The law about disinheriting was no longer on the statute book. 'I immediately phoned the bank's legal advisers,' continued our lawyer, 'and told them in no uncertain terms that they were no good at their job! And when they had looked up the law they phoned back to admit that they had been wrong – and The Salvation Army could now pick up the shares at any time convenient to them.' It was 'welcome, training college'!

On Christmas Eve Colonel Ruben Nuesch went to the bank. An hour or two later he returned with the precious shares in his briefcase.

But the story was not yet over. It would take many months before architectural plans for the new college could be finalised and construction could begin. Should we hold on to the shares or sell them?

Members of our informal advisory board were unanimous in their view. 'Sell immediately.' We did – and the resulting half a million dollars were deposited in our bank. Within weeks the share market suddenly collapsed and the oil shares plunged in value. And to cap it all: during the months that the half a million dollars were on deposit at the bank, interest rates went wild – reaching at one point 50 per cent. The cup was not only full, it was running over!

The new training college opened a year later. Mr and Mrs Vis were invited to the opening ceremony but did not feel able to come. However, their gift is honoured by a plaque in the entrance hall of the college. But Mr and Mrs Vis did accept an invitation to meet with General and Mrs Jarl Wahlström at International Headquarters, and over a cup of tea the General was able to express the Army's deep gratitude for their gift.

They probably never knew it, but their generosity had enabled God to make them part of his strategic plan for answering our prayers for a new training college.

Creative projects

For some time I had thought of writing a devotional work on what it means to be like Jesus. Any parallels drawn between his life and ours always face the dilemma that Jesus was not only human but was also divine. He can therefore seem quite out of our league – with no comparison being possible.

What I wanted to do was to explore the idea of the Holy Spirit being the common denominator. The man Jesus was *perfectly* filled with God the Holy Spirit – and it was this which made him divine. We as human beings can only be partially filled with the Holy Spirit. But it is the *same* Spirit that fills us – and we too can therefore experience something of the divine in our lives. Though such exploration can never wholly account for the uniqueness of Jesus as the divine Son of God, I felt that some helpful practical insights for Christlike living might emerge.

I prepared a synopsis of the work under the title of *The Man Perfectly Filled with the Spirit*. My thought was to offer the chapters first as a series to the international *War Cry* with publication in book form to be considered after that. The chapters therefore had to be relatively brief, and my plan was for a work of 26 chapters of about 1,200 words each, making it a series lasting six months. Major Robert Street, the editor of *The War Cry*, responded positively, and I made plans to write chapters on a regular basis over the next six months.

Summer was approaching and we had planned the holiday of a lifetime. Together with another officer couple we were going to drive down to the southernmost tip of the South American continent, the fabled Cape Horn. It was going to take many days, with much of the journey being over rough unpaved roads. The coast of Chile becomes spectacularly wild as one journeys south, with ranges of snow-clad mountains intersected by deep fjords, and it has not yet proved possible to build a road through. We would therefore have to cross into Argentina and cross back again to Chile when we reached Tierra del Fuego. It was going to be an unforgettable journey.

We had made extensive preparations, but just as we were about to depart typhoid fever struck. Typhoid used to be a killer. The cemetery in Valparaiso is full of graves of foreign sailors who succumbed to the disease when their ships anchored in the port. But modern antibiotics have transformed the treatment of the disease. However, it is not to be trifled with. It incapacitates one totally for at least a month. I had been the first to go down with it, and had never felt so helplessly weak in all of my life. Now it was Freda's turn. The journey to Cape Horn was off.

But the next three weeks became unforgettable in a different way – for both Freda and me. The boys went off to camp, and my life during those holiday weeks became centred on nursing Freda back to health and strength. But I also began writing *The Man Perfectly Filled with the Spirit*. Caring for someone you love must be conducive to writing, for the chapters began to flow. I was on a creative crest in every way. And when Freda got over the worst stage I would often sit on the bed and share with her what I had written that morning. They were precious days. And when the three weeks ended and it was time for me to go back to work, more than half of the 26 chapters had been written.

The chapters duly appeared in the international *War Cry* and in 1986 were published in book form. The book has been translated into a number of languages, and of the books I have authored it remains my favourite.

The music side was not fallow either. I set myself the task of writing a series of Scripture choruses which, by arrangement, also appeared regularly in the international *War Cry*. Of these 'Sing and make music' is probably the best known. But 'The Lord is near', based on Philippians 4:6-7, is the one I like best.

Musical *Son of Man*

The pattern of commissioning a Gowans/Larsson musical for large congress events had not been forgotten. When the USA Western Territory was planning its centenary congress for 1983, the knock on the door came once more. The Gowanses were by this time stationed in that territory.

We will gladly accept this commission, we said, as long as we can have the freedom to create a musical that can live on for general use following the congress. And that is how *Son of Man* was written. This musical explores the life, death and resurrection of Jesus from the angle of him being the embodiment of God through the Holy Spirit. Its core idea therefore parallels that of *The Man Perfectly Filled with the Spirit*.

Son of Man was one of the musicals written when John and I were at a long distance from each other. We feel that it is none the worse for that, and in fact has some of our best songs. It was premiered on 5 June 1983 in Los Angeles, and was first published by the USA Western Territory and later by SP&S Ltd in London.

During our stay in Chile Freda ventured out as a producer of musicals when she directed the Spanish versions of the mini-musical from *Hosea,* and full-length productions of *Spirit!* and *Son of Man*. In *Son of Man,* Jesus in a white poncho surrounded by the 12 apostles in their red ones made an arresting sight. Freda was to continue in the producer role when we returned to England.

Those mountains

Whenever I looked at the Andes mountains I still felt the inner pull that had drawn me to them as a boy. As a family we sometimes explored the lower reaches and valleys. But in the massive range that dominates Santiago a number of the peaks touch 10,000 feet.

On winter evenings I would sometimes sit on a hillside near our flat and watch the setting sun work its magic on the white snow.

With the help of a map and a local mountaineering book I studied the contours of the mountains until every feature was engraved on my mind. I knew which was the highest peak in the range – and the yearning to reach it grew ever stronger. I reckoned it was within my capacity, no actual scaling of rock faces would be involved, and in summer the temperature would be moderate. But it could not be done in one day. It would mean spending a night out on the mountain.

The inner pull was so strong I decided I ought to try. Freda was very understanding. I made my plans, and then early one morning while it was still dark Freda dropped me off at the highest point that could be reached by car. As the sun rose I set out with rucksack on back and followed the mountain trail as it wound its way ever upwards. I kept going at a steady pace for many hours. I felt a sense of inner exhilaration at being in the remote and barren mountain world all on my own.

But from my research I knew that the moment of truth would come when I reached a narrow ridge – the Trail of the Incas – that links two mountains. I wasn't sure it would be safe for me to cross it. And it was also the point of no return – if I crossed there was no way that I could get back before nightfall.

Early afternoon I reached the old Inca trail. I stood surveying it. A path about a foot wide stretched before me. It continued for about 300 yards to the safety of the next mountain. On both sides of this slender trail virtually sheer drops of loose stones yawned, ending in narrow ledges a hundred or so feet down. And beyond the ledges lay the void. It was not a reassuring sight, and as I studied the scene it became clear to me that if I slipped and fell the consequences would be incalculable.

I pondered my options. It did not take long. From the moment I had seen the trail I had known in my heart of hearts that to attempt to cross it would be a risk too far. After all, I was a husband and a father – and the chief secretary of the territory! It was time for 'mission abort'. So I turned back.

I knew that I had to beat the dark, so I ran and clambered down the mountain path at breakneck speed. Even then I was still an hour short of my goal when night began to fall. I was relieved to reach the road eventually, and even more relieved when, in that pre-mobile phone era, a car appeared on the lonely road and I was able to thumb a lift back to Santiago. When I let myself in to our flat late that night, it was to find Freda and the boys in bed together watching television. A happy family reunion marked the end of a great if incomplete adventure.

Where next?

Our stay in the South America West Territory culminated with a territorial congress led by General Jarl Wahlström, preceded by a zonal conference for the territorial commanders and chief secretaries of South and Central America and the Caribbean.

It was an open secret that some of us were about to have changes of appointments, and we wondered whether the General would use the opportunity afforded by the zonal conference to speak to us. He did – and during a coffee break when we sat at small tables on the terrace, he chose to have a word individually with those involved. Surreptitiously we were called one by one to join him at his table. After consulting a list hidden in his hand he gave us our orders – and asked us to keep them to ourselves.

Everyone else was of course fully aware of what was happening! At the end of the coffee time most of us knew something that we could not share, and also knew who else knew something that they could not share! Freda and I were appointed to the International Training College in London, I as principal, and we were promoted to the rank of colonel.

It would be good to return and see family and friends again. Sadly, during our four years away Freda had had to return for her father's funeral and then later to nurse her mother in her final days. But as a family we felt a wrench at leaving Chile – the warmth of its people and the beauty of the country. This long and thin country, so narrow that you can stand on the Pacific beach and seemingly just reach out and touch the snowclad mountains that mark the boundary with Argentina, stretches from the hot deserts near the equator in the north right down to the ice of the south pole in the Antarctic, with every conceivable climate and nature in between.

The Chileans say that when God finished creating the world he had a whole collection of different bits and pieces left over. So he stuck them all on the west coast of South America – and called it Chile. I think they are right!

Training Principal

We took up our appointments at the International Training College (ITC) in August 1984. The ITC had a quasi-territorial status, and as principal I reported to the General through the Chief of the Staff. Freda became the college librarian. This was a new discipline for her, but one that she soon mastered and which opened up an avenue for ministry to cadets which often went well beyond their literary needs.

Our quarters were in Bromley, and once again the corps there became our spiritual home. The transition to secondary schooling for Karl and Kevin also went smoothly. We were to live in Bromley for the next nine years, while Freda and I held three different appointments. The continuity in corps and school for our sons during their vital teenage years was an unanticipated blessing for which we have many times thanked the Lord.

Coming back to the training college was like coming home. But I soon discovered that life as the principal was very different from college life as I had experienced it before. As a young member of staff I had been right in the thick of things, literally sharing the lives of the cadets on a daily basis. I found that I missed that, and it took some time to make the adjustment.

In the interval of 18 years educational thinking had also changed. As previously mentioned, the tide is out for teaching cadets by means of lectures. As principal I was therefore no longer expected to give lectures two or three times a week. I regretted that I would not have that same opportunity for regular creative contact between principal and cadets that I recalled from my own training days. Building bridges for interaction with the cadets – both as a session and individually – therefore became one of my prime aims.

A key role of a training principal is to keep the college focused on its aim – to produce effective Salvation Army officers with a strong sense of mission and the necessary spiritual qualities and practical skills as leaders to make things happen in the world out there. A

Salvation Army training college is a battle school – it is a Sandhurst or a West Point rather than an Oxford or a Harvard.

Training the heart is therefore essential – for without fire and passion there is no 'get up and go'. Training the head is vital – the effective proclamation of the gospel and the vast demands of Christian leadership today are impossible without a trained mind. Training the hands – preparing the cadets for the vast variety of skills that they will need as officers – is crucial. Cadets are not being trained to be theoreticians – they have been called to be practitioners, co-*workers* with God.

But training time is limited, and in the rightful pursuit of excellence it is possible for those responsible respectively for the spiritual, academic and practical aspects of training to press for greater emphasis to be given to their particular aspect. This is a healthy creative tension. The task of the principal is to have a clear vision of the end purpose of training and to ensure that everyone else keeps that same focus.

Lieut-Colonel Mary Carby was the assistant principal and Major and Mrs Keith and Pauline Banks the senior training officers for most of our time at the ITC, and we could not have wished for a better team. Deep and lasting bonds were forged with the members of staff, and with the cadets of the four sessions who, as Mrs General Olive Coutts once put it to them, were 'Larsson-trained'. To see their development and then to head their commissioning celebrations in the Royal Albert Hall, as training principals then did, was indeed a sacred honour.

Musical *Man Mark II*

A musical was requested for the 1985 International Youth Congress to be held in Macomb, USA. John Gowans, who was still stationed in that country, conceived the idea and wrote the script for what became *Man Mark II*. Its message of a new humanity created in Christ is timeless and of universal application, but parts of the musical undoubtedly reflect John's experience of service in the USA. A cast was drawn from the Southern California Division, where John was the divisional commander. By now we had arrived at a good working pattern – after all, it was our ninth musical – and the music came without difficulty.

126

I was able to use some of the songs from *Man Mark II* initially in the musical presentations that I had reintroduced as part of the commissioning days in the Royal Albert Hall. But the actual premiere of the musical took place on 21 July 1985 in Macomb, and was watched by the 5,000 young people gathered for the youth congress.

One of the most powerful songs of the musical is 'When crosses come'. It became the appeal song that evening. As the young people sang together 'I'll not turn back whatever it may cost, I'm called to live to love and save the lost' 600 of them came forward to offer themselves for service as officers. I have always regretted that time-wise this song just missed the 1986 edition of *The Song Book of The Salvation Army*.

Other projects

The church growth movement was sweeping through the evangelical church during those years, and the Army around the world was waking up to its potential for our evangelistic mission. It seemed that some of the principles which had been foundational to the Army's concept of mission were now being rediscovered and trumpeted as new discoveries.

All movements of thought and trends tend to pass in time, but they often leave a legacy which becomes a permanent part of the Christian heritage. I felt that the church growth principles would become part of that heritage. But as I kept reading and hearing about the importance of these principles I found that I could not lay my hands on a concise summary of what they actually were. Nor was there anything on the market which applied the findings specifically to the Army and its mission.

The need for an Army-related work on church growth was clear. I kept hoping that some of the officers and lay-Salvationists who were spearheading the movement within the Army would find the time to write something along these lines. But they had their hands full. I didn't feel particularly qualified to attempt it myself, but as no one else seemed to be venturing out in this direction, it gradually became a conviction that writing such a book was a service to Salvationists that I could render.

So I immersed myself in the voluminous material that the church growth movement had spawned, drawing from every available source both outside and inside the Army, and then wrote the book *How Your Corps Can Grow*. In it I identify and introduce 26 church growth principles. The book has been translated into a number of languages and seems to have met the need it was designed to meet.

Another project followed. General Eva Burrows wanted to update the text of the articles of war, the declaration that soldiers study and sign before being enrolled, which is now known as the soldier's covenant. The General asked me to research the matter.

The declaration is in two parts, first the 11 points of doctrine – which would of course not change – and then a section dealing with lifestyle. I researched the text of this second section and found that, except for some very small amendments, it dated right back to the beginnings of our history.

The more I studied the wording the more inadequate it seemed to me to be. For one thing it reflected an era long since gone. For another, it left unmentioned large areas of Christian lifestyle and service integral to the commitment a soldier makes. It also seemed unduly negative, majoring on the things a soldier promised not to be or do. I began to feel that a complete rewrite was needed – but one which would retain the spirit and aims of the original. That is not what I had been asked to do – but I thought it was worth attempting, and then the General could decide whether she wanted to proceed along those lines or not.

After careful study of *Chosen to be a Soldier*, the orders and regulations for soldiers, I began drafting a new text whilst always keeping an eye on the previous one. I drafted and redrafted. There were dilemmas. Should the various statements be aspirations or promises? For example, should it be 'I will *seek to* uphold Christian integrity in every area of my life,' or should it be 'I *will* uphold Christian integrity in every area of my life'? For some points aspiration seemed more appropriate than a promise. For others – for example abstinence from alcohol – anything less than a promise would be wrong.

When I had finished my drafting I shared the text with a number of colleagues for comment and then reworked and polished again. I knew that the text would have to be translated into every language in which the Army works, and that every word would be carefully weighed in soldiership classes around the world. With regard to the 'aspiration or promise' dilemma I provided both options in the final draft for the points where I felt aspiration was a possibility, so that the question could be thoroughly aired in discussion before a decision was taken.

The General seemed very appreciative of the approach I had taken. In preparation for the International Conference of Leaders that was to be held at Lake Arrowhead, California, in 1988 she circulated the draft text for comment to all territories with the request that it be considered by small groups at all levels. This was a major process. But when it was completed, I was reassured to note that the original draft text remained remarkably unscathed.

After considerable debate at the conference and some further minor verbal adjustments, the conference recommended acceptance of the text – with the title of soldier's covenant – and the General approved it for issuing in 1989. The conference felt that all the points should be in the form of promises and not aspirations. I have sometimes wondered since whether a mixture of the two forms might not have worked.

Another creative task that General Eva Burrows asked me to tackle was a revision of the handbook *Salvation Army Ceremonies*. I formed and chaired a small group for that purpose. The new edition was published in 1989 without fanfare, but in fact included far-reaching changes. No longer could it be said that two Salvationists entering into marriage were marrying The Salvation Army! And no longer could it be thought that a child of Salvationists was being dedicated to the Army rather than to God! And no longer did the words of funeral committal include the phrase so hallowed by tradition but so open to misunderstanding and pain: '*As it has pleased God* (to promote our dear comrade to the home prepared for him in Heaven)'.

By the summer of 1988 we had completed four years at the International Training College. Counting my year as a sergeant, I had spent 12 years of my officership there. I felt at home in the place. It was in my blood! But when I received word that General Eva Burrows wished to see me, I wondered whether it might be about a change of appointment. It was. And the General managed to take me completely by surprise.

Chapter Eight

RESOLVING A CONUNDRUM

WHAT General Eva Burrows wanted me to do was to help her to find a way of resolving a problem that every General for at least the previous four decades had wrestled with, but which had always ended up in the 'too hard' basket.

The problem, in a nutshell, was the conflict between the General's international and British roles and the seemingly inextricable intertwining of the international and British administrations and their financial resources. The situation was unsatisfactory for both the international Army and the Army in the United Kingdom. The Army around the world felt that too much of the General's time and energy was devoted to the UK. And the Army in the UK felt that the attention of its leader was too often elsewhere.

The problem was complex, intractable and of long standing – a veritable conundrum. The General shared with me the acute sense of frustration about the situation both internationally and in the UK, and said that she had made a commitment at the High Council that elected her to seek a resolution. That was why we were now meeting. The General wanted me to help her resolve the conundrum.

From Colonel Henry Gariepy's biography of General Eva Burrows, *General of God's Army,* I subsequently learnt something of the General's background thinking in selecting me for the task. The colonel writes: 'The General's intuitive discernment led her to the man supremely qualified for the task. Larsson's name was a household word around the Army world. He had a background of Third World experience, was the noted author of Army books, and composer for the internationally popular Gowans and Larsson musicals. He brought to this project an articulate voice, an analytical mind, a nonconfrontational approach to sensitive issues, and an

131

intimate knowledge of the problem, having served in the UK as well as on IHQ.'

The General later told me that she was not sure how I would react to this assignment. She must have been reassured when I told her that the subject had already exercised my thinking. Some years before I had written an article about it for *Field Scene,* an internal magazine for British Territory officers. Its somewhat provocative title was 'Needed: A Full-Time Leader for the Army in Britain'. The British Commissioner of the day apparently saw it as useful ammunition for his cause. But it was not only the title but also the content that was provocative, and in the end prudence won and it was never published.

I therefore looked forward to 'having a go' at trying to find a way through, and in July 1988 we were appointed to International Headquarters. My task was to research and consult and then to draw up a strategy which would 'lead to the more effective and vigorous expression of Salvation Army ministry in the UK, whilst at the same time maintaining the strength of the General's worldwide authority and control through appropriate International Headquarters administration'. My title was 'Assistant to the Chief of the Staff for UK Administrative Planning' – a title and status deliberately chosen so that every door would be open to me in my research – and I was responsible to Commissioner Ron Cox, the Chief of the Staff.

Freda was appointed 'Co-ordinator – Married Women Officers', and reported to Mrs Commissioner Hilda Cox. In these more enlightened days when it is required that every officer must have an appointment in his or her own right, it is almost hard to remember – and understand – that it was not always so. In the UK married women officers whose husbands were appointed to a headquarters often found that their services were no longer required. The system no longer needed them. How such a vast pool of dedication and skill could have been neglected for so long is one of the mysteries of Army history, and one for which we have a lot to answer. How could we have been so blind for so long?

Freda's task was to look after this very sizeable group of women officers associated with IHQ and wherever possible to find openings for those without appointments at a London headquarters or in other expressions of Army work. In this she was singularly successful, and her accomplishment was a factor in the subsequent introduction of the policy that made it mandatory for *every* officer to have an official appointment.

A 'plus' of my new appointment was the opportunity to work closely with General Burrows. I had first met her when I attended the International College for Officers. Brigadier Eva Burrows was the newly appointed assistant principal and made a great impression on us all. Over the years she had become for me a role model of an Army leader. When she became General it seemed to me that she was everything that a General should be. I therefore looked forward to the new working relationship. And during that time the General became my mentor, and has remained so to this day.

The problem

The heading of my unpublished article written for *Field Scene* crystallised the problem. The Army in Britain was without a full-time leader. All authority necessary for effective overall leadership was vested in the General, but modern-day Generals were too busy looking after the world to be able to give the needed attention to the UK. Administratively this produced a state of near paralysis, the symptoms of which at times bordered on the mind-boggling, as what follows will help to show.

As I tried to sort out the puzzle I found myself going right back to the days of William Booth. The research confirmed to my mind that the administrative system for the UK made perfect sense when viewed in its historical context. But circumstances had changed and the system had not moved with them. I delved into a myriad of fascinating facets of Army history – and it was history with which I would later find myself personally involved. The conundrum is best understood in its historical setting.

From the moment the early Salvation Army crossed the Atlantic in 1880 and thus became an international army, all Generals have worn two hats – an international and a UK one. When wearing the international hat they have been the leader of a global movement, and when wearing the UK hat they have been in charge of the Army in Britain.

The General's headquarters was at first designed only to serve William Booth when he was wearing his UK hat, but when the Army went international an 'overseas' department was added so that it could also support him when wearing his international one. For good measure the name of the headquarters was changed to International Headquarters. But that was really a misnomer for its predominant role was always to support the General in his British leadership role. At the time of my research, two thirds of International Headquarters personnel served the work in the United Kingdom. From the earliest days onwards, all the financial resources from the UK flowed into one central pot at International Headquarters and were allocated by the General to meet the needs of both the Army's international work and the work in Britain.

William Booth was not of course a one-man band, and when wearing his British hat he delegated responsibilities along *functional* lines. As the work grew he appointed a leader for 'field' (corps) work, a leader for social work, a leader for training, a leader for 'trade', etc, just as any territorial commander does today. All of these leaders were responsible to him as General.

The work in Great Britain was for many years much larger than any work overseas, and the appointed leaders were consequently accorded high status and usually carried the rank of commissioner. In time these various branches of work in the UK began to be organised as territories, with separate headquarters, each with its complement of departments, to direct and support different aspects of service. The commissioners in charge were assisted by chief secretaries, and were governed by *Orders and Regulations for Territorial Commanders and Chief Secretaries.* This included the Managing Director of the Salvation Army Assurance Society, the Principal of the International Training College and the Secretary for Trade at SP&S Ltd.

In time the various 'territories' within the UK also established their own middle management structures across the country, all with their own series of 'divisional' headquarters. Each did it in its own way. For example, the 'field' territory had divisions headed by divisional commanders. The Men's Social Services had provinces headed by provincial officers. The Women's Social Services had districts with district officers. The Salvation Army Assurance Society had divisions led by divisional managers. The IHQ Public Relations Department developed regions with regional officers. None of the boundaries of these divisions, provinces, districts and regions matched geographically. And the Slum (later Goodwill) Department, which was part of the 'field' territory, supervised a chain of centres throughout the UK that stood outside any of these divisional structures.

The 'field' territory was by far the largest unit within the UK and because of its numerical dominance became known as the British Territory, and its leader as the British Commissioner.

The British Territory went through various experimental phases in middle management. For 25 years – from 1883 to 1908 – the 37 field divisions were grouped into 10 provinces with provincial commanders in charge to whom the divisional commanders were responsible. And for five years – 1936 to 1940 – the British Territory was divided into four separate territories along geographical lines. Each had its own territorial commander with the rank of lieut-commissioner, responsible to the British Commissioner. When the experiment was abandoned in 1940 only the Scotland and Ireland Territory retained a separate identity.

At the time when first William and then Bramwell Booth was in charge no one questioned the system of functional territories – 'armies within an Army' – in Britain, with each leader reporting to the General. They had both successfully run the Army in Britain with one hand and the Army in the rest of the world with the other.

In their era the sheer size of the Army's operation in Britain when compared with anywhere else in the world was a significant factor in the situation. In 1929, when Bramwell Booth relinquished command as General, there were more than 5,000 active officers and 150,000 soldiers at work in 1,500 corps and 220 social centres in Britain. There were 645 cadets in the current session of cadets. Even SP&S Ltd was a large operation – already by 1914 employing 650 people.

But the successful working of the system of functional territories reporting to the General depended entirely on him being able to wear his UK hat often and long enough to give effective leadership to the Army in Britain. Constitutionally and practically, the General was totally in charge – and there were innumerable matters great and small that required his attention.

Only the General could determine mission strategy and give overall leadership. Only the General could approve a property transaction, however small. The General controlled the appointments of officers to the larger corps and institutions. He issued all minutes dealing with conditions of service for officers in the UK. He approved the leaders of youth councils. Tradition even dictated that no meetings could be held in the Royal Albert Hall unless they were presided over by the General or the Chief of the Staff.

But with the continual expansion of the Army overseas successive Generals found it increasingly difficult to give the time and attention to the British scene that the system demanded. A distinct leadership vacuum began to develop in the United Kingdom.

This leadership vacuum had consequences at the cutting edge of mission. As those in charge of the various 'armies' in the UK sought to compensate for this leadership void, those branches of work began to take on even stronger separate identities. Officers commissioned to one of these 'armies' usually stayed there for all of their officership. Negotiating a transfer was as complicated as transferring to another country.

Officers working in the same community worked independently of each other. In a town one could have the bizarre situation of corps officers, men's social service officers, women's social service officers, public relations officers and assurance society officers serving the same community but in complete isolation from each other. Five separate armies in the one town – and the only leader with the authority to make them march in step and provide strategic direction was the Army's international leader, the General.

The sense of separateness was deepened by the fact that the only time that officers of the various 'armies' in the UK came together for officers' councils was at international congresses. None were held between 1914 and 1965 so the sense of isolation was acute – and with it a feeling at ground level that there was something distinctly odd about a system that allowed such lack of integration.

Frustration with the situation was felt even more acutely at the top. Questions began to be asked around the Army world. Why was the General giving so much time to the UK? And why did the UK have so many commissioners? By 1948 their number had risen to 16 – and this figure did not include commissioners at IHQ with international responsibilities. Even Campfield Press at one time had a lieut-commissioner in charge.

Within the UK the frustration was felt most acutely by the successive holders of the office of British Commissioner. As the leadership vacuum opened, all eyes turned to the British Commissioner to fill the void. But his hands were tied. He was not authorised to engage in fund-raising and had only limited authority in property matters. He had no say regarding social services, the training of cadets, or the provision of the necessary tools for the task through SP&S Ltd. Neither did his remit include contact with the media and publication of books and periodicals such as *The War Cry* and *The Musician* (later *Salvationist*). And, as already noted, all matters to do with allowances for officers and other practical matters were handled by International Headquarters. Any territorial commander in the world would consider authority on such matters to be essential for the giving of effective leadership. But in the UK the British Commissioner was not the 'territorial commander'. The General was.

Early wrestling with the problem

Matters came to a head at the commissioners' conference that General Wilfred Kitching called in 1958. The 'British problem', as it became known during that conference, was not even on the agenda, but became a subject that dominated the event.

It was clear that the General was deeply burdened by the situation. He was the third General to come to that position from being British Commissioner (Generals Edward Higgins and Albert Orsborn being the other two) and had therefore experienced personally the frustration of that appointment. He was now the General – and was required to wear the two hats. It seemed mission impossible to give effective leadership both internationally and nationally at the same time.

General Kitching knew from his own long experience all about the leadership vacuum that existed in the UK. There was even talk of the need for a 'super' commissioner to whom all other commissioners would be responsible. It is clear that all gathered in conference knew that something had to be done. But neither the General nor anyone else at that time could see a way of resolving the matter. The complexities seemed insurmountable.

Chief of the complexities they wrestled with was the constitutional one. As far back as in the Deed Poll of 1878, William Booth had laid down that the Army 'should always be under the oversight, direction and control of some one person' – and all subsequent constitutions had reaffirmed that the Army had to be under the oversight, direction and control of the General. How then in the UK situation could the General possibly give away his British hat?

A further constitutional dilemma was that the General was the *managing* trustee of all the Army's assets in the UK. This had been laid down in The Salvation Army Act 1931, which created The Salvation Army Trustee Company. It was by law, not choice, that the General had to be personally involved in every property transaction and any large financial decision. There seemed to be no way around that.

And would it be responsible for a General to relinquish control of the British assets? The General could not forget that he had an international hat to wear as well. Funds generated in the UK had always been available to the General for financing work overseas. In the inter-war years 48.5 per cent of all funds expended by IHQ to support international work had come from the UK. In the years immediately following the Second World War the percentage had risen to an astonishing 57 per cent. The UK was financing the Army world. Was it really right for the General to cut himself off from the British gold mine?

A further consideration was the very real fear that if the General did not have a specific field of action within Britain, which was his by right, there was a danger of the General in time becoming merely a ceremonial figure. The Pope is world leader of the Roman Catholic Church by virtue of being the bishop of Rome. The Archbishop of Canterbury is world leader of the Anglican Communion by virtue of being the bishop of Canterbury. William Booth became the world leader of The Salvation Army because he founded and was in charge of the Army in Britain. Though the historical parallel with the Roman Catholic and Anglican Churches is not exact, it was feared that if the General became so detached from Britain that he might as well be based in, say, Geneva, the role of the General would be changed out of all recognition.

Yet another factor at the time was the very real difficulty in human terms of dismantling a structure which involved so many leaders of high rank and status.

The momentum towards change

The difficulties and complexities faced by General Wilfred Kitching were genuine, and could not be resolved at the commissioners' conference in 1958. But that conference triggered a momentum towards change. The process was to last more than 30 years. During those years it was almost as if an unseen hand was guiding developments at each turn of events.

General Kitching himself set the process in motion immediately after the commissioners' conference by putting before the Advisory Council to the General a proposal that all the social and community operations in the UK should be brought together under one 'social commissioner'. The proposal was warmly endorsed by the council, but was not to become reality for 20 years.

However, the process had begun. The introduction of advisory boards to the UK scene in 1964 by General Frederick Coutts gave an unexpected but powerful impulse to it. The eminent personalities from all walks of life who served on these boards were dismayed to find that there was not one Salvation Army in the UK but many – and consistently recommended that the Army had to become one to be effective. General Coutts also created a Central Social Service Council in 1966 to bring together the leaders of the various expressions of social work.

The election of General Erik Wickberg in 1969 added a new factor to the momentum towards change in that he was not British. Until then all Generals, with the exception of General George Carpenter, had been British-born and were familiar with the British scene. General Wickberg was to be the first of seven successive non-British Generals who just as naturally looked on the British scene from a different perspective. Some of them must at times have wondered in their heart of hearts why they had to wear a UK hat at all. Had they not been elected to be the Army's international leader?

The momentum towards change was given further impetus by the 1969 High Council in that all candidates were asked whether they would seek to resolve the 'British problem' if elected. This same question was asked again at the 1974 High Council when General Clarence Wiseman was elected, in 1977 when General Arnold Brown was elected, in 1981 when General Jarl Wahlström was elected, and in 1986 when Commissioner Eva Burrows became

General. The pressure for change was therefore literally coming from on high.

Responding to this challenge, each successive General took initiatives that facilitated the momentum towards change. In 1972 General Erik Wickberg began the process whereby colonels instead of commissioners were appointed to the Men's Social Services, the Women's Social Services, the International Training College, and SP&S Ltd. Though these units retained some of their territorial trappings, their leaders were declared ineligible for membership of the High Council. The sale of the Salvation Army Assurance Society to the Wesleyan and General Assurance Society in 1972 in effect removed one of the 'armies' within the UK. In 1973 General Wickberg took steps to make the financing of the *international* part of IHQ more international – so lessening the need for British funds for that purpose.

General Clarence Wiseman in 1974 appointed a top-level commission to study possible ways of resolving the 'British problem'. This resulted in the creation of a Chief of the Staff's British Council so that key leaders could meet on a regular basis. General Wiseman also set up co-ordinating councils at divisional level, which brought together the leaders of the various 'armies' in each area under the chairmanship of the 'field' divisional commander.

General Arnold Brown, elected in 1977, added to the momentum by merging the Men's and Women's Social Services into one 'Social Services' in 1978. This again reduced the number of 'armies' by one.

Most significantly of all, General Brown initiated and saw through the complex legal process that resulted in the *Salvation Army Act 1980*. This new constitution distanced the office of the General from the day-to-day administration of the Army in the United Kingdom. The General ceased to be the managing trustee of The Salvation Army Trustee Company. He no longer had to be personally involved in every property transaction. In this and other ways, the *Salvation Army Act 1980* proved to be an absolutely crucial factor in the process towards change.

In 1981 General Arnold Brown set up a second commission – with a wider membership – to seek ways of resolving the problem. This was as a direct consequence of a television programme critical of various aspects of the Army's work in the UK. The need to respond to the media had again brought to the fore the lack of co-ordination between the various branches of work and the absence of a supreme leader who could speak for the Army in the UK as a whole.

This second commission was not due to report until after General Arnold Brown had left office. But in preparation for the High Council that was to elect his successor, he circulated a proposal that all of the 'armies' in the UK should come under the direction of the British Commissioner, but with International Headquarters retaining over-all financial responsibility. This sharpened the focus of the question addressed to candidates at the 1981 High Council about the 'British problem'.

General Jarl Wahlström, elected in 1981, decided to await the report from the second commission that General Arnold Brown had appointed before taking any further action. When it arrived he found that the second commission had taken a different line from that which General Brown himself had proposed. Instead of the British Commissioner assuming overall direction, the commission recommended the appointment of a National Commander who would stand above the British Commissioner and all other UK leaders – in effect creating another level of command. Shades of the 'super' commissioner mentioned already in 1958.

In the light of this conflicting advice, General Wahlström appointed a third commission of key leaders to examine these options and the many 'variations on a theme' that they were giving rise to. This third commission identified seven possible options for the way ahead, but its recommendation was neither that the British Commissioner nor a National Commander should be given overall command of the Army in Britain, but that a National *Co-ordinator* should be appointed.

The Advisory Council to the General gave qualified support to the concept of a National Co-ordinator on the understanding that it would not diminish the role of the British Commissioner and would only be a temporary measure – but predicted a rocky road ahead. The key would be the content of the memorandum of appointment that the National Co-ordinator would receive.

General Wahlström therefore appointed a fourth commission to examine in greater detail the National Co-ordinator proposal and to prepare a detailed memorandum of appointment. The General deliberately chose non-British members for this commission so that vested interests would not come into play.

As the commission wrestled with the practical outworking of the concept it soon found that in such matters the devil is in the detail. For example, to what extent would the British Commissioner and the other leaders in the UK continue to be directly responsible to the General, and to what extent responsible to the National Co-ordinator? To what extent would the National Co-ordinator give overall strategic direction to the Army's mission? Even Solomon would have quailed at these challenges.

But this fourth commission did eventually produce a draft memorandum of appointment for a National Co-ordinator. However, when this was presented to the Advisory Council to the General for review, so many alarm bells rang in the minds of the members that the council decided to inform the General that it could no longer support the appointment of a National Co-ordinator.

Having reached this impasse, and with the next High Council being only six months away, General Wahlström concluded that this was a matter best left for his successor.

His successor was none other than General Eva Burrows – elected General in 1986. She knew the British situation from the inside, having been principal of the International College for Officers, leader of the Women's Social Services and territorial commander for the Scotland Territory. After carefully reviewing the findings of the four commissions, General Burrows decided against appointing a fifth. Instead she took the line of the old adage: 'a committee of one gets things done'. And that was why in 1988 I was given the task of seeking a way of resolving this matter.

Towards a solution

The situation I found in 1988 was very different from the one that General Kitching and his colleagues had faced at the commissioners' conference in 1958. The momentum towards change already described had removed obstacles and paved the way for new possibilities. A further factor influencing the situation was that whilst the Army in the developing world had grown in the intervening years it had seen losses in Britain. Much research had already been undertaken and documented, not only by the four commissions but also by individuals who had presented submissions. The literature on the subject was therefore vast.

There was also an air of anticipation – an acceptance that things could not go on indefinitely as they were, and a feeling that the time for half-measures was over. If the job was going to be done, let it be done in a clear-cut and decisive way. The key leaders who would be involved in the process were committed to it. Among them I mention Commissioner Ron Cox, Chief of the Staff; Commissioner Peter Hawkins, Chancellor of the Exchequer at IHQ; and Commissioner Harry Read, my mentor and friend of old, the British Commissioner. Colonel Dinsdale Pender was the territorial commander for Scotland, and Colonel Margaret White the leader of the Social Services. Their openness to change was reflected by other leaders at all levels within the UK. And supremely there was a General in office with the courage and determination to make things happen.

My research and work over the next two years took me into every nook and cranny of International Headquarters and the associated headquarters in the United Kingdom, and also included research visits to Canada and the USA. No leader or other staff member was too busy to see me. Every door was wide open, every document available. Eventually I could almost recite by heart the *Salvation Army Act 1980*. Throughout I kept in constant touch with the General and the Chief of the Staff, sharing with them my thinking as it developed, and incorporating their guidance into the creative process.

Every possible option was examined and evaluated and new ones created and tested. In addition to those already mentioned, options included giving the Chief of the Staff the additional role of National Co-ordinator, or even appointing two Chiefs of Staff – one for Britain and one for the rest of the world. But in a command structure such as the Army's, co-ordination rarely succeeds, and this had been the experience of the years. Band-aid solutions no longer commended themselves.

The conviction rapidly grew that the interests of the Army's mission in the UK would best be served by the creation of a single territory, under one leader, into which all aspects of work would be incorporated. As far as possible in the unique UK circumstances, this new territory would have the same relationship with International Headquarters as all other territories in the world. The entwined international and national administrations would therefore have to be thoroughly disentangled. This vision was the seed that was to grow into the creation of the United Kingdom Territory with the Republic of Ireland in November 1990.

Two formidable barriers

But at least two of the barriers noted already in General Kitching's time were still in place. And they were formidable. The first of these was the constitutional issue. On this the *Salvation Army Act 1980* had rightly reiterated yet again that 'the Army shall be under the oversight, direction and control of the General'. So was it possible for the General to give away her British hat?

The answer was, and remains, a clear no. By edict of the British Parliament, The Salvation Army in the United Kingdom must be under the oversight, direction and control of the General. It is a responsibility the General cannot relinquish, even if she or he should wish to. The General must always be the leader of the Army in Britain. End of story? Not quite.

In the *Salvation Army Act 1980* the General's powers and responsibilities are listed in great detail in a number of clauses. The final of these clauses has 27 words, and it is on these 27 words that everything that was to take place in November 1990 hinged. Among the General's power is the power 'to entrust or delegate to and to withdraw from the Chief of the Staff, Commissioners and other officers such powers, duties and discretions as he thinks fit'.

Those words were not new, and the General had always delegated 'powers, duties and discretions' with respect to the Army in the UK. But in the past the General had delegated to a number of different leaders, not answerable to each other, but answerable only to him. The big constitutional question was whether it would be possible for the General to delegate all of these powers, duties and discretions to just one person – the territorial commander of the new territory.

Extensive consultation with IHQ's official legal advisers Messrs Slaughter and May, and with the Charity Commission, the government watchdog on charity issues, eventually confirmed that, with certain provisos, it could be done. In these consultations and in all matters constitutional I greatly appreciated the skill of the IHQ legal and parliamentary secretary, initially Captain Shaw Clifton and then Captain Peter Smith.

The second formidable barrier to be overcome was the matter of finance. Fortunately the Army's global financial situation had changed significantly from the one General Kitching had faced in 1958. Resources for international work now flowed in increased measure from the financially independent territories, and particularly from the four USA territories. The financial burden on the UK for international work was therefore no longer so disproportionate. But for IHQ to give up its fund-raising capacity in the UK would be a radical step, one that no previous General had even contemplated. But in the event, General Burrows did not shirk even from that decision.

As far as the stewardship of the resources was concerned, all the Army's financial and property assets in the UK were in the one pot – The Salvation Army Trustee Company. Though no longer a trustee, the General had a clear constitutional relationship with the company. How could the General 'oversee, direct and control' the Army's work without access to the necessary resources? And yet, unless the assets were disentangled there would be continual uncertainty as to what was international and what was British.

Could a Salvation Army *International* Trustee Company be created and the assets separated, with the General having a constitutional relationship with both companies? At first it seemed an impossible scenario, but after protracted consultations with Slaughter and May and the Charity Commission, a way was found that enabled a Salvation Army *International* Trustee Company to be created. The lengthy and complex process of separating the assets – in which a decision had to be made about the destiny of every fund and every property – turned out to be a triumph of common sense and goodwill.

The General's dual role
With the creation of the United Kingdom Territory the General did not give away her British hat. The Army in the UK continues to be

under the oversight, direction and control of the General. And it is the General who is the leader ultimately responsible for everything in the UK. There is no mention of a UK territory or a UK territorial commander in the *Salvation Army Act 1980*. The UK territorial commander is answerable to the General, but it is the General who is answerable in law if anything goes wrong. The General also has an inescapable relationship with both The Salvation Army Trustee Company – which has stewardship of all the UK assets – and The Salvation Army International Trustee Company. Though not a member of either trustee company, the General sees all agendas and minutes of meetings of both companies and has the power to intervene.

The General therefore still regularly puts on his British hat. This is mostly done behind the scenes through the direct contact he continually maintains with the leader to whom he has personally delegated his 'powers, duties and discretions' with respect to the Army in the UK. This relationship between the General and a territorial commander is unique, the key factor being that the General is resident in the United Kingdom. If one pictures the territories of the Army world as ships in a naval fleet at sea, it is the United Kingdom Territory ship that has the Admiral of the Fleet on board. And just as the admiral will have a unique relationship with the captain on whose ship he is based, so the General has a unique relationship with the UK territorial commander. It is a relationship that has to be carefully nurtured, and it therefore bypasses the normal bureaucratic processes.

The General also puts on his British hat when he reviews the agendas and minutes of the meetings of the UK Trustee Company. And from time to time he publicly puts on his British hat when, as the ultimate leader of the Army in Britain, he meets with royalty and government officials, or with the Salvationists of the UK Territory. But the General is no longer involved on a day-to-day basis with the strategic direction or administration of the Army in Britain.

Widening of remit and consultation
As it became clear early in my research that we were moving towards a separation of the international and UK structures, General

Eva Burrows saw a golden opportunity for undertaking a review of the international administration as well. At that point I had begun to concentrate on giving shape to the projected UK Territory with the Republic Ireland by the preparation of detailed plans. But the General now decided to widen my remit to a study of how the new-look, slimline International Headquarters would function and how the IHQ-related changes would be implemented.

It had always been part of the plan that at some point management consultants would be called in to review our work and to give detailed advice on the various aspects. And when I had completed my plans for the separation of the administrations and drawn up detailed proposals for both the UK Territory and the new-look IHQ, Coopers & Lybrand were awarded the review contract.

Coopers & Lybrand worked with us for a period of four months, conducting their own interviews and engaging in their own research. They confirmed the appropriateness of the plans being made, added many invaluable insights, and helped us prepare detailed job descriptions for the key appointments of both the new UK and IHQ administrations.

Planning for the United Kingdom Territory

On the UK side, I was anxious that the senior policy and strategy-setting body should not be the Territorial Finance Council as was then still customary in most territories. In the early stages of the Army's development, territorial commanders were given virtually unlimited authority. But in 1899 the first *Orders and Regulations for Territorial Commanders* was issued, decreeing that all territories must establish a Territorial Finance Council. The aim was to widen responsibility for the control of assets.

This limitation of a territorial commander's authority was not welcomed by all territorial commanders, and was a key reason why William Booth's son, Herbert, then in charge of the Army's work in Australia and New Zealand, resigned from officership.

But no top-level *policy* council was required by orders and regulations. And when, with the passage of the years, the style of leadership in the Army became more collegial, the Territorial Finance Council by default gradually took on the role of being the main strategic and administrative council for territories. This was unfortunate, for it gave the appearance that finance was the most vital factor in all policy decisions to do with the Army's mission.

I was anxious to take advantage of the thinking, initially developed in the USA following a consultancy exercise undertaken by Booz Allen Hamilton in 1968, whereby departments at territorial headquarters are grouped together under senior leaders, who together are known as the 'cabinet'. In the USA territories the 'cabinet' still functioned in an informal way. But in consultation with Coopers & Lybrand we took the concept a stage further and the 'cabinet' became a formally constituted body – the Territorial Executive Council – which was to be the supreme administrative council of the territory with special responsibility for policy and strategy. This council was to meet weekly.

In connection with the UK it was decided to leave the amalgamation of the 'armies' at middle level to a second phase. Separating the international and UK administrations was a big enough step in itself for the moment. A 'middle management commission' was in due course appointed, under the chairmanship of Lieut-Colonel Derek Elvin, and after some years all the various aspects of work in any given part of the UK were placed under the direction of the divisional commander. The full integration of the personnel function was also deliberately phased.

Scotland and the Republic of Ireland

Scotland proved to be a considerable challenge. The 'field' work there had become a territory in 1917, a sub-territory in 1922, had lost its territorial status in 1929 when a national secretary was appointed, only to have it restored in 1936. Until 1980 the territorial commander in Scotland was responsible to the British Commissioner, not the General. The arrangement creaked, for the Army in Scotland was bound in so many ways to the Army in the rest of the United Kingdom – social, training, trade, publishing, music – and, interestingly, Salvationists in Scotland often expressed a wish to be more, not less, part of the bigger Army in the UK as a whole.

General Eva Burrows had been territorial commander for Scotland. I had been the territorial youth secretary. We both appreciated the Army there and wanted only the best for it. Could

Scotland become a totally independent territory – with all aspects of work coming under one territorial commander and with the assets being further sub-divided by the creation of a Scotland Trustee Company?

The possibility was examined, but research indicated that the Army's work in Scotland could not be financially self-supporting. A Scotland Territory would have to become a grant aided territory – drawing on the international resources of International Headquarters. That was not a welcome prospect. But neither was the prospect of Scotland losing its separate identity as a unit.

In the end a middle-of-the road arrangement was arrived at. Scotland became a 'command' within the United Kingdom Territory. The four divisional commanders there reported to the Scotland Commander, whose headquarters was in Glasgow. The Scotland Commander was a member of the Territorial Executive Council and was responsible to the territorial commander. It was recognised that this arrangement would be costly and difficult to work in practice, and so it proved. The command structure was therefore discontinued in November 1994, and a Scotland Secretary appointed instead, with the divisional commanders reporting direct to territorial headquarters in London.

The Republic of Ireland is an independent country and is not part of the United Kingdom. How best to handle administratively the small but virile expression of the Army there also proved something of a challenge. The solution reached was that of a certain constitutional independence as is indicated by the name of the territory – the United Kingdom Territory with the Republic of Ireland.

Planning for a restructured International Headquarters

A key development on the international side was the plan to form an International Management Council to be chaired by the General. This was to be the equivalent of the 'cabinet' at territorial level. The received wisdom from the days of William Booth was that the General should not be part of any regular boards or councils as this could diminish his freedom of action. Obviously the General frequently met with advisers according to the issue under consideration. But for the General to be the 'chair' of a 'management council' was entirely new thinking.

Was such participation in a council shades of the idea of 'the General in council', which Commissioner David Lamb had advocated in the late 1930s? This concept had been rejected at the time but had inspired the formation of the Advisory Council to the General in 1947. Would chairing a management council fetter the General's freedom of action? Would constitutional traditionalists rise up in protest?

General Eva Burrows herself welcomed the idea of an International Management Council and gave it her approval. But when the official announcement regarding its creation was made, it was carefully explained that 'the power of decision-making will remain with the General who will be free to accept or reject the balance of views expressed in the council's discussions'. No letters of objection on the subject were ever received.

The International Management Council is the General's 'cabinet'. The form of governance parallels the American presidential system in which, following consultation with the cabinet, it is the president who takes the decisions and is responsible for them. It is not like the British system of government under which decisions are taken in cabinet and the cabinet is collectively responsible for them.

International Headquarters is very different from a territorial headquarters in that every issue it deals with has a geographical component as well as a functional one. It is not only a matter of considering a particular personnel, programme or business issue in the way that a territorial headquarters does. It is also a matter of considering how the issue under review will affect Africa and India and South America and every other corner of the world.

Coopers & Lybrand suggested that there were three options for dealing with this challenge. In the first option, the senior line of management at international secretary level would be *functional* – personnel, programme, and business – with the geographic factor being represented by 'desks' at the second level of management. In the second option, the senior line of management would be *geographical* – the five international secretaries of geographical zones – with functional support being provided at a second level of management. In the third option, *functional* and *geographic* representation would be at the same senior level of management. The third option was the one chosen, and at IHQ there are currently five geographic (zonal) international secretaries and four functional ones, all with the rank of commissioner.

Announcement and reflections

In May 1990 General Eva Burrows announced the setting up of the new United Kingdom Territory with the Republic of Ireland, the separation of the administrations and the reorganisation of International Headquarters. The new territory was to commence operation on 1 November 1990 and the reorganisation of International Headquarters was to take effect on 1 February 1991. In addition to volumes of detailed planning I had also prepared a 15-page document summarising the changes and the background to them, and this was published 'by authority of the General'. My work on the project was nearly at an end – or so I thought.

This chapter is being written 16 years after the changes that took place in 1990, and it is opportune to look back on them with the advantage of the perspective that time provides. There is no doubt whatever that the separation of the administrations has worked to the advantage of the Army's mission in the United Kingdom. Even the fears that the General's position in the UK might be marginalised have so far proved groundless, and hopefully that will always be so.

The effect of the 1990 changes on the international side has also been positive. The General has been freed up for international ministry, and International Headquarters has a much clearer identity as truly international.

If there has been a negative it is that International Headquarters no longer has the financial strength it used to have. Though reliance on UK funds diminished over the years, the existence of the British funding source, available if needed, gave a certain strength to IHQ. International Headquarters is now virtually wholly dependent for its existence and its mission on the contributions received from the territories. This could in time subtly affect how the role of the General is perceived. The restructuring plans originally included the setting up of a massive international endowment fund, and it is to be regretted that this did not in the end materialise. However, in recent years other steps have been taken which are significantly addressing this issue.

The 1990 International Congress

The announcement in May 1990 of the administrative revolution that was to take place in November of that year was made at a time when preparations for an international congress, to be held in London from 29 June to 8 July 1990, were moving into their final phase. I had been involved with planning for the congress from the earliest stages, but 18 months before the event the General appointed me chairman of the planning committee. I therefore found myself ultimately responsible for the congress arrangements and was glad to have Major Ray Houghton, with his superb organisational skills, working with me as the executive officer for the event. Time-wise the twin tasks of making preparations for the congress and the administrative changes dovetailed well together. I could juggle between them and as the congress approached devote more time to that task.

The congress had been conceived on a grand scale. As was traditional for international congresses, it was to be a 10-day event. The 5,000-seater Royal Albert Hall had been booked for the full 10 days and daytime and evening events were held there every day. In addition a college next door to the Royal Albert Hall had been booked for seminars. For the two weekends the 10,000-seater Wembley Arena had also been booked.

To home in on just one detail: having to form and pre-rehearse four distinct 750-voice choruses made up of songster brigades from British corps for the two weekends of meetings at the two venues would be enough to daunt anyone. Except, of course, Lieut-Colonel Norman Bearcroft, who handled the musical side of the congress with his trademark aplomb and cheerfulness. But what other territory could mobilise 3,000 songsters for such an event? The 'host' British Salvationists met magnificently this and every other demand made on them. But to the congress planners this was just one aspect among thousands that had to be seen to.

Ensuring a good attendance at every event over a period of 10 days was another challenge. British Salvationists were likely to attend one or other of the weekends, not both. In the run-up to the congress I sometimes wondered whether the early planning had been over-ambitious. But when the congress began I was relieved to find that this was not so.

The congress, under the leadership of General Eva Burrows, turned out to be an exhilarating experience for everyone present. At the end of it I was pleased to file the memory of it in my mind under 'mission accomplished'. But when we reviewed the event after its conclusion, we recommended that future international congresses should be centred on one weekend only and not two, and this became the pattern for the international congress that was held in the year 2000 in Atlanta.

Musical *The Meeting*
The tradition of requesting a Gowans/Larsson musical for big congresses had not been overlooked, and in the early stages of the preparations for the 1990 International Congress, John and I were duly asked to write and present yet another work. We were hesitant. Was it for us one musical too many in the series? Writing *Take-over Bid* had been as exhilarating as climbing Mount Everest for the first time. Would climbing it for the 10th time engender the same excitement? But we accepted, and ideas soon flowed. The musical *The Meeting* was the outcome.

The musical focuses on the lives and circumstances of a group of people who are attending an Army meeting. Its key point is that the meeting which will transform their lives is not the meeting at the hall but a meeting with Christ.

The Meeting was produced by a British cast under the direction of Major John Mott and was premiered during the congress in the Wembley Auditorium on Friday 29 June 1990. The musical was well received and was subsequently published by SP&S Ltd. *The Meeting* packs a powerful message and like the earlier musicals has been widely used by groups around the world.

The Meeting is the last – at least thus far – in the series of Gowans/Larsson musicals. As we look back on the era of the musicals, John and I often comment that on that great day when the book of life is opened in Heaven, we are likely to discover that we have influenced far more people through our songs than through our mainline appointments. If that turns out to be so, we will praise the Lord for the opportunity that has been ours. And we will also look out for Denis Hunter in the great crowd and thank him yet again for bringing us together.

An unexpected turn of events

Soon after General Eva Burrows had informed the Army world that a United Kingdom Territory was to be created, she shared with me that she had decided to announce before the international congress who would hold senior leadership responsibilities within the territory – the territorial commander, the chief secretary and the members of the 'cabinet' – so that the congress would not be overshadowed by speculation.

A number of names had been pencilled in during our discussions, but some of the boxes at cabinet level on the administrative chart were still blank. Commissioner Harry Read, the British Commissioner, was retiring on 1 November 1990, and this opened the way for a territorial commander for the new territory to be appointed. As to who this might be I felt was a matter for the General and for the General alone. But I saw various possibilities. Colonel Ian Cutmore was the chief secretary in the British Territory and it was envisaged that he would continue in that role in the new territory and be a bridging figure.

Some days before the international congress the General asked to see Freda and me. The fact that Freda was included in the invitation warned us that it was likely to be an 'is there any reason why you should not accept this appointment?' kind of conversation and we prepared our hearts and minds accordingly. A cabinet appointment? An appointment at IHQ? Perhaps another overseas appointment? We would soon know.

But the General never asked the fateful question when we met with her. She went straight to the point and said that after giving the matter long thought and much prayer, she had come to the conclusion that the person best fitted to head up the new territory was the person who had conceptually masterminded its creation. She was therefore appointing me territorial commander and Freda president of women's organisations of the UK Territory, with the rank of commissioner.

Perhaps it was just as well that the General never asked the 'is there any reason why not?' question, for I can still vividly recall the sense of shock I experienced as she informed us of her decision. Of all people in the world no one knew better than I the significance of the step the General was taking in appointing a UK commander. For the past 125 years the General had shared out this delegation of powers and responsibilities to a number of leaders. Now the General was about to take the awesome step – awesome for her and awesome for the person concerned – of delegating these powers and responsibilities to just one person. I knew the risk that the General was taking. And now I was hearing that the one person was going to be me!

Of course I appreciated the General's trust in me. Of course there was a part of me that felt greatly honoured that at 52 years of age I was to be entrusted with leading the largest Army territory in the western world. Naturally I expressed my gratitude to the General as best I could, and assured her that she could count on us giving the task every ounce of our energy.

But I was genuinely thunderstruck. And at times in the next few days before the public announcement was made, Freda and I even wondered whether we ought to ask to be excused. But our experience of life thus far had always been that demand creates supply – both from previously untapped resources within and from the vast resources of God himself – and it seemed late in life to start saying no to its challenges. So as officers are meant to do, we went where we were told. We said yes to life. And have always been glad that we did.

Chapter Nine

THREE DIVERSE TERRITORIES

ON 1 November 1990 the new United Kingdom Territory with the Republic of Ireland got off to a flying start. Preparations had been very thorough.

Perhaps the most immediate change was felt by the two thirds of the personnel of International Headquarters who had UK-related functions – property, public relations, editorial, most of the Finance Department, and others. For on that day they ceased to be members of IHQ and transferred to the territorial headquarters of the UK Territory. They were still in the same building, most of them still sat at the same desks and did the same jobs – but the reporting relationships were entirely new. When the third of personnel who remained on International Headquarters first met on their own they were a bit shocked to discover how small International Headquarters had suddenly become!

In the Territorial Executive Council, the 'cabinet', I had a gifted and experienced team of leaders. The chief secretary was Colonel Ian Cutmore – shortly to be promoted to the rank of commissioner in recognition of the size of the UK operation. He and his wife Nancy were delightful colleagues. The field secretary was Colonel Ray Holdstock, the social secretary was Colonel Margaret White, and the Scotland commander was Colonel Bramwell Baird. Lieut-Colonel Ivor Rich headed business administration, Lieut-Colonel Stephen Pallant personnel, Lieut-Colonel Malcolm Bale communications, and Freda was the territorial president of women's organisations.

There was a great sense of expectancy among the officers and soldiers. One had felt it in the public launching of the territory in the Westminster Central Hall when the General had spoken about the Army's work in the United Kingdom being given new wings.

I sought to set the tone for the new leadership team when we met as a 'cabinet' for the first time. I asked them, firstly, to be a 'can do'

157

team – a team of possibility thinkers that, in Charles Wesley's words, would 'laugh at impossibilities and cry it shall be done'. I wanted them to make it exciting to be a Salvationist in the UK. I asked them, secondly, to be a 'cut through' team – a team that would always be ready to cut through red tape and to encourage initiatives and innovation. And I asked them, thirdly, to be an 'out there' team – a team whose whole existence would be motivated by a desire to serve those at the cutting edge.

I told them of the British air marshal who felt that the field units 'out there' were so important that he issued standing instructions to the staff at his headquarters that only he himself could say 'no' to any request from a field unit. The staff could approve requests but any refusal would have to have the air marshal's personal say-so. I asked the UK leadership team to reflect that kind of spirit in their dealings with those at the front.

Commissioner Harry Read had brought a wonderful spirit of optimism to the UK Salvationists through his leadership as British Commissioner. Mine was the privilege to build on that. And mine was the privilege of bringing together the various 'armies' in the UK in a way that had never been possible before.

Freda and I therefore made a special point of interacting with the officers and staff of all the units which previously had not come under the direction of the British Commissioner – like the social services, Scotland, public relations, and the training college. I made sure that in public meetings these branches of service were given due recognition. The song 'Bind us together' was the prayer of our hearts. And I believe the Lord answered it.

The greatest binding together came in the annual residential officers' councils held in Swanwick. These had always been British Territory councils – for the officers who were part of the 'field' branch. Now they became the councils in which all the officers of the new territory met, albeit in five separate sessions of three days because of the numbers involved. It was moving to see officers, who perhaps had last met in such a setting when cadets, finding each other again. God blessed these councils and they were a vital part in the cementing together of the territory.

I also wanted to visit each of the 25 divisions and touch as many of the corps as possible. That was a daunting task – but an immensely rewarding one. Our weekend visits would therefore frequently follow a demanding pattern. Saturday morning we would be driven to a divisional centre, arriving in time to meet with the officers of the division over tea, after which we would lead and speak in a divisional Saturday evening event. We would then stay with the divisional commander and his wife in their home, which gave us opportunity to get to know them and the work of the division better.

On Sunday morning we would drive to the first corps of the day for the holiness meeting. After that we would have lunch at a social centre in that or some other town, visit the centre and speak to the staff. We would then drive to the next town for the afternoon meeting in the second corps of the day. Tea was often taken at yet another social centre with the same programme pattern. After tea we would then drive to the third corps of the day for the salvation meeting. Time-wise we had some close scrapes with these inter-corps journeys! Following a cup of tea with the local officers after the evening meeting we would set out for the drive back to London.

We borrowed the rule of thumb that Commissioner Geoffrey Dalziel had set himself when British Commissioner. If we could be back in London by 1 am we would return home on the Sunday evening. And just as Commissioner Dalziel had role-modelled for us, we would leave for the office at 7 am the next morning. Looking back it seems that even in the realm of energy, demand creates supply!

The sense of excitement and 'can do' was felt throughout the territory. With respect to corps work, a strong conviction came to us that we should be launching into new communities, opening new corps and outposts. There was a deep and widespread desire to shift out of anything that could seem like maintenance mode. The divisional commanders were asked to survey prospects for new openings within their divisions – and to focus the prayer resources of their division on these possibilities.

They were requested to share their findings at a meeting of divisional commanders held at Sunbury Court. No one present will ever forget the occasion. At the front of the hall was a large map of the United Kingdom. Then, following a time of intense prayer, one by one the divisional commanders went up to the map and placed flags on the communities to which they felt the Spirit was leading them. At the end, there were nearly one hundred flags on the map. And many of these communities have since seen the Army flag literally planted in their midst.

A feature of the British Territory had been the large-scale 'Celebrations of Faith' which Commissioner Harry Read had introduced. With the attendance and participation of Salvationists from new corps plants, these events became even larger and ever more exciting.

The support from the public for the Army was as always quite amazing – almost frightening. I sensed it whenever I engaged with the media. Knowing that contact with the media would be an important part of my responsibilities as territorial commander, I had asked the UK's director of media relations Captain Charles King and Pam Rhodes, a well-known television presenter, to give me training in this art.

I got off to a helpful start. Soon after I became the leader, I took part in a phone-in radio programme about the Army. After the interviewer had asked me about the Army's work and we had conversed for some minutes, he invited listeners to phone in with any comments they would like to make.

The listeners began to phone. Their comments were all in praise of the Army, and I sat there purring like a cat and enjoying the way the programme was going. But for the presenter this was not 'good radio'. I could sense he felt the need for some tension to be part of the mix. So he said over the air: 'Isn't there anyone who would like to say something critical about the Army? Here's your chance.' But the positive calls just kept coming. So the presenter repeated his request – but still to no avail. I thought to myself: 'Not many Salvationists can be listening to this programme!'

In the end the patience of the presenter snapped. 'Here's your last chance. Surely there is someone out there with something critical to say about the Army!' The last caller, a woman, came on the air. 'I just want to say,' she said, 'that my son used to be a drug addict, and had it not been for The Salvation Army he would still be one!' 'I give up,' said the presenter. But he said it with a smile.

What with the approval from without for the Army and the sense of new life at its heart, we felt that God was blessing his Army and our own ministry. The new territorial structure had given a fresh impetus to the Army's mission in the UK. But a storm was about to break.

Turbulence

In the early weeks of 1993 it became necessary for us to call in Coopers & Lybrand to investigate an investment transaction that had been causing us concern. As a result it became clear that the Army had become the victim of a fraud by persons outside of the Army and that $8.8 million US dollars had moved beyond our control. We subsequently instructed Slaughter and May to start legal proceedings.

It was a crisis of the utmost magnitude. We knew that when we informed the territory and the media, the confidence of both Salvationists and the public would be shaken. It was also a crisis for me personally. As the territorial commander I was ultimately responsible for everything within the territory. And there was an added poignancy. General Eva Burrows had taken an awesome step of faith in delegating her powers and responsibilities for the Army in the UK to just one person. I had been entrusted with those powers and responsibilities. And now this crisis. I felt that I had let her down – and had let the new territory down.

It had been with a very heavy heart that I made my way to her office to break the news to her. She was magnificent in her response. But in the course of the conversation I said that she should not hesitate to move me to another appointment if she felt that it would help to restore confidence.

We set a date and time for the public announcement, equipped a room with a bank of telephones, and brought in a team of experts to help us handle the media blizzard which we knew would break. I wanted the officers of the territory to be the first to know, and informed them about the situation in a letter timed to arrive the day before the media release.

When the announcement was made, the fact that the Army had 'lost' $8.8 million dollars predictably became the headline news the next day, and further mentions followed in succeeding days. It was bad. Very bad. But it could have been worse. The media appreciated our openness, reported the matter factually and did not add fuel to the fire by their comments. Thankfully the dominant reaction from the public seemed to be one of sympathy.

The story was to have an amazing sequel. Slaughter and May, in a worldwide asset-tracing and recovery exercise spanning 13 countries, were eventually able to recover every cent of the US $8.8. million dollars, plus an additional US $4.9 million dollars to cover interest lost and the entire legal costs for the recovery exercise, making the total recovered US $13.7 million dollars. And it was reassuring that in the wake of the crisis, financial giving by the public did not diminish but actually increased. But in the dark days of the spring of 1993 all of that still lay ahead.

Shortly after receiving the news of the fraud, the General had rightly donned her British hat and had asked Coopers & Lybrand to widen their enquiries and turn them into a full investigation into the loss of the money. In due course the General felt that a change of territorial leadership would be helpful to the situation. I knew it was right.

So after two and a half years in command of the UK Territory we received farewell orders. As the 1993 High Council was only weeks away, we were to receive our next appointment once the post-High Council panorama was clearer. I therefore attended that High Council as a commissioner without appointment. And following the High Council we were appointed to New Zealand as territorial leaders.

We will never forget the outpouring of sympathy and love towards us from the officers and Salvationists of the UK Territory during those valley days of 1993. We received hundreds upon hundreds of letters and messages. We were going to sorely miss our colleagues in the UK for whom we had such great affection – and it seemed that they were going to miss us.

The events of 1993 were for me personally the biggest crisis I had ever had to face – a crisis which Freda shared with me and in which she was my unfailing support. But I discovered an inner steel in my make-up that I had not previously realised was there. Perhaps I intuitively knew that handling adversity was part of saying yes to life.

Six years later at the 1999 High Council I referred to what had happened in 1993, words that capture some of my inner feelings of those days:

The events of 1993 were not easy for Freda and me personally. I had to decide how to react inwardly. Was I to crawl into a corner within and just lie there and wait to die? Or was I to pick myself up, dust myself off, and keep going? I chose the latter. I began to notice in my biblical and biographical reading how many people, including those in the Lord's service, had been through difficult patches, and had emerged the stronger after such experiences.

I took particular comfort from the apostle Peter. I am so glad that after the events of Holy Week he did not crawl into a corner and hide. He resumed his leadership role in the Early Church – but never made a secret of the fact that he had had a failure in the past. I took Peter as my role model. And in the years that have passed since then, Freda and I have positively looked forward to each new challenge, and have in a marvellous way experienced the wonder of God's grace.

The appointment to New Zealand would mean the break-up of the family home. Karl was 21 and was already undertaking media studies at Bournemouth University. Kevin was 20 and was about to embark on a degree course in music at Colchester Institute. When it came to the last evening together we asked the boys how they would like to spend it. They suggested we should watch a video and hired in the light-hearted film *Sister Act*. So on the last night together we laughed a lot.

But the evening was tinged with sadness. And for me there was an added inner turmoil. For though I knew deep down that all families face a moment of parting, and that for officers' children it is often the parents rather than the children who move away, and that our boys were no longer children but young men, I also knew that things could have been so different. To this day I can't watch *Sister Act* without the memories of that evening returning.

New Zealand, Fiji and Tonga

We arrived in New Zealand with a sense of anticipation for all that was to lie ahead. The process of inner healing was speeded by the warmth of our welcome – and by the stunning beauty of the country. New Zealand is without doubt one of the most spectacularly beautiful countries on earth.

The chief secretary, Colonel Arthur Thompson, had in an imaginative way arranged for us to have our evening meals for the first few days in the homes of different officer families. With these social occasions, the contact with officers and staff at territorial headquarters, and the encounters with other Salvationists, we quickly felt totally at home and within a short time got to know many of the young people of the territory as well.

Most of the houses in Wellington are built on the sides of hills, and are made of wood in preparation for the 'big one' – the earthquake that it is feared might one day hit the city because it is built on a fault line. Our quarters were situated on the crest of a ridge, and the large panoramic windows overlooked a sweep of suburbia, with the airport and the blue-green water of the bay beyond, and the scene framed in the distance by a background of majestic mountains rising to the skyline. Healing during those first days flowed from that scene, and inspiration ever after.

We welcomed and continue to applaud the more-relaxed lifestyle we found in New Zealand. That was even reflected in the adventure of getting to know the corps and centres in that diverse country. Saturday has traditionally been family day in New Zealand so our weekend visits were often concentrated on just the Sunday.

Taking an early Sunday morning flight from the airport that we looked down upon from our windows in order to get to a holiness meeting somewhere in New Zealand became a frequent pattern. It never ceased to amaze us that we could leave home at a comfortable hour on Sunday morning, catch a flight to Christchurch on the South Island, change there for an onward flight to Dunedin in the far south, and still be in time for the holiness meeting. Had the Wellington city authorities not imposed restrictions on Sunday evening flights because of noise we would have been able to fly back that same evening after the salvation meeting.

The island countries of Fiji and Tonga, which are part of the territory, opened up for us the wonders of the Polynesian world. Fiji is a volcanic island and is dominated by a high central mountain, with the jungle sloping down to the exotic beaches. Soon after our arrival, we led the 20th anniversary celebrations of the Army in that country. It was heartwarming to see the large group of Fijian officers and soldiers.

The islands that make up the Kingdom of Tonga are, in contrast, as flat as pancakes – pancakes dotted with palm trees. The work in Tonga was only seven years old when we arrived in the territory and was still a work in progress. On one of our visits the officer in charge had arranged officers' meetings – three full sessions. We were seven officers in total. We got to know each other well that day! The Fijian and Tongan people come from different branches of the Polynesian heritage, the Tongans in particular being noted for their warlike attributes. But what warmth and friendship we met in both countries!

The Salvation Army is part of the very fabric of the New Zealand nation. It arrived at the time when the country was becoming established and has therefore 'always been there' and is highly respected. In the Army's earliest days the work among the Maoris prospered. But in one of those inexplicable changes of appointment that cause historians such grief, the officers who had been so notably successful in that ministry were moved to another appointment, and the work languished and has never reached the same peak again.

Since those early days the nation of New Zealand has become a secular society, very advanced in its societal thinking, in which the Army has maintained its strength. This the Army has achieved partly by remaining itself and partly by having the flexibility to adapt to changing circumstances.

The Army of the future

It has been said that whenever some wave of thinking hits the worldwide Church, New Zealand catches it full force. Perhaps it has to do with the rugged individualism of the Kiwis, as the New Zealanders call themselves, and perhaps with the country's geographical isolation. So when the wave of the charismatic revival hit in the 1970s, New Zealand bore the brunt of it, and the Army experienced in an acute way both its highs and its lows.

During our years in the country, the wave that was buffeting us was the conflict between traditionalists and 'contemporaries' – especially with respect to styles of worship. This was of course a wave that was lapping the shores of the Church worldwide, but in New Zealand it had the force of a tsunami. There was a wide gulf fixed between those who held that only songs printed in and sung from *The Song Book of The Salvation Army* could have God's blessing, and those who equally strongly held that songs were meant to be sung 'off the wall' and that any song in the song book was by that very fact disqualified!

But this was really the tip of the iceberg. The greater underlying conflict was the extent to which it was right for the Army as it approached the 21st century to shed its traditional way of doing things and adapt itself to the times – perhaps in the process becoming even a new creation.

This of course is a fundamental concern for the Army worldwide, and it exercised us greatly. Military armies that do not adapt to changing circumstances no longer win any battles. In William Booth's day, armies went to war with soldiers on horseback wearing scarlet uniforms. Any army that tried that today would become the laughing-stock of the world. Times have moved on. The argument from the contemporary wing was that unless The Salvation Army adapted itself radically to changed circumstances it too was in danger of winning no more battles – and possibly even becoming a laughing-stock.

In her day, Catherine Booth had given forceful backing to what she termed the 'adaptation of means'. But how far was it right to shed the baggage of the years? What are the essential 'core values' of the Army that we must die to defend, and which are the 'means' which we should adapt or even shed?

There was a strong wind blowing in support of the Army losing its distinctiveness and for it simply to merge into the Christian scene as yet another gospel mission. I have sometimes likened this to a 'Christian Mission' syndrome in our midst – the seeming desire of some for the Army to revert to what it was before it became The Salvation Army.

The situation in New Zealand was serious. This was no theoretical matter. Corps were tearing themselves apart on these issues. It was becoming a polarisation between officers and soldiers, with soldiers generally being more in the traditional mould than the officers. In fact, there was no shortage of officers willing to plant *new* corps where there would be no established Salvationists and they would have total freedom to experiment without the encumbrance of traditional trappings.

It was also a polarisation between generations – with the young naturally being the ultra-contemporaries. The young people were magnificent in their dedication and mission zeal. But they did not want to commit themselves to the Army by becoming soldiers in the traditional way – and least of all did they want to become officers.

Core values

Seeking to define and promote the Army's core values was therefore a matter of highest importance for our mission. I gave much time to this matter, and wrote extensively on the subject. The enforced concentration on this theme was to be of great value to me in later worldwide responsibilities.

I found that it is relatively easy to define the essential core values of the Army – its passion for mission, its pragmatic approach to evangelism, its social concern expressed in down-to-earth practical ways, its basic dynamism as befits a church which is also a movement, its doctrines, its emphasis on holiness, its informal worship style. What is much harder to define is what is *unique* to The Salvation Army, for most of the Army's core values are also among the core values of other denominations within the Christian Church. Is it only the quasi-military aspects that one is left with as unique to the Army, and if so, how essential are they to what the Army is?

I came to the conclusion that the quasi-military aspects are an intrinsic part of our identity, and that the way forward is not to seek to escape that heritage but to seek to adapt it to the temper of the times and maximise its advantages.

I also concluded that what makes the Army unique is its particular ethos – a word which the dictionary helpfully defines as 'the distinctive character, spirit and attitudes of a people'. There is an indefinable distinctiveness at the heart of Salvationism. It is the unique way in which all that we believe in, all that we are, and all that we do and stand for as an Army are blended together – even though few of these ingredients are in themselves ours alone. It is the particular way that our attitudes and convictions and passions as a movement have developed. And it is when you add all of these intangible factors together that you end up with that unique, distinctive and indeed beautiful something – the ethos of a people called Salvationists.

Earlier generations spoke of this ethos as the 'Army spirit'. They may have had difficulty putting into words what they meant – but in their hearts they knew exactly what the term described. It is this ultimately indefinable 'ethos of the Army' which is the supreme 'core value' of The Salvation Army – the core value that must never be lost, and which must be taught by word and example to each new generation.

But the challenge in New Zealand was to apply these insights in practical terms. For example, to what extent is uniform-wearing a necessary part of the Army ethos? The Army is the most visible part of the Christian Church. Would we lose something vital to the Army ethos if we lost this visibility? My own strong conviction is that we would. But the challenge was how to carry the hearts and minds of those who saw visibility as something peripheral to what we are. Throughout the process the aim was to accept the need for change, but not to lose anything essential to the Army's ethos. And we always recognised that in practical matters there could be legitimate divergences of views.

The process of adapting the Army to changing circumstances will in one sense never end – for outer circumstances will always be changing. It is how the Army's ethos is best applied in each age that is the crucial point.

A key aspect was of course the matter of worship style. To what extent is the Army's traditional approach to meetings a necessary part of the Army ethos? And that brings us back to the 'worship war' between traditionalists and 'contemporaries', which we found raged in some corps – and which again, of course, was not a phenomenon known only in New Zealand.

It is very clear to me that the distinctive Army style of worship is a very precious part of our heritage. To be part of an Army meeting at its best is a most moving, uplifting and powerful experience. But it is also clear to me that every tradition needs to be continually renewed if it is not to settle into a deadly rut. I therefore welcome the infusion of new inspiration that has come through the 'praise and

Above: Addressing the Salvation Army world on the web at the end of the 2002 High Council

Left: The two Johns in concert as General and General-elect at the Gowanses' farewell and our welcome

Below: With Chief of the Staff Commissioner Israel L. Gaither and Commissioner Eva D. Gaither

Above: Visiting a village in Bangladesh

Left: Thanking the pilot of the Missionary Aviation Fellowship on our return to Nairobi from Western Kenya

Below left: Commissioning Cadet Min Naung in Myanmar

Below right: Greeting Peter from the Home of Joy in Uganda

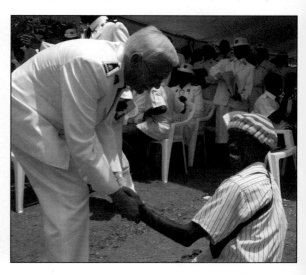

Top: Dancing in Papua New Guinea

Above left: Counselling in Korea

Above right: At the piano in Atlanta, USA

Right: Preaching in Sydney, Australia (photo: Anna Thompson)

Left: With President George W. Bush at the White House in Washington (White House photograph)

Below left: With the Princess Royal at the opening of the new International Headquarters

Below right: At a London congress, junior soldier Gary Pitt has his passport in hand, ready to travel anywhere with us

Right: With Pope Benedict XVI in Rome (photo: Arturo Mari, courtesy of *L'Osservatore Romano*)

Above left: Celebrating the Army's 70 years in Singapore

Above right: A refreshment break in Zimbabwe

Right: Meeting the media in Brazzaville, Congo

Above left: With young people in Finland

Above right: With two American children

Right: With young people at an Army school in Hong Kong

Left: Greeting Salvationists in India

Below: Being welcomed Indian style

Below: Witnessing with the young people of the European Youth Congress in Prague, Czech Republic

Bottom left: Salvationists kneel at the world's largest mercy seat during the All Africa Congress in Harare, Zimbabwe

Below: Getting a football match under way at the All Africa Congress as the Gaithers and Freda cheer me on

Above: Yes to life, and yes to each other (Photo: David DeJonge)

Right: Responding to the congregation's greeting at the Farewell Salute in the Westminster Central Hall, London, at which the members of the 2006 High Council were also welcomed

The Larsson family in Los Angeles, Christmas 2006.
Karl and Sarita are standing behind me. Kevin and
Jacqui are behind Freda, and we are holding their
two children Ethan and Aidan.

worship' style of singing. Some of these songs are beautiful beyond words. They will become classics and part of the Christian treasury.

But what a tragedy it is that the introduction of such singing around the world has sometimes been accompanied by denigration of the treasures that previous generations and centuries have created – and in the case of the Army, denigration of our own culture of song. For most Christians the classic hymns and songs are a cherished part of their mental furniture – words that have brought them close to God for as long as they can remember. What needless hurt has been caused when that furniture has been smashed as if by vandals. God does not want to destroy what he himself has in the past inspired. He wants to renew, he wants to *add* a new dimension. It was never meant to be 'either/or'. It was meant to be 'also/and'.

The debate I have described taking place in New Zealand was passionate, but it was a mission-driven passion. On all fronts, social and community service as well as evangelistic, the Salvationists of the territory were seeking to find better and more-relevant ways of fulfilling their mission. It was like being at the vortex of a creative flow. It was bracing and it was exhilarating.

God's nature

We fell in love with the beautiful nature around us. Freda and I had always been avid walkers. But in New Zealand we were introduced to the joys of 'tramping' the forest and mountains trails, and serious walking has remained a permanent part of our lives.

The mountains of the Rimutaka Forest Park that we looked out on from the windows of our quarters were not of Andean height. Even the summits were clothed with vegetation. But from the moment I walked into our home I felt their pull. I soon identified Mount Matthews as the highest point and determined to reach it some day. It was just under 3,000 feet, about the same height as Scafell Pike, England's highest peak in the Lake District.

I knew that getting to the foot of the mountain from the nearest car access point – which would include fording two thigh-deep rivers – would add time pressure. So on the Saturday morning when Freda dropped me off at the nearest point to the mountain it was still pitch black. Armed with a flashlight I set off on the forest trail. Three hours to the foot of the mountain and three hours up to the top. The summit was engulfed in cloud – but never mind! Three hours down and then three hours back along the forest trail. Freda had returned and was waiting for me in the car. Afterwards when I looked at Mount Matthews from the quarters' window I often relived the elation of that day. It was a satisfying feeling of 'been there – done that'!

The General phones

After three years we were due for homeland furlough. I had had opportunity to return to Britain for the 1994 High Council, which elected General Paul A. Rader. Karl and Kevin had both been able to come out to visit us – Kevin even working in New Zealand for a time. But it would be good to spend time with them back home and with other members of the family and friends. And we also planned to have some time in a caravan in Wales.

Whilst enjoying our caravan life in Wales in the summer of 1996 we had a message: would I phone the General. We set out to find a public phone. We eventually found one of the classic old red phone boxes planted on the wayside in a remote corner of the countryside.

The conversation was brief and to the point. General Paul Rader said: 'I am appointing you territorial commander of the Sweden and Latvia Territory, and Freda as territorial president of women's organisations.' I thanked the General – and that was about it. But that brief phone call had turned our world upside down – as is so often the case with such phone calls – and we therefore took a photo of the phone box to commemorate the occasion.

It was not a time for the old question, 'Is there any reason why you should not accept this appointment?' Army leaders are expected to go where appointed. That is one of the commitments of leadership. The General must be able to make the disposition of his top leaders in the way that he considers best for the Army's mission. And Sweden was my own country, so the prospect of returning there was welcome.

But whether an appointment is welcome or not, I believe in the Army's appointments system. I also welcome the increased measure of consultation that now takes place wherever possible. This enables the Army better to match personal giftedness and personal convictions about spheres of service with available appointments. But consultation has to be handled with great sensitivity on the one side and great understanding on the other. For having engaged in consultation it is ultimately the Army that has to make the decisions – and sometimes 'the exigencies of the war' do not match our own wishes.

Being practical and action-oriented by nature, Freda and I immediately packed up our things and headed back to London. We drove straight to Foyles bookshop in Charing Cross Road – reputedly the largest bookshop in the world. We needed to arm ourselves for the new battle.

I had left Sweden precisely 50 years before, and was now returning at the age of 58. I had not used the Swedish language during those 50 years and was not sure if anything of it was left in my mind. Perhaps it was in some remote corner. For Freda it was going to mean starting from scratch on a second new language. We bought a substantial selection of 'teach yourself Swedish' books plus dictionaries and grammars, and then within a few days were on the plane back to New Zealand.

We had been given three months warning about the change of appointment, and during those weeks I set time aside daily for language study. I discovered that our first public engagement in Sweden would be the weekend after our arrival – an inter-divisional congress during which I would be required to give seven Bible messages. I knew I had to preach in Swedish. Anything else would be soul-destroying to the Swedish Salvationists. A Swedish-born territorial commander who could not speak Swedish? Unthinkable!

I therefore prepared the full text of the seven messages plus any 'responses' to introductions that the programmes appeared to require. This was an unaccustomed discipline for me, for I like to speak freely from brief notes. I then arranged for this material to be translated into Swedish.

I next took lessons in Swedish pronunciation. By a happy coincidence the territorial music secretary in New Zealand at the time was Swedish by nationality. We spent many hours together as I read the talks to her, annotated difficult words, and tried to imitate her pronunciation. But it all paid off in the end!

And then it was time to say goodbye. There were so many things we were going to miss. We were going to miss the country. So much so that we even considered settling there in retirement.

And we were going to miss working with Colonels Hillmon and Lorraine Buckingham, who had become chief secretary and territorial secretary for women's organisations during our time there. We were going to miss the effervescent leadership team at territorial headquarters, miss the officers and soldiers of the territory. We were going to miss 'tramping' the trails. We were going to miss our home on the crest of the ridge which had come to mean so much to us. And we were going to miss working in that most dynamic part of the world – the 'Pacific rim'. But other adventures lay before us.

Sweden and Latvia

We arrived in Sweden on 1 October 1996. We knew that the first engagement upon arrival was to meet with the staff of territorial headquarters over coffee. I assumed that some words from me would be required, and on the flight from London I had jotted down some thoughts with the help of a Swedish dictionary. I had put the notes in my briefcase. I still had no idea whether I really could speak Swedish or not. When we arrived in Chile there had been a 24-year gap with Spanish. But now the gap was of 50 years.

We were met at Arlanda airport by the chief secretary, Colonel Gunnar Nilson, and his wife Berit – two people who were quickly to become our friends and with whom it proved a delight to work. In the sorting out of the luggage I found that my briefcase with the precious notes was in the other car. 'No problem,' said Gunnar. 'We'll be travelling in convoy.' But I had broken the first rule of international travel for speakers: never be parted from your notes.

When we arrived at THQ there was no sign of the other car. But as everyone was waiting in the meeting room we went straight in – confident that the briefcase would soon catch up with us. Speeches of welcome were made. Flowers were presented. It was getting near my turn to respond. Still no briefcase. And then Gunnar called on me to speak.

I knew that everyone present wondered just as much as I did whether I could still speak the language I had spoken when living on that same building half a century before. I took a deep breath. I opened my mouth. I began to speak. And the words I needed simply poured out. I discovered that I had a totally unexpected freedom in my mother tongue. I was able to venture down paths of thought that I had not even pre-prepared in my mind. I found myself relating easily with the audience, and I could sense their pleasure that this native stranger could communicate with them in their own language.

That built up my confidence for the next weekend – the inter-divisional congress. Though this time I kept a close eye on my notes when speaking I nevertheless had liberty, as the preachers of old used to say, when I gave my seven messages. The warmth of the response was reassuring and encouraged us. I did, however, remind the officers in the officers' meeting that when I last lived in Sweden my reading had mainly been Donald Duck and Mickey Mouse and that I therefore had some catching up to do!

Mastering a language is downright hard work and there are no short cuts to be had. During my years in Sweden I continually had to keep working away at the language – always carefully preparing even my 'contact words' (a useful Scandinavian term) for the early part of meetings. Preparing such 'spontaneous' words ahead of time for situations one had not yet experienced was sometimes as challenging as preparing the main message.

Freda enrolled in the state-sponsored language course that all immigrants who want a work permit are required to take. Her fellow pupils were recent arrivals from Afghanistan, Iran, Palestine, Kosovo, and just about every other country to the east of Sweden. All classes were totally in Swedish, for that was the nearest there was to a common language. It was immensely demanding – a 'five-afternoons-a-week' course spanning several months. But with her characteristic 'can do' approach, Freda was soon venturing out in Swedish both informally in conversation and on the platform.

Innovation

Coming from New Zealand to Sweden, we had moved geographically about as far as it is possible to go – from the extreme south to the extreme north. But in a surprising number of ways, the two countries were replicas of each other. Watching the news on television or picking up a newspaper, we found that the same issues were being debated. Both countries were extremely advanced in every way – technologically, intellectually, culturally. Social welfare legislation covered every area of life. And both countries were secular to the core.

It was therefore no surprise to find that the Army was grappling with many of the same challenges in both settings: how to reach the hearts and minds of a secular generation with the gospel, and how to work in tandem with the state to solve social problems whilst at the same time pioneering new services. It was also reassuring to find that just like their Kiwi colleagues, Swedish Salvationists had a vision for the whole world.

The Army in New Zealand has kept before it the ideal of tithing its personnel for work overseas. Swedish officers and lay personnel have served in their hundreds around the world – and the tradition is still strong. In 1990 the Swedish territory again showed its spirit of mission by re-establishing and then maintaining, at great financial cost, the Army's work in Latvia. For Freda and me, frequent visits to Latvia opened up the Baltic world to us.

Innovative ways of reaching out with the gospel were a marked feature of the territory and took many forms. I was therefore not surprised when the field secretary, Lieut-Colonel Hasse Kjellgren, mentioned that a number of young people in Stockholm wanted to form a corps of their own – a youth corps – which would have the specific aim of reaching the youth of the capital with the message. I readily gave my agreement.

I was excited because a corps by young people for young people would take the concept of niche corps within the Army into a new area. Niche corps are designed to attract and minister to a particular group of people within society. In church growth thinking this is summed up by the 'homogenous unit' principle – namely that in evangelism one needs to take advantage of the fact that birds of a feather like to flock together. It is probably the most controversial of the church growth principles, but the Army, with its pragmatic approach to evangelism, has not been slow to see its value.

Niche corps have included corps designed to reach out to specific socio-economic groups like the goodwill corps in Britain, to specific language groups like the Chinese or Korean or African corps in the USA, or to specific interest groups like the corps for college students on or near college campuses in various parts of the world. And now we were going to experiment with a corps by young people for young people. Exciting!

The controversial aspect of niche corps is of course that a Christian congregation is meant to be fully inclusive. Everyone without exception should be made welcome in the family of God. With that there can be no argument. So niche corps are but means to an end, and are usually of a temporary nature. That is how it has been in Army history. Corps designed to reach one socio-economic strata have in time reached a much wider group, and corps that have reached out to one language group have in time merged into the local culture and have adopted the local language. But in the meantime they have met a specific need in an innovative and effective way.

None of us had any illusions that it would be different with a youth corps. Young people soon become young marrieds, then young parents, and before you know it, young middle-agers and beyond! They are not likely to want to transfer to another corps. But the validity of the 'like attracts like' principle was abundantly confirmed for us. Powerful forces are released when young people are set free to reach out to their own generation in their own way.

The youth corps was going to be called 'Corps 393' – the next number in the list of corps opened in Sweden during the history of the Army there. It was deliberately a neutral name that did not tie the corps to a specific location or even a specific age group. I was asked to preside over the launching of the corps in the Stockholm Temple Corps, which has a very large hall complete with gallery.

It proved to be another unforgettable event. As I walked towards the hall the pounding pulse of the electronic music from within could be heard two blocks away. Entering the hall was like arriving at a rocket launch. Vast screens and giant sound speakers dominated the scene. Huge celebratory banners and posters added both a festive touch and a call to action. Young people in colourful tee shirts and blue jeans milled everywhere – with precision and with purpose.

The hall was full to capacity with well-wishers – of all ages. It seemed that everyone wanted to show their support for the young people. Seated in the front centre block were the retired officers of Stockholm – a large and formidable group, steeped in tradition. I wondered how they were reacting. But I felt a lump in my throat when I saw them beating out the rhythm with their feet, clapping their hands and singing for all they were worth! Perhaps a hearing aid or two had surreptitiously been switched off. But what did that matter? I was proud of them.

The launch was as good as anything seen at Cape Canaveral. It was powerful because young people were being set free to do their own thing in the service of the Lord, powerful because youth was speaking to youth, powerful because every other generation was there in support, and powerful because the ear-piercing high-tech music was so absolutely right for that occasion. I was sure that as Catherine Booth looked down from the battlements of Heaven she was smiling in approval at this 'adaptation of means'. She might even have been tapping her feet – perhaps urging William to join in.

It was a memorable launch to what has become a remarkable ministry. Corps 393 has lived up to the high hopes that were vested in it that Sunday afternoon. A decade later some of its founder members may be a bit older, but its focus on mission to the youth of Stockholm remains as intense and effective as ever.

Faithfulness

But while innovation and verve and vigour were one part of the picture, sheer dogged faithfulness was the other. In the 50 years that had elapsed from the time when my grandfather – Commissioner Karl Larsson of 'work for the night is coming' fame – was the territorial commander, the forces of secularism had taken their toll on the Army in Sweden.

The breadth of scope and sheer quality of all its operations were as evident as always. But numbers were not what they had once been. There were large corps, but there were also corps that had become small and where just holding on was a victory. I wanted to hug these often elderly comrades who week upon week kept the doors of the Army open. I told them that I sometimes wished I had a suitcase full of 'Orders of the Founder' that I could hand out to them as we travelled through the territory.

I think of the elderly lady 'field sergeant' who was in charge of one such small corps. The corps had once had a band, and the band had conducted open-air meetings in the town square. But now only she and a handful of soldiers were left. Yet each week she would bake buns and make coffee, and then she would go down to the town square and set up a table. As people passed by she would offer them free coffee and a bun.

'That is how I get in touch with people,' she said to us. 'And as we talk I share with them what the Lord has done for me.' Is not that the kind of spirit that would have commended itself to William Booth?

We felt a strong calling to the ministry of encouragement. I kept reminding these my friends that there is an ebb and a flow in history, there are high tides and low tides, but it is the same God who is in control, and who holds the whole wide world in his hand. If we have been called to serve him at a time of low tide for the Christian message, then all that God expects of us is that we do our best and remain faithful.

I kept emphasising that we are not to go around feeling a burden of guilt as if the lack of visible results is somehow our fault. It was sometimes heartrending to hear these old saints of God saying, 'If only we had done more. If only we had prayed more.' They carried a heavy burden of failure.

But I sought to convince them that it was unreasonable to think that the whole of western civilisation has turned against God because of some personal shortcomings on our part. We are up against principalities and powers over which we have no control. And God does not want us to go round weighed down by guilt. It is his work, not ours, that we are engaged in. We can safely leave the final outcome to him.

Most of all I kept reassuring my colleagues that *this* is just as much the day that the Lord had made as all the days of the past – and that God wants us to rejoice and be glad in it! Despite the challenges we are facing, it is OK to be glad!

Habakkuk got it right in his time when he exclaimed: 'Though the fig tree does not bud and there are no grapes on the vines, though the olive crop fails and the fields produce no food, though there are no sheep in the pen and no cattle in the stalls, *yet will I rejoice in the Lord, I will be joyful in God my Saviour'* (Habakkuk 3:17-18, *NIV*).

I saw hearts lifted and burdens shed when at a congress I shared with them my own free translation of that passage:

Though there is indifference to the gospel
and people seek the values of the world,
though there is little spiritual fruit to be seen
and the harvest is small,
though new people do not come to the meetings
and no one has got saved for a long time,
yet will I rejoice in the Lord,
I will be joyful in God my Saviour.

I hold the officers and Salvationists of Sweden – and indeed the officers and Salvationists of the whole of Europe – in the highest esteem. They are now in the very frontline of mission. And just as adversity can reveal unsuspected personal qualities, so the challenges the Army in Europe is facing are bringing out a superb response from the Salvationists. I will not be surprised if in future years the Army worldwide will be taking its lead from Europe when it comes to creative and innovative ways of reaching out with the gospel in a secular age.

A new task awaits

During our time in Sweden I became chairman of the Advisory Council to the General. The council consisted of five London-based commissioners and five commissioners from further afield, and we met thrice yearly at International Headquarters for three or four days. Membership of the council familiarised me with a number of the issues that the General was currently facing around the world, and was therefore a helpful preparation for what was yet to come.

Attendance at the 1999 High Council, called to elect a successor to General Paul A. Rader, was a very different experience for Freda and me, for unlike the High Councils in 1993 and 1994, Freda was to be a member of the council. This was due to the changes introduced in 1995 whereby married women officers now hold rank in their own right. Membership of the High Council has traditionally been 'all commissioners and all territorial commanders', and by virtue of Freda being a commissioner we were to share the experience together.

At the High Council I was nominated to become a candidate. After reflection and prayer I came to the conclusion that not crawling into a corner because of the events of 1993 included saying yes to this challenge as well. Five members accepted nomination, Colonel Shaw Clifton, Colonel Israel L. Gaither, Commissioner Earle Maxwell, Commissioner John Gowans and myself. After the first ballot the two colonels withdrew, and after the second ballot I withdrew. It then became an absolute cliffhanger between Commissioners Earle Maxwell and John Gowans – with Commissioner John Gowans eventually emerging as the next General of The Salvation Army.

A couple of days later John phoned. Would I become his Chief of the Staff?

Chapter Ten

GOWANS AND LARSSON – AGAIN

GENERAL John Gowans was the 16th General in the line of succession that had started with William Booth. In the corridor outside my office as Chief of the Staff hung the photos of all the previous Chiefs, so I counted them up. The turnover had obviously been greater. As I took up my appointment on 1 August 1999, I was the 21st Chief of the Staff. Freda was appointed World Secretary for Women's Organisations and World President of Salvation Army Scouts, Guides and Guards.

What a distinguished heritage I was entering into! The greatest of the great was of course Bramwell Booth. He was also the youngest to become Chief of the Staff and the longest serving.

Already by the age of 14 Bramwell was doing the accounts at headquarters for his father. By the age of 16 – in 1872 – he was clearly his father's right-hand man in the management of The Christian Mission and was responsible for supervising a whole range of its activities. Whenever his father was away from London, Bramwell reported to him daily by letter. When The Christian Mission became The Salvation Army in 1878, Bramwell began to be called Chief of the Staff. If one reckons from the time that he was 16 until the death of his father in 1912, Bramwell Booth was second in command for 40 years.

If ever there was an executive match made in Heaven it was the relationship between William and Bramwell Booth. They were almost opposites in temperament and personal characteristics – Bramwell taking more after his mother – but as a duo team their respective gifts complemented each other perfectly. If William was the apostle Peter to the early Army, Bramwell was its Paul. It was Bramwell who ensured the permanence of his father's prophetic and visionary legacy. And it was Bramwell who created the role of Chief of the Staff – and it is to his example that all succeeding Chiefs have looked.

A curiosity of Salvation Army administration is that the unique working relationship between William and Bramwell Booth was adopted as the pattern of leadership for all territories. Every territory has the equivalent of a William Booth and a Bramwell Booth in its territorial commander and chief secretary.

A chief secretary in a territory does not have quite the same independence of authority as the Chief of the Staff. Many matters that territories are required to refer to International Headquarters are 'for decision by the Chief of the Staff'. But the relationship between the territorial commander and chief secretary in a territory is clearly based on the William and Bramwell Booth model. In many ways the arrangement is unique to The Salvation Army.

The exact nature of the relationship in the sense of who will do what is largely undefined in *Orders and Regulations for Territorial Commanders and Chief Secretaries*. This allows leaders to work the relationship in accordance with their respective giftedness. The system is by now well tried and usually works well. But territorial commanders do not themselves choose their chief secretaries, and not all duos have had the 'of one mind' affinity that characterised the original father-and-son team. The working relationship between a General and his Chief of the Staff will also differ according to the personalities involved. For that reason there is no written memorandum of appointment for a Chief of the Staff.

Looking at the photos on the wall I observed that the shortest-serving Chief of the Staff was Commissioner Norman Duggins. General Wilfred Kitching appointed him in 1961 when Commissioner William J. Dray retired. Soon after entering office, Commissioner Norman Duggins conducted a spiritual day at the International Training College. I was a member of the staff at the time. He spoke about the Holy Spirit, basing his message on the whole of Romans 8. The impact he made that day remains vivid. Many of us thought we had spotted the next General.

Imagine the shock to the Army world when only some weeks later Chief Duggins collapsed as he conducted the holiness meeting in Paisley Corps and died the next day. He had only been Chief of the Staff for two months. General Kitching then chose Commissioner Erik Wickberg to be his Chief. Erik Wickberg served not only General Kitching for the remainder of his term, but was also Chief of the Staff to General Frederick Coutts.

When elected General himself, Erik Wickberg showed administrative courage in the appointment of his Chief of the Staff. He selected an officer who only six years previously, at the age of 50, had been the territorial youth secretary in his native Canada, had never been a divisional commander, nor a chief secretary, nor a territorial commander. He chose Arnold Brown – secretary for public relations at International Headquarters – and gave him the rank of commissioner to go with the appointment.

There must have been astonished gasps somewhere along the line. From being one of the boys Arnold Brown had been catapulted past all the commissioners at International Headquarters into the position of second in command of the international Army. But the General's choice was not only brave, it was inspired. For far too long this outstanding officer had been held back at territorial headquarters in Canada, despite repeated requests from International Headquarters for him to be released for wider service.

The problem was that he was so gifted that he had become indispensable to the territorial leadership. But when General Frederick Coutts was in office he had cut through all of that and, despite even a last-minute plea from the territorial commander in Canada, he had insisted that Brigadier Arnold Brown be appointed to International Headquarters. 'Decision taken. Brown proceeds to London' read the terse telegram from IHQ. And now, only six years later, here he was – the new Chief of the Staff!

I was later to discover, both as Chief of the Staff and General, that when International Headquarters reaches out its hand to fast-track a leader for the future, a frequent first reaction from territorial leaders is: 'Absolutely right – but please not yet. This officer is irreplaceable.' At times we acquiesced, but mostly we placed first the long-term interests of the territory concerned and of the global Army. I myself always kept the Arnold Brown saga before me. He should have been brought into the mainstream of leadership in Canada and also made available to the world long before he was. We usually found that leaders understood and accepted with good grace when we had to insist on an officer being released for international service.

I was honoured that General-elect John Gowans had asked me to become number 21 in the line of Chiefs of the Staff. Perhaps it took some courage on his part to appoint someone who was so clearly identified as a friend. But for myself I felt that the working relationship we had developed in the course of writing the musicals had set a useful pattern and that our respective gifts fitted well together.

I also felt confident that our friendship would survive any minor strains that might arise from time to time in the new working relationship. With the musicals we had been two equals. When we had reached difficult points we had each advanced our views, and on the rare occasions when we could not reach a common mind, one or the other had gracefully yielded.

But the relationship between General and Chief of the Staff was going to be quite different. We might discuss and reason and explore some matter together, and we might agree or disagree about a proposed course of action – but it would always be the General who in the end decided. We both understood that, and we both understood that the usefulness of such explorations of ideas behind the scenes depended on them remaining private between us. Our working relationship therefore rose to new heights of creativity – as did our appreciation for each other. And working with John never failed to be stimulating and invigorating.

A world view

The General and Chief of the Staff meet every morning whenever they are both at International Headquarters, and electronic communication now enables them to be constantly in touch even when one or both are out of the country. Email has revolutionised the conduct of Army business as much as it has transformed business practice everywhere. The new medium demands an immediacy of access and response that previously would have been unthinkable. The day of dictation to secretaries or dictaphones has virtually gone. In has come the laptop and the instant reply.

As the 'e' wave began to roll in the 90s, International Headquarters in consultation with the territories initiated exploration into the most useful electronic system for the Army to adopt universally. Once a decision had been arrived at,

International Headquarters insisted that all territories adopt the same chosen system, and as a result the Army early on became a world leader in the field of international intranet and database systems. There will come a time when the General will be able to address in person every corps in the world. And it will come sooner than might be thought possible today, for the developing world is leapfrogging generations when it comes to the development of such technology.

A big change for me personally was that the whole world had suddenly become my parish. Emails would pour in from the remotest parts of the globe, and I quickly had to become conversant with the history, geography, politics, and the current challenges facing the Army in over a hundred different countries. Fortunately International Headquarters is designed to provide quality functional and geographic support to the General and the Chief of the Staff.

But it was a long way from that first appointment in Sunderland Southwick and Washington, when my area of responsibility was delineated to the last street on the local map hanging in the officers' room. Woe betide an officer who at house-to-house collecting time crossed the street if the other side belonged to another corps! With the youth appointments that followed, my horizons had expanded to cover whole countries, and even more so when I became a chief secretary and territorial commander. But now it was the whole world – and not only the countries in which the Army was already at work, but even the countries into which it might expand in the future.

Freda and I knew that we needed to keep fit to handle this global assignment. Much travelling would be involved. New Zealand had well and truly given us the walking bug. In Sweden we had found that the only way to safeguard time for a walk each day was to do it first thing in the morning. So that is how we had begun each day – whatever the weather. There is something infinitely beautiful on a dark winter morning to be the first to leave one's footprints in snow that has fallen through the night. We decided to establish the same pattern in London whenever we were not away travelling. And so for the next seven years – during my term as Chief and General – we set the alarm for 5 am and then went straight out for a two-mile walk whether it was wet or dry.

The role of International Headquarters

Having had a hand in designing the shape and function of the 'new-look slimline' International Headquarters that resulted from the separation of administrations in 1990, I was especially interested in finding out how things had developed in the nine years since then.

I was pleased to find that the structure had stood the test of time, and also pleased to note the fine tuning that had taken place. The basic blocks of functional and geographic international secretaries with their respective departments supporting the General and the Chief of the Staff were there. The International Management Council was still the central forum for the transaction of business and the setting of policy and strategy, but its name had been changed to International Strategic Planning and Management Council. Some years later it reverted to its original name.

Still in place was the key concept that the zonal departments are the 'gateway' departments between the territories and International Headquarters. A territory does not need to concern itself with who handles what at International Headquarters. All matters can be directed to the zonal international secretary who then assumes responsibility for routing the matter correctly and ensures that it is dealt with.

But all systems need to be continually checked for relevance and effectiveness, and with the General's blessing I instituted a review of the role and function of International Headquarters. I set up an inter-disciplinary group for that purpose and chaired its weekly meetings. We defined the mission of IHQ as follows. 'International Headquarters exists to support the General as he/she leads The Salvation Army to accomplish its God-given worldwide task to preach the gospel of Jesus Christ and meet human need without discrimination.'

No mission statement ought ever to be set in stone – our mission statement was in fact built on the statement previously issued in 1992 – but it helped us to clarify both to ourselves and others why International Headquarters exists. For one thing, the mission statement links inextricably the role of IHQ with the leadership role of the General. For another, it makes clear that the leadership role of the General has everything to do with 'mission'.

And a key role of International Headquarters is therefore to be the dynamo that inspires, directs, supports and resources mission around the world.

We broke down the outworking of that role into a series of bullet points, which became an extended version of the mission statement. We said that International Headquarters assists the General –

- To give spiritual leadership, promote the development of spiritual life within the Army, and emphasise the Army's reliance on God for the achievement of its mission.
- To provide overall strategic leadership and set international policies.
- To direct and administer the Army's operations and protect its interests – by means of appointments, and delegation of authority and responsibility with accountability.
- To empower and support the territories and commands, encourage and pastorally care for their leaders, and inspire local vision and initiatives.
- To strengthen the internationalism of the Army, preserve its unity, purposes, beliefs and spirit, and maintain its standards.
- To promote the development, appropriate deployment and international sharing of *personnel.*
- To promote the development and sharing of *financial resources* worldwide, and manage the Army's international funds.
- To promote the development and international sharing of *knowledge, expertise and experience.*
- To develop the Army's ecumenical and other relationships.

To accomplish these goals, the General uses his powers of delegation and IHQ works as a team. It is a small team. When we eventually moved into a new building it was the smallest IHQ building the Army has ever had. This was not because the Army internationally had got smaller. On the contrary, the Army is bigger today than it has ever been. The smallness of the IHQ team is due to the separation of administration that took place in 1990 and the 'slimline' changes introduced at that point. It has also seen continual downsizing ever since. But it is a remarkable team because of the diversity of its range of skills – and it has to handle challenges big and small.

The continuing challenges

A continuing challenge for International Headquarters is to preserve the Army's unity amid the diversity of its constituent parts. The Army is the most closely knit church in the world – even surpassing the Roman Catholic Church in this regard. It is the same Salvation Army everywhere in the world. All territories have the same mission, accept the same doctrines, are governed by the same set of directives in the form of internationally binding orders and regulations, and their officers and soldiers sign the same covenants. And yet at the same time there is a great diversity between territories. This diversity is essential. The Army must adapt to the local culture and circumstances if it is to achieve its mission. It is how to keep in balance these two ideals of unity and diversity that will always be a challenge to International Headquarters.

Linked with this is the need to empower the territories. The mission action is of course 'out there' – not at International Headquarters. And that is why a key role of IHQ is to empower and support the territories and inspire local vision and initiative. This is accomplished by delegation of authority to the local leadership – with that leadership in turn being accountable to the General. So within the constraints of unity accepted by all, territories are granted considerable autonomy.

The sharing of financial resources is another key concern of International Headquarters. Numerically, two thirds of the Army today is found in Africa and South Asia. But two thirds of the financial resources are in the Western world. When it comes to the sharing of financial resources, the story of The Salvation Army is one of remarkable international generosity and mutual support. International Headquarters facilitates this process through the International Self Denial Fund, to which all territories contribute, and the quite remarkable system of 'projects'. About two thirds of territories receive grant aid in some form or other.

If the sharing of financial resources is a remarkable story, so is the continuous sharing of personnel. The complexities involved seem to grow greater as the world becomes smaller! Again,

International Headquarters plays the leading role in facilitating that process. Another responsibility of IHQ is to encourage and monitor the development of personnel in all countries where the Army is at work.

Yet another crucial role of IHQ is to facilitate the sharing of knowledge, expertise and experience. This is sometimes achieved by making the right link-ups between people – linking need with supply wherever it is to be found. At other times it is achieved through the sharing of written material. The previously mentioned international intranet system has a vast database capability that is opening up possibilities in this regard that our forefathers could not even have dreamt about.

The General and International Headquarters are in fact the glue that binds the international Army together! A useful way of picturing the role of International Headquarters is to imagine the office of the General and IHQ as no longer being there. At a stroke, The Salvation Army would be a very different Army. Instead of being one Army marching in one direction, it would begin to become a collection of armies each doing its own thing. Soon it would no longer be The Salvation Army as we know it today, and as William Booth meant it to be. Always the visionary and the realist, the Founder knew what he was doing when he laid the Army's international foundations as he did!

As Chief of the Staff my role was to be the leader of the General's staff at International Headquarters. Our task as a multi-disciplinary team was to ensure that the General had all the support and resources that he needed to lead the Army to accomplish its worldwide mission as it marched into the 21st century.

International Commission on Officership

The International Conference of Leaders held in Melbourne in March 1998 had expressed serious and ongoing concerns in relation to the recruitment and service of officers. This had led the conference to recommend that a commission be established 'to review all aspects of the concept of officership in the light of the contemporary situation and its challenges, with a view to introducing a greater measure of flexibility into the concept of officership'.

General Paul A. Rader accepted this recommendation and established an International Commission on Officership of 23 members of widely different ages, experience and cultural background. The commission met for a number of week-long working periods under the chairmanship of Commissioner Norman Howe. It presented its findings in the form of 28 recommendations some days before General Rader retired from office. One of the first tasks awaiting General John Gowans on taking office was therefore to consider these recommendations and his response to them.

Officership in The Salvation Army, as the commission noted, 'is a complex subject which has developed its own spirit and character, established its own traditions, created its own literature, and impacted on lives in a wide variety of cultures'. In drafting its recommendations the commission therefore identified four factors related to officership that it judged to be foundational to its work: 'the concept, covenant, conditions, and context' of officership.

Some of the commission's recommendations were broad and foundational and dealt with leadership structures and models. For example, 'we recommend that territories continue to move away from authoritarian models of command and develop consultative models of leadership, characterised by consistency with gospel values, servant leadership, cultural relevance, flexibility, increased and wider participation, and mutual accountability'.

There were also more-narrowly focused recommendations favouring a wider age span for entry into officership, greater flexibility in training for officership, and the strengthening and enriching of officer service through opportunities for personal development. Other recommendations in this category included the need for leadership development, the appointing of younger leaders, and the increased releasing of the resource represented by women officers, both single and married.

Some of the recommendations dealt with potentially contentious issues. These included the question of whether it should still be required of married couples that both spouses be officers, whether it should still be required that officer service be for life, and whether 'tent-making' – the taking of outside jobs – should be permitted for officers in exceptional circumstances. The commission also recommended that a review of the rank system be undetaken. All in all, plenty for any new administration to get its teeth into!

As a first step the General embarked on an extensive process of consultation regarding the 28 recommendations that had been made. There are well-established systems for consultation with territorial leaders. But in addition the General approved a proposal that every officer in the world – active and retired – should have the chance to comment on the 28 recommendations. That launched us into what was to be the largest consultative process ever undertaken in the Army's history.

We engaged the MORI organisation – one of the most respected firms in the field of international opinion polling – to help us set up the process and to analyse the responses. Early in 2000 the recommendations and a questionnaire were sent to territories for distribution to each of the then 25,000 active and retired officers worldwide. There were formidable barriers of language and geography to be overcome if all officers were to have the opportunity to say whether they agreed, disagreed or had no opinion on each of the recommendations. Some officers were two or three walking days away from the nearest postal link.

The cooperation from the territories was exemplary. The enthusiasm became contagious. Here was an opportunity for every officer in the world to communicate direct with the General! MORI provided expert guidance so that the highest standards of professional polling were maintained – and when more than 12,000 completed forms were returned the firm was astounded. The scale of response was far higher than they had ever experienced. Seventy-four per cent of all active officers in the world took part. Some officers felt that they wanted to elaborate further on the responses they had made, and more than 500 separate submissions – some of them very substantial – were received.

We aimed to announce and discuss the results of the consultative process at the International Conference of Leaders to be held in Atlanta, Georgia, in June 2000, just prior to the International Millennial Congress in that city. This tight timetable gave a useful urgency to the process.

The conference was a 'one subject' conference. The only item on the agenda was consideration of the recommendations of the

International Commission on Officership and the responses received from officers through the consultative process.

But it was one subject divided into 28 parts. And as each recommendation was reached, the global response to the three options of 'agree, disagree, no opinion' were shown in percentage form on the large screen which dominated the conference room.

Most recommendations that the commission had made received overwhelming backing from those officers around the world who responded. With some recommendations one could almost sense the 'surely not in *my* part of the world' reaction from a number of leaders. But the next set of slides would show the breakdown of the figures zone by zone – and these zonal results were often very surprising. Where relevant we also displayed separately how men and women officers, and active and retired officers, had responded.

The consultative tool may have been basic and not given to much nuancing, but it nevertheless gave an unprecedented information base for the discussions at the conference and for the decision-making process.

Immediately following the conference, and before the congress, the results of the global consultation were made available to all officers around the world. Officers with access to the electronic intranet system received the results in a matter of hours. For others it was a longer process.

About seven weeks later, on 24 August 2000, the General announced his decision on each of the 28 recommendations in a letter sent to all active and retired officers. Part of my task in my working relationship with the General was to produce for his review the first drafts of such communications. This turned out to be a 20-page document of 8,800 words: 'The Recommendations of the International Commission on Officership – The General's Response and Action Plan'. In it the General set out not only his decisions but also something of the background, discussion and 'next steps' relative to each recommendation.

'I have directed the Chief of the Staff to follow through with the implementation of the various points in the plan on my behalf,' wrote the General. And that was to occupy many hours of my time in the months ahead.

Implementation was complex given the diversity of the subjects touched on in the recommendations. Some matters could be dealt with by changes to international orders and regulations. But others dealt with organisational habits and entrenched attitudes for which different ways of influencing thought and action had to be identified. An important aspect was that each territory was required to establish a broadly based 'officership task force' to consider the spiritual and practical issues arising from the recommendations of the international commission in relation to that territory. The final reports from these task forces were to be sent to International Headquarters for the General's attention.

In the course of the history of The Salvation Army many commissions have been set up to consider a variety of subjects. Some have been more influential than others. The remit of the International Commission on Officership was to seek ways of 'introducing a greater measure of flexibility into the concept of officership', and it is likely that future historians will view this commission as having been one of the most influential in terms of the changes of facts and thinking that it brought about. The leadership of General John Gowans in this regard will always be remembered as a significant feature of his term of office. General Gowans made the interests of the Army's mission the paramount consideration in his decisions, and on certain key issues, where views diverged geographically, he was prepared to favour diversity over uniformity if the mission would thus be furthered. For example, whether officers could be married to non-officers became a matter for territorial discretion.

The 2000 International Millennial Congress

When General John Gowans entered office we found that the foundations of the Atlanta International Millennial Congress to be held in June 2000 had been well laid. It was to be centred on one weekend only, not two, and was to take place in a venue large enough to accommodate the 20,000 delegates, thus obviating the need for concurrent events in other halls. It was the first international congress – apart from two youth congresses – that was to be held outside England.

Though the venue was Atlanta, it was nevertheless an 'IHQ event'. From the onset, under the direction of the General, we gave very careful oversight to every aspect of the congress. We focused especially on the main events to be held in the large, modern auditorium shaped like an egg.

A splendid innovation was that speakers addressed the audience from a large round platform in the centre of the arena with the congregation seated all around them. Remembering to turn from time to time in order to address different parts of the audience was the new challenge for speakers. But continuity was maintained throughout by the speaker's image being projected onto large screens above the platform that faced in all directions. The steps of the circular platform formed the mercy seat.

A memorable feature of the congress was the centrality of the preaching from the Word of God. Ample time had been safeguarded for this by careful planning and ruthless pruning of other items. A further memorable feature was the way that the mercy seat was used by hundreds of delegates in every meeting.

The congress to mark the entry of the Army into the new millennium proved a triumph in every way. It was an investment in the future and a time for celebration. During the weekend it was announced that for the first time in the Army's history the number of soldiers had passed the million mark! It was a time for new vision and a time for new commitment. Such events leave indelible impressions on all those privileged to attend – and made a special impact on the host American Salvationists who were there in their thousands. No part of the Army world is more generous towards the support of the Army around the world than the USA territories, and here was opportunity for first-hand contact with the international Army as never before.

The '101' building

Another pending issue that had awaited the General on taking office was the matter of the IHQ building at 101 Queen Victoria Street. It was to occupy our attention throughout the term of office of General Gowans and also well into my own term as General. A book could be written about the many twists and turns of the '101' saga!

When the UK Territory was set up in 1990 it was announced that 'the territorial headquarters of the new territory will at first share accommodation with International Headquarters at 101 Queen

Victoria Street', but that 'an early item on the agenda for the new territorial administration will be to commence the planning for securing a separate territorial headquarters building'.

Early in 1999 the territory duly moved into a separate headquarters building in Newington Causeway, on the other side of the River Thames, whose street number is coincidentally also '101'. In the 1990 separation of international and UK assets, the 101 Queen Victoria Street site and building had become part of the international trust. However, the strong historic link of the UK operation with the site was recognised by inclusion of a proviso, that should the site ever be sold or redeveloped, a portion of the proceeds would be assigned to the UK trust. This proviso was honoured by the transfer of a substantial sum from the international trust to the UK trust to help finance the purchase and refurbishment of the new territorial headquarters building. The '101' site and building therefore now belonged entirely to the international trust.

The imposing building that housed International Headquarters was not old – it had been built and opened as recently as 1963. But it was very much a building of its time, reflecting not only the thinking but the technology of its era. To bring it up to date would require a vast investment of funds – funds which we did not have. And with two thirds of the personnel now having moved to the new UK headquarters building, the '101' building was also too large for our use. But the way it had been constructed made commercial letting of parts of it almost impossible. So we were faced with a classic dilemma. The international trust was in possession of a valuable asset. But it seemed that the only way the trust could raise the necessary funds to take advantage of that asset was by selling it.

Protracted discussions with outside experts and our internal advisers followed. We did not, of course, start from scratch. General Paul A. Rader and his team had already looked at various options. And throughout the long process – for me it would be a full five years – we were blessed with a team of advisers of the highest calibre to guide us on each aspect of this multidimensional process.

Heading the internal team was Commissioner Brian Taylor, international secretary for business administration. The commissioner poured not only his expertise but his whole heart and soul into the project. Sadly, he was unexpectedly promoted to Glory just before the building opened. Heading the external team was Andrew Chadwick, of Chadwick International, a brilliant architect whose practice specialises in space economy and design. It was Andrew, more than anyone else, who helped shape our dreams and helped us to turn them into reality.

There were many angles to consider. Should we sell the 101 building and site and relocate out of London – say to Nottingham, William Booth's birthplace? Or should we relocate to a London suburb – perhaps somewhere near Heathrow airport – or relocate to a smaller site within central London? All options were carefully considered.

At one time a delegation of us, headed by the General, set out in a minibus to view possible alternative sites in the centre of London. Some of the sites that we saw might, at a push, have served our purposes, but some were almost unbelievably awful – down alleyways tucked away behind railway bridges. All of them were vastly inferior to the '101' site. The tour was an absolutely necessary part of the process, for it became the catalyst that convinced us that if we were going to stay in London it had to be on the '101' site.

It was not only the lack of a suitable alternative within London that drove our thinking. We were also conscious of the Army's long link with the '101' site, of it being a prime site in the City of London, and, supremely, that the Army is not a business, it is a people – a people at whose head stands the General. A business, especially in these days of modern communication and transport, can locate itself virtually anywhere with little loss. But a people headed by a leader, an international people scattered across the globe, needs a central and visible physical focal point where its leader is located.

In the nature of things, not a large proportion of the one million Salvationists would ever visit London. But it was vital that those who did should not find the General housed down an obscure backstreet – or even in some London suburb or up country. The General had always had his headquarters right in the heart of London. We became convinced that in the larger interests of the international Army this must remain so, and that somehow or other we had to find a way of staying on the '101' site.

The idea of the Army itself developing the site with a mix of headquarters and commercial letting had had to be discarded for lack of funds. But we then explored the possibility of a developer taking on the scheme and putting in the necessary funding. The seemingly insurmountable problem with this solution was that the site was not large enough. We required 50,000 square feet for our purposes, and that left too little of the site for a financially viable development project.

But then a breakthrough occurred – the first of many. Reliance Bank, owned 51 per cent by the international trust and 49 per cent by the UK trust, was housed in the '101' building. At this point in the process the bank came up with a proposal that it should acquire a separate property more suitable for its special needs. Provision for Reliance Bank had always been part of our space planning for any new scheme at '101', and this change of course led to a recalculation of our needs. With space no longer being needed for the bank and with some other quite substantial adjustments we made, we found that we could manage with 35,000 square feet. It was this breakthrough that opened the way towards a viable development scheme.

A number of developers presented schemes and various financial options were considered. One developer wanted us to occupy the east end of the site, but we were determined that headquarters must be at the west end of the site. In that way it would face St Paul's Walkway, the extraordinary route that links St Paul's Cathedral with the Tate Modern art gallery over the Millennium Bridge – a walkway used by five million people a year. After many ups and downs, twists and turns and seeming cul-de-sacs morphing into throughways, the exploration ended with the signing of a contract with Hines, a large privately owned real estate company.

In return for a 150-year lease of two thirds of the site for a commercial building, Hines undertook to build a separate new headquarters for the Army on the remaining third of the site at virtually no cost to the Army. After 150 years, during which time an annual ground rent will be received, the two thirds of the site and whatever building is on it at that time will revert to the Army. The journal *Property Week* called it 'the kind of property deal that most occupiers dream about'. Mine was the responsibility as the Chief of the Staff to sign the contract on behalf of the Army – a document of well over a hundred pages.

When it came to the design of the new headquarters it was clear from the onset that this must be more than an ordinary office building. Here were 35,000 square feet of possibility! The General himself chaired and inspired the thinking of the design team. Andrew Chadwick injected ideas and concepts and helped us to see how our hopes and aspirations could be expressed in concrete and glass. He painted the scene for us of the tent of a Roman general always being at the centre of the camp, and suggested that the General of The Salvation Army should not be hidden away on some distant executive floor.

We wanted the building to be efficient without being ostentatious. We wanted it to symbolise not only the caring mission of the Army, but the fact that the Army is a spiritual movement. We wanted the building to communicate transparency and openness. We also wanted it to be a welcoming building – to the public passing by and to visiting Salvationists. Andrew Chadwick summed up this vision for the building in three phrases: modern in design, frugal in operation, and evangelical in purpose. Those three phrases were to shape the design of the new International Headquarters.

After a sojourn of three years at Denmark Hill, while the old building was demolished and the new one built, the new International Headquarters at '101' was ready to be opened officially by the Princess Royal on 9 November 2004. By then I had been General for two years and had led our project team during that period – investing what must have been in total hundreds of hours to the supervision of every detail of the building's design.

As we looked on the building that day with its striking lines, its transparency and light, its welcoming aspect and the central chapel symbolising the spiritual nature of the building, it seemed to me that the three phrases – modern in design, frugal in operation, and evangelical in purpose – had become a reality. The building has since won a number of architectural design awards.

The story of the new IHQ building is incomplete without some background information I shared at the official opening. The fact that International Headquarters was able to enter a new building in 2004 was because of the generosity of one person more than a century before.

When William Booth moved his headquarters to Queen Victoria Street in 1881 the Army did not own the freehold to the land. Gradually, adjoining sites were acquired until the full site as we know it today was occupied by the Army. But it was a concern to William Booth that the Army did not possess the freehold.

He therefore in 1891 approached a friend of the Army, Mrs Elisabeth Orr Bell, and suggested she might like to give a donation that would enable the Army to purchase the freehold. The sum involved was huge: £70,000 – £4.5 million in today's terms – and all that her donation would be acquiring was a piece of paper! But she did not demur. She there and then donated the money.

Picture it in today's terms: Mrs Orr Bell listens as the General outlines the need, she goes over to the desk, takes out her cheque book, writes a cheque for £4.5 million, hands it to the General, and then walks away!

But it was that ownership of the freehold that was to give The Salvation Army a gleaming new International Headquarters 113 years later. As I said at the opening, the new building could well have been called the Elisabeth Orr Bell Memorial Building.

The 2002 High Council

The three years and three months as Chief of the Staff passed quickly. There was a sense of anticipation about each day. What would it bring by way of good or bad news? What steps to strengthen the Army and its mission worldwide could be taken that day? What storms might blow up somewhere around the world and catch us by surprise? 'Consecrated to the unexpected' is as useful a motto for those at the administrative apex as for those at the frontline of service.

The years had also given to Freda and me the opportunity to visit parts of the world that were new to us – Africa and India in particular. They had been satisfying years, and with the Gowanses due to retire in November 2002 we would have six months left before our own retirement on my 65th birthday. Perhaps I could be a useful 'bridge' for the incoming General, or, if the new General wished to choose his or her own Chief of the Staff immediately, I could take on some writing assignment.

Part of the constitutional responsibility of a Chief of the Staff is to summon the High Council four months before the retirement date of the General, to meet around six weeks later. Summons were therefore despatched on 12 July and the High Council met at Sunbury Court on 30 August 2002.

Every High Council is a high spiritual experience for those who attend. Commissioner Brian Taylor had been elected president, and he appointed Commissioner Brian Morgan as chaplain to the council. This proved to be a singularly inspired choice, and as the chaplain led us in worship and prayer we felt that we were indeed standing on holy ground.

Freda and I were not unmindful of the fact that I might be nominated as a candidate for the Generalship. With the retirement age of the General being 68, that would give us a term of service just short of three and a half years. We had thought and prayed about it and had determined what our response would be if it happened. We both felt that the doctrine of availability had to be operative. If asked we would respond that we were available. We also determined that if elected we would see this as the next and culminating adventure in God's service, and that if not elected we would make the very most of our final six months of service and then move with a sense of anticipation into the next phase of life – retirement.

Nine members of the council were nominated. Nominations are by secret ballot and the number of votes received by each nominee are not disclosed to the council. However, by a recent amendment to the orders of procedure of a High Council, each nominee before accepting or declining nomination may ask the president privately how many nominations he or she has received. The information given to me by the president reinforced the conviction that I should accept. Of the nine nominees, only three of us accepted nomination: Commissioner Shaw Clifton, Commissioner Hasse Kjellgren and me.

In my speech to the High Council I said that one of my chief aims if elected as General would be to encourage the process of renewal. I said that I believed that The Salvation Army was going through a time of most remarkable renewal. This Holy Spirit-inspired process had been happening for some years, and had been happening worldwide. It did not mean that the Army was not facing challenges, difficulties and even threats – but that the Army was being renewed even where circumstances were adverse.

'One can tell that renewal is taking place,' I said, 'because so much good is happening in the Army world today. There is so much openness to new thinking and new methods, so much creativity and innovation and adaptation, so much questing after the fullness of the Spirit, so much more wanting for the Army to rediscover and return to its roots, so much more passion for mission among Salvationists – that one is led to conclude that what we are seeing is a movement of the Spirit. God is at work. He is renewing his Army! Of course the process of renewal is still patchy. Of course there is still a long way to go. Of course the process produces tensions. But I believe a process of renewal is happening. The Army is experiencing a *renaissance!*'

When it came to the time for voting, Freda and I had a profound sense of peace in our hearts. Our times were in God's hands, and from our personal perspective, whatever the outcome it would be fine with us.

We entered into the first ballot. When the president announced the result I found that I had achieved the necessary two thirds majority in the first ballot – and had therefore been elected the next General of The Salvation Army.

There comes a moment when theorising about 'what might be' suddenly changes into hard fact. I can remember the awesome realisation hitting me in that moment that I was about to step into the shoes of William Booth himself. But escape was still possible.

At this point of a High Council the president asks the officer who has been elected whether he or she is prepared to accept office. By a curious constitutional proviso, the person elected can delay his or her response. In my case it could have been up to 72 hours, but through an amendment to the constitution since then it has now been shortened to 24 hours. During that time the High Council cannot be dismissed in case the response should be negative.

It is difficult to imagine what could motivate someone elected as General to ask for a delay at this point, but it is not hard to picture the cataclysmic effect that a delay would have on the members of the High Council and on the Army around the world. Fortunately no one elected as General has ever wished to take advantage of this route for delay – or escape. And in response to the president's question I duly responded affirmatively – and was therefore declared to be the General-elect.

Some of the most hallowed moments in a High Council occur at this point. The president calls the General-elect and his wife to the platform. The General-elect signs the official documents and then speaks to the members of the council.

The long tradition of High Councils is that once a new General has been elected everyone closes ranks – even those who have voted for someone else – to accept the General-elect as the person chosen by the High Council as a whole. Every member in turn has a personal moment with the General-elect and his wife. Prayer is offered. And then the doors are opened.

As the doors swung wide on that Friday 6 September 2006 and Freda and I stepped outside, we found General John Gowans and Commissioner Gisèle Gowans heading the group of well-wishers awaiting us. With the cameras carrying the scene live around the world on the web, I was welcomed as the 17th General of The Salvation Army and Freda as the World President of Women's Ministries.

Chapter Eleven

WHAT'S THE GENERAL FOR?

THE first task that awaited me as General-elect was to choose my Chief of the Staff. There was no doubt in my mind as to who I wanted it to be. It had to be Commissioner Israel L. Gaither, territorial commander of the USA Eastern Territory.

I had admired Israel Gaither from afar for a number of years. We first met in 1997 at a territorial headquarters retreat in the USA where Freda and I were the guest speakers. Then in 1999 we were fellow candidates for the Generalship at the High Council and got to know each other even better. In my years as Chief of the Staff, Israel Gaither had been the territorial commander for the Southern Africa Territory, and I had appreciated his fine mind and visionary leadership. Here was a leader with his focus firmly on mission, and a leader who could make things happen. So Israel Gaither was the one and only name on my mental short list. There was no Plan B.

The only problem was that Commissioners Israel and Eva Gaither had commenced their ministry as territorial leaders of the USA Eastern Territory just five weeks previously. With my term of office commencing on 13 November 2002, they would only have three months as leaders of their home territory before having to set off again. I knew the territory loved them, and I knew that they appreciated being there. They had just been reunited with their family after three and a half years' absence on service overseas. Was it fair to even ask them?

But the conviction that it should be Israel Gaither was strong. He had all the necessary qualities. I knew that our hearts beat as one. And it was right that Israel and Eva Gaither with their complementing gifts should be released for ministry to the global Army. I was convinced that that must be the overriding consideration.

As is frequently the pattern at High Councils, the candidates had been asked whether they would consult with a number of commissioners before choosing their Chief of the Staff. I had undertaken to do so. I also knew that once the final 'amen' is said at High Councils and the General-elect is presented to the Army world on the web, the councils tend to break up quickly, with members heading for airports to catch flights home. I wanted to speak to Israel and Eva Gaither before they departed, and therefore knew that I had no time to waste.

So while the members of the High Council were having refreshments and getting ready to leave, I consulted individually with a number of senior leaders and sounded them out about my proposed choice. The immediate and warm endorsements the proposal received were an additional confirmation to my own heart and mind.

Freda and I and Commissioners Israel and Eva Gaither therefore met in one of the anterooms at Sunbury Court and I shared with them my thinking. The request came as a shock to them. Their hearts and minds were absolutely focused on their home territory which they had just been called to lead – even to the extent that Israel Gaither had chosen not to accept nomination for the office of General at the High Council that had just closed. So I sensed the personal agony that my request was causing them. We prayed together. They returned home to think and pray further over the matter. I was delighted when some days later they were in touch to say that their answer could only be yes, and that they must leave everything else in God's hands.

'Dare I show my face here with you tonight?' is how I began my video message some weeks later to the congregation gathered at the Centennial Memorial Temple in New York City for the farewell meeting of the Gaithers. The response from the congregation confirmed the esteem and affection in which they were held – and also the sense of pride felt that one of their own was going to be second in command of the international Army. The USA Eastern Territory's loss was the world's gain. And as I look back over my term of office as General I am more than ever convinced that one of my best decisions was the first that I took – to ask Israel L. Gaither to be my Chief of the Staff.

Transition

A London hall had been booked for the welcome of the new General. The public retirement meeting for General John Gowans and Commissioner Gisèle Gowans was to take place in the evening meeting of the Day of Celebration held annually in November. I suggested that if the morning meeting could be devoted to the passing of the torch to the new team, then there would be no need for a separate welcome meeting at a later date. This became the plan we worked to and the booking of the other hall was cancelled.

In the morning meeting of the Day of Celebration held on Saturday 2 November 2002, General John Gowans welcomed me as the incoming General and Freda as the World President of Women's Ministries, together with Commissioners Israel and Eva Gaither as the new Chief of the Staff and World Secretary for Women's Ministries.

The afternoon meeting took the form of a 'Gowans and Larsson' feature about the musicals. Wearing our grey uniforms for the occasion, John and I sat alone on the platform – with me at the piano – and spoke about the musicals and led the congregation in singing songs from them.

In the evening meeting it was my privilege to present the retirement certificates to John and Gisèle and on behalf of everyone present – and indeed all Salvationists around the world – to wish them God's blessing as they entered into the next phase of their lives.

For my address in the morning welcome meeting on that day I had decided to focus on a theme which over the years had become a passion for me and which was to dominate much of my speaking and writing as General – namely the vast potential of that unique gift of God to the world called The Salvation Army. Since those days of hard thinking in New Zealand about the core values of the Army and the way that as an Army we are in danger of being diverted into something we were never meant to me, the conviction had hardened within me that God wants us to be ourselves, and that we are at our best when we are truly ourselves.

Curiously it was an event in Sweden, during our time of leadership there, which acted as the final catalyst in my mind. One weekend we visited a corps which was celebrating its hundredth anniversary. Following the Sunday evening meeting a coffee fellowship was held for the soldiers and friends of the corps. Ministers of others churches in the town had also been invited, and it was suggested that some of them might want to bring words of good wishes to the corps on its anniversary. What one of them said wrote itself indelibly on my mind.

'I envy The Salvation Army its name,' he said. 'You have your mission and your dynamic written into your name!' He continued: 'As you know, I am the priest of the Swedish church, the Lutheran church, here in this town. We Lutherans are good people. But I have to ask myself, what does the name Lutheran convey to people about who we are and what we do? All it tells them is that we are linked with someone who lived nearly 500 years ago.'

He looked along the line of his colleague ministers seated in the hall, and then added: 'And you, my friend, you are the Baptist minister. Now you are also good people. But what does the name Baptist say to the man in the street?' He homed in on yet another colleague. 'And you, my friend, are the minister of the Methodist church. Now, you are very good people, William Booth came from being a Methodist! But tell me, what kind of a message does the name Methodist send out to people? I fear it is not a very enlightening one. Don't you wish,' he added, 'that you were called The Salvation Army?' Everyone laughed. He then made his point again: 'That's why I envy The Salvation Army its name. You have your mission and your dynamic written into your name!'

When in 1999 Roy Hattersley published his biography of William and Catherine Booth, *Blood and Fire,* I noticed his description of the classic moment when William Booth gave The Christian Mission its new name. With a stroke of his pen, William Booth changed the heading of an article written by the young George Scott Railton from 'We are a Volunteer Army' to 'We are a Salvation Army'.

Roy Hattersley describes this as a moment of whimsy on the part of the Founder. But to my mind Roy Hattersley got that point wrong. To us Salvationists it was not a moment of whimsy but a moment of divine inspiration. For 'from that moment', as W. T. Stead wrote about the early Army, 'its destiny was fixed – the whole organisation was dominated by the name'. New strategies to match the inspiration of its name were devised with breathtaking speed. Old methods were discarded or adapted and new ones invented. Writes the official historian, Robert Sandall: 'An irresistible spiritual offensive swept over cities, towns and villages in every direction, and set the whole country ablaze.'

The change of name took place in 1878. By 1886 – just eight years later – the 50 stations of The Christian Mission in Britain had become 1,006 corps of The Salvation Army, and the 88 evangelists of the Mission had become an astonishing 2,260 officers. The result of a moment of whimsy? Never! That was the moment in which our mission and our dynamic were written into our very name.

Basing my thoughts on Paul's appeal to the Christians in Rome to 'not conform to the pattern of this age', I challenged Salvationists in the welcome meeting to dare to be radical in their personal following of Christ, and to dare to be radical about everything that our name 'The Salvation Army' stands for. I called on them to value the uniqueness of the Army. I urged them to stop looking enviously at other traditions or even back to Christian Mission days. 'Let's dare to be different,' I said. 'God has raised us up for a purpose. And we are at our very best when we are most ourselves!'

With the inspiration of the words of the Lutheran priest still ringing in my ears, I urged Salvationists everywhere never to forget the depth and width and breadth of the word 'salvation' – the mission word in our name. 'Our mission is nothing less than salvation for the whole world,' I said, 'and every one of us is called to be a stakeholder in the evangelisation of all peoples.' I went on to exhort Salvationists never to forget that this salvation is for the whole person, not only soul, but mind and body as well – and that we minister to the total person because that is what Jesus did. 'We must not allow anyone to divert us from this duality of mission,' I warned.

I went on to add: 'This salvation is also salvation to the uttermost. We are a Holy Spirit movement. We hold a radical doctrine of holiness. We believe that there are no limits to what the power of God can accomplish in the life of a believer. And this salvation is also salvation for the disadvantaged. Jesus said that he had been anointed "to preach good news to the poor" – and the Army's special mission is to reach out to the poor and needy in society.'

As I held up before my hearers the wonder of everything contained in the word salvation, I challenged every Salvationist – myself included – to dare to be true to that vision.

I then turned to the word 'Army', the word that defines our style. 'The word army,' I said, 'tells us that we are an action people. We are not a sit-back-and-wait movement, but an activist, dynamic, get-up-and-do force that proclaims the gospel and stands up for right. The word army also reminds us that we are a mobilised people – an army mobilised for God in which everyone has a part to play. A Salvation Army corps is not a flock with a pastor, but a force with a captain. Every corps is a mission team.

'The word army,' I emphasised, 'also keeps before us that we are called to be a visible force. Through our uniforms we are the most visible part of the Christian Church – and we must never lose that visibility. Furthermore, the word army tells us that we are prepared to adapt – to fight the battles of today with the weapons of today.'

I shared with the congregation how Roy Hattersley had been invited to be interviewed at one of the Celebration Days following the writing of his biography of William and Catherine Booth. In the final question the interviewer had asked Lord Hattersley if, following the many months of delving into the Army's history, he had a word of advice for the Army of today. He paused. Roy Hattersley would not for a moment think of himself as standing in the prophetic tradition. But the words that he next spoke came with all the authority of an Old Testament prophet: 'Salvation Army,' he said, 'be what you were called to be, and do what you were called to do.'

'Our name tells what we are called to be and what we are called to do,' I concluded. 'Our mission and our dynamic are there. Now let's dare to be true to the vision God had when he raised up The Salvation Army!'

Into action

The public welcome meeting had been held 11 days before I was due to enter office. The Gaithers had flown over especially for the occasion. It was now the day before we were due to take over, and they had arrived back and were settling in at their quarters.

The Army, through long and possibly over-frequent experience, has got the matter of transitions off to a fine art. We waved goodbye to General John Gowans and Commissioner Gisèle Gowans at 4 pm on Tuesday 12 November, and then, together with our personal staff, we began the physical moving of effects to ready the offices for the next day.

Early on the morning of 13 November 2002, Freda and I together with Commissioners Israel and Eva Gaither arrived at International Headquarters – then still at Denmark Hill – and entered our fully prepared offices. Not a beat had been missed. And as a foursome, Israel and Eva and Freda and I began our work.

During my years as Chief of the Staff, I had been most ably assisted by my private secretary, the ever-efficient Major Jeanne van Hal from The Netherlands. The major was there on the opening day to once again initiate a new Chief of the Staff – her third – into the intricacies of that role.

In the office of the General I inherited Colonel Laurence Hay from New Zealand as executive secretary to the General. The colonel combined that role with the secretaryship of a number of key IHQ councils together with responsibilities for research and planning. He was a walking encyclopaedia of every aspect of Army administration – in fact the epitome of the indispensable man. His knowledge and wisdom were to be at my disposal throughout my term of office.

Captain Stephen Yoder from the USA Central Territory became my private secretary and was also Freda's secretary. We chose not to have an ADC who always travelled with us. This was partly because Steve was a married officer with a young son. But from time to time Steve accompanied us on our world travels. And whether in the office or with us on our journeys, Steve brought his speciality of cheerful proficiency to every task.

Historically it is comparatively rare for the Chief of the Staff to be elected General by a High Council. Only three of my predecessors had been so elected, Edward Higgins, Erik Wickberg and Bramwell Tillsley. But there can be no better preparation for the office of General. It meant that I was conversant with every detail of the issues facing the Army. It had been good to work with General John Gowans. But now the ultimate judgment on all matters would be mine.

I have always kept before me and applied to myself the old Rabbinic saying: 'On the judgment day the Lord will not say to you:

"Why have you not been Moses?" He will say to you: "Why have you not been John Larsson?" I had always wanted to avoid that scenario, and had said to the High Council that I would be me.

That was my determination as I took over the supreme leadership role. Over the years I had developed a collegial style of leadership and I wanted to develop that even further as the General. I can't claim any great originality in that. The age of consultative leadership in the Army dawned many years ago. But the outworking of the vision has varied greatly according to the personalities involved. I was therefore pleased that in the planning for the new International Headquarters I could proclaim the message of collegiality not only in word and deed but also in wood and glass.

The boardroom at the new International Headquarters is a circular room with glass walls that is dominated by an imposing round table which seats 24 people. It is here that the General meets with his top leadership team. The shape of the table enables everyone to hear and see clearly. But the significance is far deeper than that. Being round, the table has no 'head'. Everyone has an equal opportunity to be seen and heard, and the contribution of every participant counts.

When the building was being planned the architects started referring to the boardroom as the 'rotunda', and the name stuck. And the rotunda is in fact a statement in wood and glass about contemporary Salvation Army leadership. The Salvation Army is still under the oversight, direction and control of one person just as William Booth determined it should always be. That person is the General. But it is a General who sits with his immediate team at a round table and who listens and consults before he decides.

Why a General?

Some time into my term of office the UK Territory arranged for me to be interviewed by a junior soldier for a video to be shown at a territorial congress at which Freda and I would be the guests. Thirteen-year-old Gary Pitt from Northampton was the chosen junior soldier.

The cameras had filmed Gary riding his bike in his neighbourhood and sitting down at his computer to prepare his questions, and had recorded his comments on the mission ahead.

The camera team had followed him on the train to London and the bus to International Headquarters. They were there to watch him arriving, being shown round, and having lunch with Freda and me. And here we now were in my office. From his backpack Gary pulled out his long list of questions, and for the next 20 minutes the conversation flowed while the cameras rolled.

His questions were delightfully pointed and uninhibited. And in his first question he went with effortless charm straight for the jugular. 'What's the General for?' he asked. I smiled, and to give myself a couple of seconds to gather my thoughts I repeated the question out loud: 'What's the General for?' But my mind was yelling: 'Everyone knows what a general is for! Did anyone ever ask Napoleon what he was for?' Yet here I was being pressed to say exactly why The Salvation Army has a General!

In my response I focused on the responsibility of leading an Army at work in 111 countries, and how it is the General's task to set the strategic direction and enable resources to be shared so that the Army can accomplish its mission. I also spoke to Gary about the awesome responsibility of being the Army's spiritual leader.

Gary wanted to know how often I received policy advice from young people, whether our military style was a turn-off to people these days, what I thought about uniform-wearing and much more. He also asked me where I would like to take him to see the Army at work.

I told him that I would love him to come with us to Africa. I said I would like him to experience one of the great gatherings of 10,000 or more white-clad Salvationists praising the Lord together. The next day I would want to take him out to one of the villages to see the Army engaged in its practical work, providing education and health services and ministering to those in need. He would then, I said, see the full wonder of the Army at worship and at work – as happens in every country where the Army serves.

Quick as a flash, Gary dug into his pocket, produced his passport and said that he was ready to go at any time! We next met on the platform at the congress following the showing of the video. We exchanged some further words, and then, to the great amusement of the congregation, Gary again pulled out his passport and reminded me that he was ready to come with us – anywhere and at any time!

The video interview with Gary summed up for me the role that now was mine. And as I looked around International Headquarters I was reminded that, in the words of its mission statement, it 'exists to support the General as he leads The Salvation Army to accomplish its God-given worldwide task to preach the gospel of Jesus Christ and meet human need without discrimination'. I had for the last three years been part of that supporting team. My task was now to lead the Army to accomplish its God-given mission.

Preparing for visits

Leading the Army and being its spiritual head cannot be done from behind an office desk. A general has to be out with the troops. And within the first few weeks we visited the three 'Bs' of Belgium, Bangladesh and Buenos Aires in quick succesion. This spanning of the globe was to set the pattern for our term of office – Freda and I wanted to be at the frontline as often as we could. We set ourselves the goal of visiting as many territories and commands as possible during our allotted span. With a few exceptions we managed to visit them all.

Official preparations for a visit by the General follow a carefully laid down sequence of events as set out in the relevant guidelines. An agreed date is established. Then many months before the visit the territory submits for comment and approval an outline of the proposed daily schedule and a list of the main events. At a later stage detailed draft programmes for each meeting follow. These are carefully checked by the General's office before being submitted to the General for approval.

The territory then prepares a comprehensive brief that contains the minute-by-minute daily schedule, the meeting programmes plus a welter of other helpful information. This includes the contact number for the General on a 24/7 basis. Copies of the brief are distributed widely not only within the territory but also at International Headquarters so that key leaders always know exactly where the General can be reached at any given time. Crisis management is part of the General's job. And though most crises can be handled at least initially at other levels, the General must always be within reach.

The content of the public meetings is a careful blend of ingredients. A basic ingredient is of course opportunity for

Salvationists to celebrate in worship through music and song, drama and testimony. In some parts of the world contributions by government, civic and church leaders seem also to be a 'must'. And then there is the ingredient of the messages from the Word of God that the General and his wife bring.

But when it comes to timing, getting the blend right each time can be a challenge. Salvationists enjoy celebrating together, but many have made great effort to hear the international leaders, some travelling for days on the back of trucks or by river boat or by foot, and will be disappointed if there is not adequate time for this to happen. Territories are therefore asked to not overcrowd the programmes in order that the General and his wife can have sufficient time for their messages. Where translation is involved the time allowed for the message has to be doubled – or the message halved.

Territories usually achieve near miracles in getting the balance right. But once a supporting speaker or a worship group are on their feet there is little that the meeting leader can do about time control. So a General must always be ready for the unexpected. If time has run out, a message that may have taken many hours to prepare has to be cut to the bare bones. Not chopped so severely that no meat at all is left on the skeleton, leaving disappointed those who have travelled long distances. But shortened enough to keep the day's schedule within reasonable bounds. I recall that in one memorable meeting I did not say a word until three-and-a-half hours had passed. By that time people were beginning to leave. I succeeded in arresting their departure by being vivid – and short.

At other times the feel of the occasion or the nature of the congregation may be the unexpected factor, requiring a different message to be mentally prepared and given on the spot. Flexibility, adaptability and acceptance became my internal watchwords for all such situations. I actually found it intellectually stimulating to seek to rise in a fitting way to the demands of each occasion, whatever unexpected feature the event might have thrown at me. I had obviously come a long way from being the young man in Chile who shied away from the morning open-air meeting because he might be asked to speak.

Personal preparation for these visits involved many hours at the computer. Generals do not employ speech writers, and preparation of messages is therefore one of the great demands made on the world leader. I once heard General Wilfred Kitching say that he aimed always to have his preparation completed six weeks in advance of any event, and that he felt inwardly pressurised if the timeline slipped. As one who has always liked to get close enough to scent an event before beginning to prepare for it, this was a wise ideal to keep before me.

Seeking to set the good news in a context that will be familiar to the audience is a key factor in preparation. Local references or anecdotes in a message will build bridges into the hearts and minds of those listening. But finding the material with which to build such bridges makes it own demands, especially when the group of listeners is unknown and still 10,000 miles away. To that indispensable pre-preparation has to be added the inspiration of the moment. Fortunately the promise of Jesus is that the right words will be given to us when we need them. And in my own experience that has often proved to be so in a way that can only be described as the work of the Spirit.

As far as practical preparation for our journeys are concerned, Freda and I got that down to a fine art. Freda prepared a permanent and comprehensive list of everything that had to be packed. With that as our guide, it became a simple and mentally undemanding matter to work our way through it each time.

The territorial brief included details of the uniform required. Navy, grey or white. For reasons of economy we forewent the biscuit-coloured uniforms worn in some parts of Africa, and wore white there instead. But in this international Army diversity rather than unity seemed to apply in the matter of uniforms, and it was of course vital that the international leaders be dressed correctly to the last detail when they stepped from the plane. Take the white uniform, for example. Long sleeves or short? With or without blouse or shirt? Collar open or closed with tie or brooch? Trousers and skirt white or navy? Shoes white or black? With or without hat or cap? If with, navy or white? Hat to be worn outdoors, indoors or both? Enough potential pitfalls there to alarm any protocol officer.

Women's uniforms tend to be more exotic, and Freda took pride in wearing the sari in India, the shalwar kameez in Pakistan, the graceful long skirt used in Myanmar and Fiji, and any other national or local variation of the Army uniform.

The cap for men is of course a predominantly Western feature. When as Chief of the Staff we visited India for the first time, I was anxious to observe the right protocol with regard to the cap. We were arriving late at night but knew that there would be a large contingent to greet us at the airport. Would the men officers be wearing caps? The international secretary thought not. But the trumpet gave an uncertain sound. Caps are not an expected part of the uniform, he explained, but some officers who have one take a pride in wearing it. And it could just happen that with the Chief of the Staff arriving, officers will have gone to the trouble of securing one! So it was with some trepidation that I left my cap at home. And it was with relief that I noticed, when the doors of the Mumbai airport swung open, that there was not a cap to be seen anywhere!

Arriving on location

In seven years of international travel as Chief of the Staff and General we spent many hours at the main airports of the world and became connoisseurs of their strengths and weaknesses. In Britain the General is one of three religious leaders accorded VIP status at Heathrow and Gatwick airports. For departures Steve Yoder drove us to the VIP lounge, and at Heathrow he then drove us right to the foot of the aircraft where we were escorted up a private stairway to the air-bridge in order to enter the plane. On our return, we would see from the window of the plane the car awaiting us at the foot of the bridge, and as the doors swung open Steve would be there to welcome us back.

Wherever feasible, similar arrangements would be made for our arrival and departure in other countries, and where not possible, every care would be taken to ease our travels. In some parts of the world it is still traditional – and possible – for large contingents of Salvationists to greet the international leaders at the airport when they arrive and depart. Only a heart of stone would not be deeply moved to hear the sound of the band playing and hundreds of voices singing 'Joy, joy, joy, there is joy in The Salvation Army' – even at one o'clock in the morning.

We greatly appreciated the care that was taken for our welfare wherever we went. Every courtesy was extended. We often commented how good it was to be undertaking our task in the era of purified water in plastic bottles. The bottled water explosion has been global, and it seems that even in the most remote jungle clearing a bottle of water will now await the intrepid traveller. When we thought of how William Booth had visited India for nearly three months in 1896 and had lived primitively, often travelling by oxcart between villages, we wondered how he had survived without the blessing of bottled water! I count as one of many blessings that in the seven years of international travel I had no health upsets whatever – not even a headache.

The territory being visited would usually assign an officer to be our 'local ADC'. These young officers were the brightest and best, knew everybody and everything, and were our indispensable guides. Sometimes it was day and night service. In one territory we found that the local ADC would be sharing our hotel suite with us. And it turned out just fine. We became attached to many of these officers. Had the world been smaller it would have been good to bring them all together at IHQ at the end of our term so that we could renew acquaintance and they could meet each other.

Another group of admirable officers were our translators. We could handle English, Spanish and Swedish, but beyond that we needed assistance. The Army is blessed in the number of skilled translators it has – translators who are frequently called into service on ecumenical occasions. It was quality assistance that we received.

Speakers are very much in the hands of their translators. It is not just a matter of interpreting the words accurately and instantly phrase by phrase. Good translators enter into the very spirit of the message and convey its essence through their body-language, the pitch and inflection of their voice, and the pace of their words. It is an art in itself. There were times when the 'flow' between speaker and translator reached such a pitch that it seemed as if the translators had become extensions of our own personalities.

A symbolic role

In our international visits it was almost disconcerting to discover how highly respected and regarded the office of the General is. I use the term 'office of the General' deliberately, for the respect and regard has little if anything to do with the personal qualities of the person who currently happens to occupy that position. It is the position of the General – not the individual – which is the 'glue' that binds the Army together.

In the remoter regions of the world, Salvationists will often make great sacrifices to meet and hear the international leader. When we once travelled by car from one territory to another in India, we encountered large groups of Salvationists waiting for us in each of the villages on our route. Some of them had walked through the night just to see the General for a few moments. In each village we would stop, ascend the platform that had been erected, receive words of welcome and the traditional garlands, respond with words of love and encouragement, and then pray for them and their families. On our way back to the car we would shake as many of the outstretched hands as possible. The total time for the stop would be around 20 minutes. We would then drive on to the next village where the next group would be waiting. And the Salvationists would then begin the long trek back to their homes.

We discovered that in some parts of India it has become traditional to preface the word 'General' with the words 'our beloved'. This prefix to the rank has become almost automatic. Just as one has Major-Generals and Lieutenant-Generals so one has Beloved-Generals. 'We welcome our beloved General,' they would say. 'Our beloved General will now lead us in a song.' 'Our beloved General will now speak.' There was something heartwarming about it, for it was more than a formula of words. Long may the custom live on! At one point I did wonder, with a smile, whether I ought to issue an edict that at International Headquarters the prefix 'beloved' must always be used when speaking to or about the General! But I concluded that the tradition would not travel well.

The respect for the office of the General took other forms as well. After an officers' councils in Kenya, we were told that a captain had returned home to find that his wife had given birth to a baby boy during the meeting. So they named him 'John Larsson'. I felt very honoured. When I told the story to colleagues back at IHQ, one of them went one better. 'That's nothing,' he said. 'When General Clarence Wiseman once visited an African territory the same thing happened – but it was twin boys who were born. So the parents named one Clarence and the other Wiseman!'

I was later to learn that in some parts of Africa it is not unusual for parents to name their children after officers they admire from afar. In one country we were introduced to a number of John Larssons, some of them already teenagers. Someone suggested a group photo of just John Larssons, but that never materialised.

Meeting the Salvationist family

Most visits to territories by the international leaders are for congresses or commissionings with united officers' councils. In some places it is not unusual for the public meetings to be attended by many thousands – often seated on the ground in large marquees. Such occasions remain vividly engraved on our minds. But occasionally arrangements were made for us to journey into rural areas to meet with smaller groups and see the Army at work there. Because they were rarer occasions, such visits stand out even more clearly in the mind.

We will not soon forget the visit to an Indian village corps. While still a mile from the community we were met by an escort of Salvationist motorcyclists who, with banners aloft, escorted us to the civic welcome. Seated on an ornate structure built on top of a decorated tractor, we were then ceremonially driven through the village as the villagers stood outside their houses and waved. At the Army hall the women were inside, seated on the floor, and the men were outside, standing and listening through the open windows.

What made the occasion especially poignant for us was the plea by one woman Salvationist – a mother. 'General, our young people are denied higher education and jobs because they are Christians. Please, General, can't you arrange for our young people to have education abroad so that their development is not hindered because they are followers of Jesus. Please, General, help our young people.' My heart ached for her – and for the young people of the corps, and for all young Christians for whom following Christ is costly.

We especially appreciated visiting parts of the world where it can be tough to be a Christian. I think of Myanmar – formerly Burma. The sight of 1,000 uniformed Salvationists coming together – each being handed a bottle of water before entry to every meeting – was nothing less than a miracle. To commission new officers, some of them setting out the next week to open the work in new areas of that country, was more than an honour. It was a sacred privilege.

The response to the altar call at the end of the proclamation of the message by the General – the Army's spiritual head – can in some parts of the world be almost overwhelming. I determined long ago never to seek to arouse guilt in my hearers when speaking. People have plenty of burdens in life without the preacher adding to them. I therefore always seek to present the gospel in uplifting and encouraging terms – literally good news. That meant that it was doubly moving to see people coming forward to the place of prayer for their deepest needs to be met in Christ.

Sometimes in the larger gatherings they would come in waves of many hundreds, followed by another wave and yet another. It was impossible for each person to be counselled personally. So when I conducted the prayer meetings, I would always pray personally for each wave of seekers as if I was ministering to each person individually at the mercy seat. I would pray a similar prayer again as each new group came until every seeker had received my personal prayer on their behalf.

Meeting friends of the Army

Visits to countries will sometimes involve meeting with heads of state or heads of government. There are no universal rules to govern such occasions. Consecrated to the unexpected is yet again the only guideline. The visit may be a courtesy call, or the local Army leaders may wish a substantive issue to be raised with a head of government.

The protocol may range from the ultra-ceremonial – with an equerry giving precise instructions before entry as to where each member of the party will sit, how the head of state is to be addressed, the order in which speeches will be made, how the exchange of gifts is to be handled, and how the interview is to be terminated – to the almost surprisingly relaxed. The visit to the Oval Office in the White House to see President George W. Bush was most definitely in the second category, with all the arrangements characterised by warmth and efficient yet friendly informality. Sometimes the head of state or government will be flanked by an array of ministers, sometimes the group is much more intimate. This influences the tone and content of the meeting. Translation is often involved.

Such visits are demanding in the sense that all of one's antennae are poised throughout to pick up the vibes and mood of the occasion and to sense the direction in which the meeting is flowing. However grandiose the occasion, I always reminded myself that national leaders are as much human beings as anyone else, and that the key is to be natural with them. Hopefully one will clearly sense who will take the initiative to end the meeting and when the right moment for that will be. I always offered a concluding prayer and invariably sensed that my prayer for the nation and for the leader personally was appreciated. We had some memorable meetings and met some very charming and impressive people. How rich the Army is in its friends!

Many of the Army's friends serve on our advisory boards around the world. When meeting a board for the first time I would usually tell them about sessions of cadets having a name, and give them the sessional name of 'The Enablers'.

When visiting Korea, the Myongji University kindly conferred on me an Honorary Doctorate of Literature in recognition of my creative output in the realms of music and the written word, and as a way of honouring The Salvation Army for its mission and ministry.

Media attention is an integral part of visits – in some parts of the world more than in others. Interestingly it was in Brazzaville, in the Republic of Congo, that the media were most active. It seemed that each morning, afternoon or evening during our visit we could hardly arrive at the next venue or depart from it without some cameraman swinging into action and a mike being thrust towards us for comment.

Fortunately, the media everywhere are usually positive and friendly towards the Army. The question most frequently asked – even within minutes of arriving in a new country – is: 'What do you think of our country?'

An important verb
To dedicate is an important verb for anyone called to be the General of The Salvation Army. In my officer service I have dedicated many children, and also buildings and indeed fascinating objects for God's

service. I think of the fishing boat I was asked to dedicate in Tonga. In an enterprising programme, the Army had a number of boats that were hired out very cheaply on a 12-hour basis to fishermen who could not afford their own boat. Each morning these boats would return with the fish caught during the night, and the fishermen would then sell their catch on the quayside.

But as General my repertoire for dedications was to be extended even further. As, for example, when visiting the India South Eastern Territory I was asked to dedicate a wind turbine that generated electricity. We drove into a windy valley graced by a number of such turbines, and there stood this gleaming new pylon with rotor blades at its apex. The words 'The Salvation Army' were emblazoned on it. It was making its own witness. And the Army was going to do its part to provide much-needed energy to that area.

Everything had been prepared for the dedication ceremony. We sat on a platform some distance away from the wind turbine. It was a very hot day and the platform was covered by a canopy. In front of us, about 100 yards away, was a great crowd of people also seated under cover. The programme began with speeches and items, and when my turn was getting near I enquired of the officer in charge whether there was anything specific I had to do when it came to the actual moment of dedication. Was there a ribbon to be cut or a string to be pulled to unveil a plaque?

Everything had indeed been thought of. The officer handed me a remote control on which all the buttons except one had been covered with tape. They were not going to risk the General getting it wrong! He pointed to a large freestanding object at the side of the field about halfway between the platform and the congregation. It was at least 10 feet tall. But one could not tell what it was, for it was completely enveloped in a drape which hung like a shower curtain from a circular frame. 'At the right moment,' he said, 'please point the remote control at the curtain, and press the button firmly – once.'

At precisely the right moment I did as I was bid. I pressed the button firmly – once. A second passed. Then another. Nothing happened. I resisted the temptation to press the button again! I knew that it might undo any good I had done by pressing it in the first place! And then, to my relief and to everyone else's delight, the circular curtain began slowly to lower. And as it descended a stone monument with a very large plaque became gradually visible. I felt inwardly rebuked for my lack of faith. Right in the midst of what to us seemed the remotest of remote locations, the ceremony had been a triumph of modern technology! Just as the pylon itself was state-of-the-art technology in the service of meeting human need.

Renewal and world evangelisation

In April 2003, about six months after I had become General, I met with the team of IHQ commissioners at Sunbury Court for three days of strategic planning. Those three days were to prove more significant than any of us were aware as we gathered together.

Our theme was the one I had chosen for my term of office: Renewal. In the opening session I commented that in the time of Isaiah, the people of God were forever thanking him for what he had done in the past. They praised him for the way he had opened the Red Sea for them and delivered them from their enemies.

But the trouble was that they were so busy looking back that they could not see what God was doing in the present. They were suffering from a Red Sea mentality. To listen to them, it was as if God had retired from active service after delivering them from Egypt! And God became so exasperated with his people that through Isaiah he said: 'Forget the former things; do not dwell on the past. See, I am doing a new thing! Now it springs up; do you not perceive it?' (Isaiah 43:18-19, *NIV*) This was my theme Scripture for the whole of my term of office.

I shared with the team how, when Freda and I were the territorial leaders in the UK, we were invited to be present at a special commemorative service that was to be held in Glasgow Cathedral following the first Gulf War. It was to be a gala event. The Queen was to be present, as was the prime minister, all ministers of the government, the full diplomatic corps and all the senior officers of the armed forces. Everybody who was anybody was to be there. And because of the fine work done by Salvationists in support of British troops we had also been invited. The invitation included transport by military aircraft to Scotland.

At the appointed hour – 5 am – Freda and I presented ourselves at the regimental headquarters in London. It was already milling with government ministers, diplomats and military officers. A fleet of buses was waiting and precisely on the minute indicated by our programmes, the sirens of the police motorcycle outriders sounded and we set off through the still dark London streets towards Heathrow airport. The buses drove straight on to the runway, and there ahead of us loomed the outline of an enormous Royal Air Force transport aircraft.

Within moments we had boarded and exactly on time the aircraft took off. I looked around at our distinguished fellow-passengers, the government ministers in sober suits, the generals and admirals in full dress uniforms, and the diplomats resplendent in the diplomatic uniforms of their country. But something was very odd. The seats on the military aircraft all faced backwards. So there we all were, all of us sitting looking towards the rear of the aircraft. This intrigued me.

I wondered whether the passenger seated next to me would know why. I could tell that he was an admiral, and by the amount of gold braid on his uniform, probably a very senior one. But there were dozens of admirals around, so I played for safety in my opening gambit.

'What part of the Royal Navy are you responsible for?' I asked. He smiled. 'Well – actually, all of it,' he replied. I was obviously seated next to the First Sea Lord himself. He ought to know.

'Why is it that we are all sitting facing backwards?' I enquired. 'Here we all are, being hurled forward at 600 miles per hour to where we are going, and yet all of us are looking back to where we have been.'

He was amused. 'There's a very good reason,' he replied. 'Studies have been made that show that if the plane were to crash, passengers would be more likely to survive if they are seated backwards. So the seating is designed to protect our military personnel. We keep telling the commercial airlines, but they say that passengers want to sit looking forwards.'

So it was in case we crashed! But the picture stuck in my mind – all of us sitting there in the plane looking in the wrong direction. And it seemed to me that it mirrored in modern terms what Isaiah had found with the people of Israel. They kept on looking back. It was almost as if they were walking backwards into the future. They kept praising God for all that he had done in the past – the Red Sea and all that – but God wanted them to turn round and see that he was still alive, still performing wonders. And that is why he was telling his people through Isaiah to forget the former things and not dwell on the past. 'Turn round, face forward, look around – see, I am doing a new thing! I am still performing wonders today!'

I could picture it happening in a moment in an aircraft, with everyone's seat suddenly being turned round. Changing the attitude of a whole people was going to take longer. The people of God were still looking back when the Messiah came – and missed him. The Church is constantly tempted to look back and to think that God was more powerful in the past than he is now. And so is the Army.

At our Sunbury gathering we spent time in prayer and discussion, focusing on the new things that the Lord was doing in his Army. As we talked together we kept being reminded of how the Army was 'overflowing' into new countries. We all had stories to share as we looked at the world panorama. No two situations were totally identical, but a frequent pattern was of Salvationists migrating to neighbouring countries, perhaps because of civil unrest or in search of a new life. In their new location they would meet together on Sundays, hold meetings, sing Army songs, make a Salvation Army flag – and then write to International Headquarters to say that they had started the Army in a new country and could the General please send officers!

We had tended to be resistant to such pleas – for financial reasons. Supporting the work we already had was a constant concern. Was it responsible to add to that burden? There were also large areas within countries where we were already at work which had not yet been reached. Should we really be crossing borders into new countries? But the more we thought and the more we prayed the more it seemed to us that here was God performing wonders in our midst – and we were missing them. He was saying to us, 'See I am doing a new thing' – and we were not seeing it. And as for resources, the conviction grew – in the already oft-quoted words – that demand would create supply.

Patrick Johnstone, the head and inspiration behind WEC (Worldwide Evangelisation for Christ) International and author of the encyclopaedic handbook *Operation World*, was our facilitator the next day together. WEC International exists to introduce Jesus to people around the world who have the least opportunity to hear about him. Its members live and work by faith. And God has mightily blessed their ministry. The invitation to Patrick had come about through a seeming chance encounter at a railway station where he had met Commissioner Paul du Plessis. But there was nothing chance about that encounter. I have described some catalyst moments. This was another.

As Patrick shared with us that day, the conviction became a certainty. God was indeed doing a new thing in our midst. It was time for us to turn ourselves around and see what was happening in the world – and to recognise that the spontaneous overflowing of the Army into new countries was a movement of the Spirit. From that time world evangelisation, always a key concern, became our absolute number one priority.

Many consequences flowed from those Sunbury days. A direct result was that some months later I appointed Commissioner Paul du Plessis to be Commissioner for World Evangelisation. Paul gave an unprecedented thrust to the whole subject, awakening Army leaders everywhere to the challenge through his skilful and passionate expositions and communications.

The subject became priority number one also at the International Conference of Leaders that was to follow in May 2004. A world evangelism database was created. The memorandum of appointment of the international zonal secretaries was widened to include *every* country in their geographic zone, not only the countries where the Army is already at work. And a number of exploratory visits to new countries were made and every report of spontaneous overflowing was followed up.

At the suggestion of African leaders, most of the territories and commands on that continent were linked officially with one or more neighbouring countries where the Army is not yet at work, in readiness for expansion when the time is right. Poland and Lithuania were added to the list of new countries where the Army is established – bringing the total number to 111. Recommencement of the work in Nicaragua was authorised – thus giving an Army presence in all countries of the mainland American continent.

The list of possible new countries continued to grow and the matter of prioritisation became acute. We did not have resources to enter every new country listed. Should we enter those where the fields were ripe unto harvest? Or was God calling us to witness for him also where the soil was hard and stony?

As my time in office drew to its end, this was still – and will always be – a work in progress. Under the inspirational guidance of Paul du Plessis, a comprehensive document entitled 'The Journey Ahead' was drawn up by the General's Consultative Council – a council in which all territorial leaders participate in person or by electronic means – for presentation to my successor as a possible working plan. On entering office, General Shaw Clifton followed through with characteristic vision and verve.

Patrick Johnstone proved influential in yet another way. On the day that he spent with the IHQ leadership team at Sunbury Court, he and I stood conversing during one of the breaks. He asked me where our membership strength lay. I told him that these days two thirds of our members are in Africa and South Asia. He looked round the group of leaders as they helped themselves to refreshments. Every one of them was a westerner. He then quietly said: 'Your leadership team does not reflect your world membership.'

Sometimes you have to hear the self-evident verbalised for it to strike home. For some time we had been seeking to internationalise the staffing of International Headquarters. But it had obviously not reached the top echelon of leaders. Patrick's comment became the tipping point in my mind. Within a few months I had appointed a Japanese international secretary to head up the South Pacific and East Asia zone, an Indian international secretary to head up the South Asia zone, and an African international secretary to head up the Africa zone.

Chapter Twelve

CULMINATING EVENTS

DURING the autumn of 2003, adherency as a form of membership of the Army became the issue of the hour. It had been boiling up for some time. In a nutshell, the question was how best to recognise as part of the Salvation Army fellowship those persons who come to faith within the Army, or who are already believers when they come to the Army, but who do not wish to be – or for some reason cannot be – soldiers.

In some territories the number of people in this category had been rapidly growing. They had become adherents. But these adherents wanted to be more than just 'supporters' of The Salvation Army. They wanted to belong. But as the adherency declaration did not include a Christian commitment, adherents had never formally been recognised as members of The Salvation Army. Yet many of them were believers who participated in the worship, fellowship and ministry of the local corps. And they wanted to be *members* of the Army. So acute was the issue in some parts of the world that corps officers were devising their own membership formulas.

The Army has had adherents from its earliest days – possibly from as early as 1886. By 1900 there were already 12,755 adherents worldwide. But perhaps with diversity taken a step too far, the term had never been defined internationally. Adherency therefore meant different things in different places at different times. So the situation that faced us worldwide was that some adherents were committed Christians active in the corps, some were still seekers after truth, some were new converts in a pre-recruit stage, some were 'supporters' of the Army without it being their place of worship, and some were simply adherents of the Army for government and census purposes.

To say that all adherents were members of the Army would have been to declare that one need not be a Christian to belong to The

Salvation Army. So that was ruled out. If we built a form of Christian commitment into the membership declaration it would allow any adherents, from now on, to be considered members of the Army. But this solution had a danger.

The danger was the creation of two types of membership – one making great demands and the other not. Soldiers make commitments as to belief and lifestyle in the soldier's covenant. The requirements for adherents would be much less. We felt it imperative that soldiership should be the primary form of Salvation Army membership. We did not want soldiers to gradually become a small elite within a corps – a kind of special service force. If we now declared adherents to be members of the Army, were we not putting soldiership at risk? Would some say: why be a soldier if there is a less-demanding way to be a Salvationist?

We wrestled with these issues through the General's Consultative Council. I came to the conclusion that, despite the danger of two forms of membership, it was right at this time of our history to build into the adherency declaration a simple personal statement of faith and aspiration to a Christian lifestyle so that adherents could be considered to be members of The Salvation Army. But in order to preserve the primacy of soldiership we stopped short of making adherents full members. They could become 'adherent members'.

The new international definition became: 'An adherent member of The Salvation Army is a person, who while not entering into the soldier's covenant, believes in the Lord Jesus Christ and seeks to follow and be like him, participates in the worship, fellowship, service and support of a local Salvation Army congregation, and identifies with the mission of The Salvation Army.' This definition was to apply to all *new* adherents, but any existing adherents who so wished could sign the new declaration.

Only time will tell how the pattern of Salvation Army membership will develop in the future. It is entirely likely that the matter will have to be revisited in due course.

Deliberations
The General presides over week-long zonal conferences in each of the five zones attended by the territorial leaders and chief secretaries and their wives of that zone. Such conferences are

usually held on a three-yearly basis, and play an invaluable role in the exercise of consultative leadership.

During my term of office I presided over such conferences in Dhaka (South Asia Zone), Singapore (South Pacific and East Asia Zone), Johannesburg (Africa Zone), Madrid (Europe Zone) and Dallas (Americas and Caribbean Zone). The Dallas conference covered Latin America and the Caribbean. We met separately in Washington with the USA national leaders and the leaders of the four American territories in one of their regular thrice-yearly conferences. Pan-American conferences are held only rarely. The leaders of the Canada and Bermuda Territory tend to get left out of the regular pattern of zonal conferences, and we therefore made a point of spending a number of days with their territorial leadership council.

It is customary for a General to convene at least one full International Conference of Leaders during his term of office, and together with the IHQ leadership team we met with all the territorial and command leaders in New Jersey, USA, from 29 April to 7 May 2004. With the over-arching theme of 'Renewal', the conference subjects ranged from the visionary, like world evangelisation and every corps being a mission team, to the practical, like finding the necessary financial and personnel resources to implement the vision.

During the conference the 'Partners in Mission' scheme was given its official launch. By this scheme all territories and commands are directly linked with other specified territories for a period of years, with all of them being both givers and receivers by way of resources and inspiration.

Since becoming General, I had become increasingly convinced that the Army should be more active and more high-profile in the combat against human trafficking for sexual purposes – an appalling international scourge of the 21st century. I therefore asked all territories to focus on this issue, and we set up an international support system for our campaign.

At the conference we concentrated especially on the resource of prayer. During the years leading up to our coming together there had been a seemingly spontaneous reawakening to the importance of prayer. Territories were planning 24/7 prayer events, and holding prayer walks, prayer concerts and prayer breakfasts. Prayer rooms were being set aside in corps buildings. At the conference we sought to take hold of and promote this worldwide movement of the Spirit.

Using the words of Jesus I also challenged the conference to 'go and make disciples'. With our senior and junior soldiers and our adherent members I saw the possibility of the Army reaching the two million mark in the not too distant future. The Lord's command was clear: 'Go and make disciples.' What he was calling us to was a renewal of our focus.

The conference prepared a statement that summarised our hopes, aspirations and commitments. It was a very hallowed and moving scene when on the final evening the delegates put their names to the declaration. Freda and I stood by the small table in front of the platform, and with a background of quiet music and singing, the leaders in turn came forward, the married leaders as couples. After a moment of prayer they each signed the declaration and then we greeted each other with a hug. It is in such precious moments that Heaven comes down to earth – and the memory of them lingers in the heart and mind.

Music and gospel arts

Another emphasis I wanted to give as General in connection with the theme of 'Renewal' was the need for our worship meetings to be renewed. As a part of this, I hoped that we might catch a new vision of how our rich resources of music and other gospel arts might be further developed in the service of evangelism and worship. I was therefore very pleased when I was able to set aside Colonels Robert and Gwenyth Redhead to spearhead this aspect. They were respected by all sides of the music and creative arts spectrum, and their two-year ministry throughout the world made a vital and lasting impact. My hopes were realised.

In July 2004 Freda and I had the opportunity of meeting with music leaders and other delegates from all around the world in Toronto, to take part in an International Music and Other Creative Ministries Forum, under the direction of the Redheads. There was a time when as an Army we seemed to worship at the altar of music. In some corps, if you were not a musician you might as well not join! Fortunately the pendulum has swung, but in some places it has swung too far. Musicians there are almost in bad odour. I hoped that my convictions about music in the Army, built up over a lifetime, would encourage the delegates.

I told the music leaders that the Army needs *more* music. Not less. That simple truth had been brought home to me many years ago through the inspired insight of a young Salvationist. I was with a group of teenagers and we were discussing the Army's future. I ventured the suggestion that perhaps when Church historians studied the first hundred or so years of the Army's history, they would conclude that music had been given a disproportionate prominence in its activities. Should there be less emphasis on music in the Army? That was the question.

'Less music?' asked the young man, as if he could not believe his ears. 'But why on earth would we want to cut back on the greatest way of communicating that we have? Music is the thing that everyone has in common!

'What do people do when they wake up in the morning?' he continued. 'They reach out and switch on music. They listen to music over breakfast. They travel to work with music. Many listen to piped music all day as they work. And then in the evening they return home to the sound of music, and as often as not spend the rest of the day with music – when watching TV or listening to recorded music, or when going out with friends. God has given the Army an enormous advantage by entrusting it with the gift of music. It has a ready-made road into everyone's heart and mind. It has been given a universal language.

'You're not suggesting,' he added reproachfully, 'that we should give up all of that, are you?' The words tumbled out with passion and eloquence – and with irresistible logic. It was one of those moments of insight when the obvious suddenly becomes startlingly clear. And it really is self-evident. If music is one of God's gifts to the Army, we don't want less of it – we want more!

What we need is music that will speak to *every* heart. Music that will speak to the traditionalist and appeal to the non-traditionalist. Music that will inspire the believer and capture the non-believer. Music with which the young can identify, and music that will entrance the older generation. Highbrow music, popular music, classical music, contemporary music, music for voice and music for brass, music for the keyboard and for the guitar, and music for the drum and timbrel! No heart must be left out of reach!

Does that mean that every corps will end up as a music society? Does it mean that those who are not musically gifted are relegated to the outer edges of the corps? No – and three times no! It must never be so. God gives different gifts to different people – and all are equally valid and equally important.

The corps programme must provide not only for the expression of musical gifts, but for the expression of *all* God-given talents. The training and opportunities for service and fellowship provided for the evangelists, pastors, carers, teachers, youth workers and every other giftedness in the corps must be at least as good as those provided for the musicians. It is when *all* parts of the body flourish that the Body of Christ is truly healthy – and we see corps life as God means it to be.

So let there be more music in the Army. Let there be performed music – music to which others listen. One has only to look around the contemporary music scene to see the impact that famous singers and their bands make on millions of listeners. And this is powerfully mirrored by the contemporary Christian music scene. But especially let there be more participative music – music in which everyone takes part. Particularly let there be more congregational singing in our meetings. And let it be good congregational singing, the kind of singing in which everyone present can heartily join!

Thank God that the end of the worship war is in sight! More and more the traditionalists and the 'contemporaries' are recognising that they both have been wrong when they have said that it must be *either* songs from the song book *or* songs from the computer! More and more both groups are saying: 'Every style has something to offer in evangelism and worship, so let's enjoy each other's music!'

In the world of Christian congregational singing the pendulum is most definitely swinging back to the centre. From its storeroom the Church is now bringing out treasures both old and new. And it is being enriched beyond measure. That is something for which to praise the Lord!

And let there be more joy in our music! Of course there is a place for plaintive music that tugs at the heartstrings. But the authentic note of Salvation Army worship is joy! Soul-saving music does not have to be dirge-like. Souls can be won with the note of praise!

When leading a congress in a country whose beautiful national music is characterised by a certain sweet sadness, I was asked to play the piano in the music festival. As per my custom with such requests, I chose a chorus on which to improvise as inspired in the moment. For that festive occasion I had chosen a cheerful chorus, and I found I had freedom. So as the inspiration flowed the arpeggios rippled, the chords cascaded and the rhythms pounded. The final notes were greeted with a mighty ovation.

As I was saying my goodbyes after the meeting, a lady said how much she had appreciated my playing, but then, after a moment's hesitation, added: 'Are you really allowed to play that kind of music in an Army hall? It seemed, well ... like jazz! I thought that music in God's house was meant to be solemn.' She seemed genuinely relieved when I assured her that *all* music belongs to God!

In my response to her I had echoed none other than William Booth himself. When he was once asked whether he thought secular music belonged to the devil, he answered: 'If it did I would plunder him for it, for he has no right to a single note of the scale. Every note and every melody and every harmony is divine and belongs to us. So consecrate your voice and your instruments, bring out your cornets and harps, and organs and flutes, and violins and pianos and drums, and everything else that can make melody. Offer them to God, and use them to make all the hearts about you joyful before the Lord.'

As I shared my convictions about Army music with the music leaders in Toronto, I wanted to affirm them in their giftedness and special role in the ministry of the Army. I could sense it happening. They got the message. Let our music be joyful. And let's have more of it!

Meeting human need

We have got used to the idea that radio and television will bring the tragedies of the whole world right into our homes. But as General I found myself listening to the early morning radio news with a new sense of urgency. The Army spans the globe with its emergency relief services, and whenever the newscaster announced a new disaster somewhere in the world – whether natural or man-made – my first thought was whether this was an emergency that called for action on our part.

I knew that the territories would be equally alert and would respond rapidly and effectively to disasters within their borders – as occurred in Mexico, Lesotho, Spain, and in the USA with the Hurricane Katrina tragedy. But I was especially alert to disasters that were too big for a territory to handle with its own resources, or emergencies that crossed borders, or which had struck in countries where we were not already at work.

A continuing tragedy was that of HIV/Aids. Resources of expertise and funding for our teams at work in many parts of the world flowed out continually from International Headquarters. The situation in Africa was especially poignant and in November 2003 I called for all Salvationists around the world to add the resource of their prayers for our work in seeking to prevent and deal with the effects of HIV/Aids in that continent.

At that time 17 million Africans had already died through HIV/Aids-related illnesses. Every 25 seconds someone in Africa was infected, joining the 29 million already infected. In some countries as many as one in every three people was HIV-positive. And 12 million children on that continent had already been orphaned because of Aids. We needed all the resources we could get to do our part in meeting this stark human need.

Wars bring in their wake unspeakable tragedies of individual human suffering. In December 2002 we undertook a winter relief programme in Afghanistan. In January 2003 we were at work in sub-Saharan Africa where the combination of war and drought threatened 40 million people with starvation. In April 2003 teams of Salvation Army personnel entered the south of Iraq.

By August of that year our extensive relief operations in Iraq had largely become centred on Al Amarah. With the kidnappings of non-Iraqi personnel that began to take place, the international support services had eventually to be physically based in Kuwait. But with a display of the resourcefulness for which the Army's international emergency services have rightly become famous, Muntajab Ibraheem Mohammed, a citizen of Al Amarah, became the 'on the spot' team leader for the 40-strong group of personnel working on behalf of The Salvation Army in that city.

Under Muntajab's leadership, and with the support of the international emergency services team, the Army constructed more than 400 homes, 30 schools, 20 vocational training centres and five clinics in that area. Water pumping stations were refurbished, and sewerage, drainage systems and street lighting were installed through large sections of the town. Extensive training programmes for local personnel were established. When Muntajab visited International Headquarters in October 2004, I admitted this modern-day hero to The Salvation Army's Order of Distinguished Auxilliary Service – the first Muslim to receive that award.

Just before Christmas 2004, Freda and I toured the IHQ building to wish the staff well for the festive season ahead. When we came to the international emergencies services, whose personnel are often away dealing with crises in the far corners of the globe, I noticed that most of the members of the team were at their desks. 'There are obviously no emergencies around the world just now,' I commented jovially. But a few days later, on 26 December, that was to change dramatically. The Indian Ocean tsunami struck.

The Army's reaction to this international tragedy of unprecedented proportions was immediate. Unlike many other agencies, we had people on the scene in many of the locations. In the best tradition of the Army, they swung immediately into action. The first bulletin outlining the measures taken by these local Salvationists went out from IHQ the very same day. In time the extensive international response became the largest in our 140-year history. Through the international emergency services section at International Headquarters, the call went out for volunteer workers and for funds. Within days, the first international teams of personnel and resources were on the way.

No sooner had they left before an historic summit meeting was held at IHQ, under the chairmanship of the Chief of the Staff. This brought together territorial commanders of the countries affected by the tsunami with territorial commanders of territories which had the much-needed resources. As a result, generous pledges of financial and personnel support were made with respect to the emergency programmes in Indonesia, India, Sri Lanka and Malaysia.

This meeting laid the foundations for a relief and reconstruction operation that was to last for many years. Food, clothing and medical aid were dispensed. Support programmes of every kind were established. Hundreds of fishing boats were replaced. Thousands of fishing nets were distributed. The new houses constructed also ran into their hundreds. 'The Salvation Army is here to stay,' was the oft-repeated message to those whose livelihoods had been destroyed. And we have been true to our word.

Inauguration of Pope Benedict XVI

The tsunami tragedy launched us into 2005, the final full year of our term of office, on a note of high drama. It was to be a year of many significant events, of which I highlight a few. One of them was participation in the inauguration of Pope Benedict XVI in Rome in the month of April.

No one can predict how long a papal conclave will last. It is therefore difficult to plan ahead for the public inauguration of the new pope. Pope Benedict was elected on a Tuesday evening. Within hours it was announced that his public inauguration would take place in St Peter's Square in Rome the next Sunday morning. It was anticipated that the inaugural mass would be attended by half a million people, many of them coming from other countries. It was obviously going to be something of an organisational feat. By Thursday an invitation reached me as the General of The Salvation Army to be a guest at the event together with Freda.

It was the first time that the General had been invited to the inauguration of a pope. It took only a moment's reflection to decide that this was an invitation I must accept.

The moment's thought was because of the changing relationship The Salvation Army and other Protestant churches have had with the Roman Catholic Church in recent decades. When I was a boy in South America there was a deep 'us and them' gulf between the evangelicals (as Protestants in Latin America call themselves) and the Roman Catholic Church. We were on opposing sides – and the evangelicals saw Roman Catholics as people needing to be saved from the errors of their ways. And vice versa.

But things began to change dramatically in the 1960s through the influence of Pope John XXIII and the Second Vatican Council. When I returned to Chile in 1980 it was to find that the 'us and them' chasm had been bridged. We were all on the same side now. Roman Catholics and evangelicals were working and witnessing together to reach secular society with the gospel.

However, the speed of change by which 'foe' had become friend was still proving bewildering to some. And as so often happens with processes of change, the process was not uniform everywhere. Much depended on personalities. It was going to take time. And meanwhile, in some evangelical hearts, as much in Europe as in Latin America, the fear lingered that the Roman Catholic Church was out to swallow up all other churches.

But having seen and been part of the ecumenical *rapprochement* that had taken place, and being convinced that the things that unite us are greater than those that divide, I wanted to seal this attitude publicly and at the highest level. So that is why Freda and I headed for Rome on the Saturday of that week.

The next day, Sunday 14 April 2005, we gathered with the leaders of other world churches and the 500,000 pilgrims in the great celebration in St Peter's Square. The General of The Salvation Army was placed in the front row facing the raised platform on the steps of St Peter's, where sat the new pope and all the cardinals of the church.

As in the spring sunshine the mass began, I was struck not only by the history and beauty of the location but also by the sheer joy and freedom of everyone present. In some ways it was like being in a Salvation Army meeting!

This was confirmed when Pope Benedict ended his stirring words, which had been interrupted again and again by applause, with an appeal to the young people of the world. 'Do not be afraid of Christ!' he said. 'He takes nothing away, and he gives you everything. Open wide the doors to Christ – and you will find true life.' A high-ranking representative of the Billy Graham organisation said to me afterwards: 'My boss could have given that message.'

The next day, Freda and I had opportunity to converse with the Pope following a private gathering with Christian leaders and representatives of different faiths. During the course of our exchange, I thanked the Pope for his Christ-centred message of the day before, and he expressed his hope that all Christians everywhere would work together to meet the challenges of a secular society.

State of the Army

In February 2005 the Army had received a nice pat on the back from the internationally renowned global strategy and technology consulting firm Booz Allen Hamilton – the firm that had helped the Army in the USA with its administrative structure in the 1960s.

The company had asked leading scholars at respected universities across the USA to nominate institutions which had 'adapted, endured and prevailed' – standing the test of time and successfully reinventing themselves to meet changing conditions. The aim was to seek to discover why some institutions endure for decades, even centuries, while others disappear into history.

Along with Oxford University, the Olympic Games, the American Constitution and six others, The Salvation Army was named as one of the world's top ten enduring institutions. Booz Allen Hamilton said that The Salvation Army was iconic in its ability to motivate and inspire its people. 'The Salvation Army's skill is in creating the culture and expressing the values that makes its own endurance possible.' In our own language: we had remained true to our mission and style.

There could have been no better background to the address I was asked to give at the new International Headquarters in May 2005. The event was entitled *An Evening with the General,* and would give guests an opportunity to see the new building, share refreshments and hear about the international Army. Just as the President of the USA gives an annual 'state of the union' address to Congress in Washington, with the nation watching on television, so I was to give a 'state of the Army' address in miniature to those assembled at International Headquarters, which Salvationists worldwide could later watch on the web. UK Salvationists had been invited to apply for tickets on a 'first come first served' basis and within a short time the event was a sell-out.

On the day, when the guests had completed their tours of the building and enjoyed fellowship over refreshments, they settled down for the address. A recent television quiz programme in the UK gave me just the opening I needed. A woman contestant had been asked the question: 'Which is the largest army in the world?' I shared with my audience that if I had been asked that question I would not have been sure of the answer. Was it the Chinese army? The Russian army? Or the American army? But quick as a flash the contestant had replied: 'It's The Salvation Army!' And that was the correct answer!

I then went on to survey the state of The Salvation Army globally in its mission of taking Christ to the world and bringing the world to Christ. My assessment of the state of the Army was upbeat, the Lord was renewing his Army, but I warned that there could be no room for complacency. God had yet more to do in our midst. The needs of the world continued to be cataclysmic. And the war was still far from being won.

Youth Year 2005

Soon after becoming General I announced that the year 2005 would be 'A Year for Children and Youth'. Echoing William Booth, I wanted to 'pay a thousand, nay ten thousand times more attention to the children' of the world.

I wanted the year to be centred not so much on celebratory occasions for the young as getting our mission and ministry to children and youth right for today. The lead-up to the year was therefore as important as the year itself, with territories urged to consider how better to meet the needs of disadvantaged young people, and how better to reach out, attract and hold the young in order to lead them to faith, discipleship and service for Christ. I was particularly anxious that our programmes for junior soldiers and corps cadets should be given new life – 21st-century life.

What you focus on you improve, and I believe that the focus on our ministry to children and youth in 2005 did just that for the Army around the world. The response in some parts of the world was quite amazing. The sophistication of many of our youth programmes and the material provided for them is most impressive these days. As part of the preparation for 2005, IHQ produced a discipling programme for the young entitled *Discovery*. I was encouraged to learn that 25,000 young people began using this material, and that 13,000 copies of a new course for junior soldiers were issued.

A highlight of the year was the European Youth Congress held in Prague, capital of the Czech Republic, for four days in August. When the organisers asked if we could be present I consulted our diary. It would be Brazzaville one weekend, Prague the next, and Tokyo the following. But we had not the slightest hesitation in saying yes.

Sharing those days with the 800 delegates drawn from 26 countries will be one of the indelible memories of our term as international leaders. A scintillating programme of plenary sessions and group activities had been prepared. Young people milled everywhere. They witnessed to the citizens of Prague on Saturday, and worshipped by a lakeside on Sunday morning. Freda and I shared these activities with them, and each meal was taken with a different group of young people. It was exhilarating, encouraging and deeply moving.

Jeff Lucas, the internationally famous Christian communicator who was one of the speakers, writes in his own characteristic style in *Lucas Out Loud* about our presence at the congress. He comments light-heartedly on the herding instinct that makes us humans want to conform to national or age-group type, and then adds:

But today I saw a couple of refreshing jailbreaks from the herd. I have watched as the World Chief of the Salvationists, General John Larsson, and his wife Commissioner Freda have been hard at work here. As leaders of the largest army in the world, the distinguished-looking couple could have easily made a brief appearance – the social equivalent of patting these eight hundred young people on the head, and then disappeared back to the elite seclusion often enjoyed by denominational big cheeses.

Not these two. Over the last four days, they have laughed with and listened to hordes of grinning youth who could barely disguise their delight because their Head and First Lady are among them. This afternoon, in the sun-baked Old Town Square, the General spoke at an open-air gathering with warmth, compassion and clarity about the Lord Jesus. A few moist eyes were evident among the tourist crowd during the event, and the Army youth cheered their silver-haired hero on.

All Africa Congress

With a weekend's break for preparation following the visit to Japan, it was now time for the September 2005 All Africa Congress – the first of its kind.

Africa! An amazing continent. The second largest in the world, with 830 million people speaking more than 1,000 languages, and the oldest known site of human habitation. Christianity came to Africa before it came to Europe. And today 45 per cent of Africans are Christian. The growth among evangelical churches remains phenomenal. It is the continent most open to the gospel.

The Salvation Army in Africa has been part of this movement of the Spirit. At the time of the congress, 41 per cent of the Army's senior soldiers were in Africa, and 66 per cent of its junior soldiers – and those percentages are likely to have increased since then. As I said to the delegates, with a mighty heave more than half of The Salvation Army might be in Africa within the next few years. Including St Helena, the Army at the time of the congress was officially at work in 18 African countries. But 'come over and help us' requests from Salvationists and friends had already reached us from eight more nations.

The concept of an All Africa Congress to celebrate this development and to look to the future came from the African leaders themselves, and it was one we warmly endorsed. Zimbabwe was chosen as the venue because of its location and because the Army there had the infrastructure to handle such an event.

Everyone in Africa was familiar with territorial or divisional congresses lasting one weekend to which people would walk or be transported by buses and trucks. But a five-day international event involving complexities of cross-border travel and different languages was going to be a new logistic challenge. Zimbabwe as a nation was going through a difficult period at that time. The congress came near to being cancelled on more than one occasion when seemingly insurmountable obstacles appeared to block the path ahead. But a way around was always found, and we decided to step out in faith.

Our faith was richly rewarded. The event was in every way the amazing event that an amazing continent deserved. The Zimbabwean Salvationists were superb in their organisation, and when on the Sunday thousands upon thousands of Salvationists marched into the National Sports Stadium in Harare for the final meeting, the drums and the hallelujahs could be heard miles away!

On the reviewing stand with Freda and me stood the Chief of the Staff, Commissioner Israel L. Gaither with Commissioner Eva Gaither, and the International Secretary for Africa and Zonal Secretary for Women's Ministries, Commissioners Amos and Rosemary Makina. As we looked out on this great assembly of Africans from so many nations, we rejoiced in all that God had done in our midst during those days. And we prayed that it would not be long before the prayer of the congress theme chorus would come true: 'Africa for Christ!'

China

The 21st century is going to be the century of China. That vast nation is developing at a breathtaking pace. I was concerned that our work there is so restricted. As mentioned earlier, in China the Army bird with its two wings of evangelistic and social mission is only permitted to fly on one wing. But the Army is being effective. As one Chinese officer so beautifully put it to me, speaking metaphorically: 'We are really flying on two wings, but one wing is invisible!'

When all foreign missionaries were expelled from China in the early 1950s it was thought that it would mean the end of the Christian Church in China. It was estimated that there were around three million Christians in China at that time. The communist government decreed that all churches must be self-governed, self-propagating, and self-supporting. In other words, there must be no outside control and no missionaries or funding from outside China.

This gave birth to the Three-Self Movement as the official Christian church, and it became – and remains – government policy that there will only be one official Christian church in China. Separate denominations are not permitted. When the missionaries left, most Christians became members of this one official church, and the various denominations in China merged into it.

When the doors of new China opened to the world in the 1980s it was revealed that far from declining, the number of Christians in China had grown enormously to around 50 million. Most of these were members of the official church. But many were members of

242

underground, and therefore officially illegal independent churches that seemed to be spreading like wildfire. As I looked to China I saw a country where the Christian Church was expanding rapidly. Estimates of 120 million believers were being heard. And I wanted The Salvation Army to be part of that exciting scene.

The opening of the doors in the 1980s had enabled the Army to return to China with community services and project work. The extent of our project work since then – building schools, digging wells, opening roads, establishing training programmes, running child-support programmes, even providing feeding programmes – has been quite amazing. The Army's name and shield is to be seen on building after building. In fact in some villages the white cotton sacks with the red shield in which the Army provides rice are prized possessions. They make excellent curtains! So when one walks down the street the red Army shield is to be seen adorning window after window. We have a presence in China!

The social wing of the Army bird is strong in China. We are welcomed and respected by both government and the people as an international NGO – a non-governmental organisation. And we are witnessing for Christ with our hands. It is the other wing – the church wing of the Army – which is the challenge. It is still government policy that there will only be one official Christian church in China – run on the three-self principles. It seems that the Army would somehow either have to fit under that umbrella – which General Albert Orsborn rejected already in 1952 – or be an illegal underground operation, which would of course be out of the question.

But the mushrooming of the Christian Church in China was ever before me. And I also watched carefully how the Roman Catholic Church was handling the dilemma. As already touched upon, the Roman Catholic Church and The Salvation Army are the two most strongly-knit international churches. The Vatican had resolutely refused to recognise the part of the Roman Catholic Church in China that had crept under the official church umbrella. But the Vatican was now seeking for the Roman Catholic Church to be officially recognised as an independent church in China. Could we somehow latch on to their coat-tails?

Early in 2005 I therefore established a high-powered China Mission Task Force at International Headquarters. The remit I gave them was of seeking for any and every possible means whereby The Salvation Army's work in China might be extended and we might fulfil our total mission – evangelistic and social. My aim and hope was for the bird to be able to fly on two wings.

I also arranged to visit government officials in Beijing in September 2005, following the 75th anniversary celebrations of the Army in Hong Kong. The Army is strong in Hong Kong, and with Hong Kong becoming part of China in 1997, The Salvation Army there has become something of a Trojan horse within mainland China – another positive development for our cause.

When Freda and I arrived in Beijing, accompanied by Lieut-Colonel Alfred Tsang, the officer commanding in Hong Kong and a China specialist, we were accorded the full red carpet treatment. Representatives of the government Bureau for Religious Affairs were at the airport to welcome us, and their hospitality throughout the visit knew no bounds. They seemed genuinely pleased that the General of the international Salvation Army should honour them by visiting China. We also had opportunity to see the still imposing former territorial headquarters building and compound where my grandparents had once lived and worked.

We held a series of meetings with top-level government and NGO officials. Some of these were with the full pomp and circumstance which the Chinese reserve for such occasions – with the two principals sitting side by side in imposing armchairs at one end of a vast room and their advisers being ranged down on each side of it.

In these meetings we were left in no doubt about the appreciation felt towards the Army – as an NGO. But what was surprising to me was the open recognition of, and appreciation for, the Army as a religious movement. The government representatives warmly welcomed me as the leader of an international Christian church.

But they welcomed me warmly precisely because I was a foreigner. Indeed, visiting Salvation Army officers are often asked to preach in churches – as long as they come from abroad. But whenever I moved the agenda to the possibility of there being Chinese Salvationists I detected an immediate hesitation. With the utmost courtesy they would reiterate in carefully chosen phrases designed to cause the minimum of offence that government policy is to have only one Christian church in China.

And that is where I had to leave the matter when I came to the end of my term as General. Efforts of course continue. With China everything is long term. But my hope and dream of seeing the Army fully established in China remain undiminished. I long for that invisible wing to become visible!

High Council Welcome and Farewell Salute

As I would be 68 on 2 April 2006, and my retirement would be at midnight of the day before, the High Council to elect my successor was duly summoned on 1 December 2005.

One hundred members met at Sunbury Court on Tuesday 17 January 2006 for a three-day pre-High Council conference over which I presided. This gave me the opportunity to render account for my term of office and also to focus on the challenges ahead.

For my keynote I selected 12 themes. The delegates then divided into eight groups to discuss these themes further. They were also asked to list in priority order the five subjects they considered most important for further discussion in the plenary sessions that were to follow. By that method I and everyone else would discern which topics were of the greatest corporate concern.

I record the themes I dealt with as they give an insight into matters that were of current interest at the time:

1. World evangelisation
2. Reaching and discipling children and youth
3. Membership of The Salvation Army
4. Combating human trafficking
5. Training for officership
6. One-spouse officership
7. Developing our personnel resource
8. The rank of lieut-colonel
9. Resolving the financial challenge
10. The General's Consultative Council
11. The sacraments
12. Being what we are called to be as an Army.

There was remarkable agreement between the groups in identifying the five most important subjects for further discussion.

In order of priority these were: Being what we are called to be as an Army; World evangelisation; Reaching and discipling children and youth; Combating human trafficking; and Developing our personnel resource.

When the conference drew to its close on Thursday evening, Freda and I returned home. The General and 'the commissioner who is the spouse of the General' – as the amended *Salvation Army Act 1980* puts it – are not members of the High Council.

The High Council itself commenced on Friday 20 January, and the following day the public welcome meeting was held in the Westminster Central Hall. As the General, I was to lead this.

There is value in getting 'two for one', and just as Freda and I had combined our welcome as international leaders with the retirement of the Gowanses, we decided to combine our public farewell with the welcome meeting to the High Council. That would avoid having two big meetings later on – a farewell to us and a welcome to the new General – only a week apart.

As the commencement time neared, the Westminster Central Hall was filled to overflowing, and the cameras were ready for the live web broadcast to Salvationists worldwide. As the International Staff Band played martial music, an international kaleidoscope unfolded as the members of the High Council entered and were rapturously received. The first part of the meeting then focused on the welcome to the High Council and the ministry of the worldwide Army.

The second part of the event included a farewell salute to Freda and me. The Chief of the Staff, Commissioner Israel L. Gaither, and Commissioner Eva D. Gaither captivated the congregation with their generous joint tribute to us.

One of the highlights in this segment for Freda and me was a video and live presentation that our sons Karl and Kevin had prepared. Kevin had arranged a brilliant musical salute based on my music and had recorded the accompaniment. On the night, he conducted the massed songsters as they performed his composition. Karl had prepared a video that synchronised with the music, and this was shown on the large screen as the songsters sang. The video featured our international visits and aspects of our lives, and when the official reporter later described this creation by Karl and Kevin as 'spectacular', we as parents agreed wholeheartedly! We were proud of our two sons, and were glad that they had travelled from Los Angeles to be present.

With my message in the third part of the meeting, the focus returned once more to the High Council. Just as an extended piece of music will often recapitulate the opening theme in its final movement, I chose to speak about the Army and its God-given mission as I had done in our welcome meeting. Addressing both the members of the High Council and the Salvationists and friends present I said to them that the word of the Lord to The Salvation Army today was 'Don't turn back!' I could sense the congregation was with me as I developed this theme, speaking from my heart:

'No one who puts his hand to the plough and looks back is fit for service in the Kingdom of God,' said Jesus (Luke 9:62, *NIV*). He was speaking to individuals. And we all as individuals need to heed his words. But I can hear a voice from Heaven calling out to us as an Army and saying: 'No church – no Army of mine – that puts its hand to the plough and looks back is fit for service in the kingdom of God.'

But can a church really look back? Can the Army really turn back from its calling, from its mission, from its passion? Yes. It is possible. For the Army – like every other church – is engaged in a cosmic struggle with the forces of evil.

Secularism shouts at us: 'Turn back – come back to the *real* world.' Unbelief envelops us. 'Turn back,' it says, 'there's nothing out there – don't put your trust in things unseen.' Materialism gnaws at our fibre. 'Turn back,' it says, 'take what is yours, lay up treasure on earth.' Worldliness whispers: 'Turn back, don't try to live by the values of the Kingdom – the values of this world are OK. Enjoy!' And nominalism breathes in our ears: 'Turn back – you're being too passionate, too committed, too sacrificial in your service. Leave the saving of the lost to others. There are lots of nominal Christians – it's alright.'

And most subtly of all, in this cosmic battle the forces of evil say to the Army as a whole: 'Turn back – and settle down! Forget about aggressive Christianity. Forget about going for souls and going for the worst. Forget about being a rescue brigade at the very gates of Hell. Forget about standing up for what is right in society and battling against what is wrong. Trust in your good standing with governments and the public. Trust in your good name. Don't do anything to threaten that. Trust in pounds sterling and dollars. Trust in programmes. Trust the visible – not the invisible. Don't take any risks. Be a nice worshipping community. Forget about being a radical, Spirit-filled force whose aim is to turn the world upside down.'

Yes, as an Army, we are engaged in a cosmic battle for our very soul. And when the voices cry out 'turn back' there can be only one reply: 'We are *not* going to turn back! Whatever it may cost. For we are called to live to love and save the lost!'

With all of our determination, and by faith, and in his strength, we as an Army must shout out that we are *not* going to turn back from being what God raised up the Army to be! He has called us to be a holy people of God. He has called us to dare to be different in our lifestyle. He has called us to be a people mobilised for God. He has called us to care for the poor, feed the hungry, clothe the naked, love the unlovable, and befriend those who have no friends. He has called us to rescue the perishing and care for the dying. And, whatever it may cost, we are *not* going to turn back from being what God raised us up to be, and from doing what God has called us to do!

Final weeks

On the day that the High Council would be voting to elect the next General, Freda and I returned to Sunbury Court to await the result. A happy custom has arisen in recent decades whereby the first person outside of the council itself to greet the General-elect is the General in office.

Commencing with the 2002 High Council, Salvationists in all parts of the world have been able to watch that moment live on the web. Traditionally the doors of the council room have swung open and the General-elect, followed by the council members, has stridden out into the sunshine to be greeted by the General and the well-wishers who have gathered. But with the 2006 High Council being a winter one a new arrangement had to be made. This time the doors swung inward, and it was the General and the group of well-wishers who did the striding as they entered the council chamber.

And there, before the eyes of the Army world, I welcomed General-elect Shaw Clifton and Commissioner Helen Clifton – the first international leaders to have served in all of the Army's five geographical zones – to their high offices and prayed God's blessing upon them.

The final weeks in office included a three-island tour – for Freda and me a nostalgic one – to Fiji and the North and South Islands of New Zealand. But the main focus was on ensuring a smooth transition to the next administration. The fact that the General-elect was London-based made it possible for us to meet a number of times as well as having almost daily contact by email and phone.

On the final day at International Headquarters the traditional Thursday morning family prayers took the form of a retirement meeting in our honour led by the Chief of the Staff. Commissioners Israel and Eva Gaither had been appointed national leaders of the Army in the USA and their own farewell meeting had been held the week before.

It was an intimate event. My sister, Lieut-Colonel Miriam Frederiksen, spoke. Miriam had been appointed to International Headquarters some months previously to understudy Colonel Laurence Hay, and was shortly to become the executive secretary to the new General. Freda's sister, Major Brenda Sterling, also spoke. She had travelled from Zimbabwe for the occasion, where David with Brenda headed The Salvation Army Leaders' Training College of Africa. Retired General John Gowans and Commissioner Gisèle Gowans were also present, and it was fitting that John should present us with our retirement certificates.

In our speaking Freda and I gave praise and thanks to God for the ministry he had entrusted to us for so many years. In my case, if I include my year as a cadet, it adds up to 50 years. We thanked God for colleagues and friends we had met on our pilgrimage. And I thanked God for inspiring me to say yes to him, and to say yes to life in all of its richness and diversity. What a satisfying adventure life had proved to be! We also said that we now looked forward to a change of ministry – for that is how we anticipated retirement. And that is how it has turned out to be.

Our very special guest was Commissioner Denis Hunter, aged 86. As these pages have recorded, he has been very influential in our service for God. I wanted Denis to have the last word on our active service as officers in the form of the final prayer.

Denis slowly mounted the low platform with the aid of his walking stick. Then with a characteristic flourish he handed me the stick to hold as he launched into a fervent prayer of thanksgiving and praise to God.

When he ended he had another surprise up his sleeve. His were not to be the last words. As I gave his stick back to him, he asked me to go to the piano and announced that in this celebration of our service for God, the very last words would be words of Jesus. He then called on us all to sing the benediction from the musical *Takeover Bid*. And as the congregation lifted their voices, Freda and I lifted not only our voices but also our hearts to God as we sang with all the passion of our beings:

> For thine is the Kingdom,
> And thine is the power,
> And thine is the glory
> For ever and ever.
> For ever – and ever –
> AMEN!

INDEX

A

Adherency, 227–28
Adnams, Ernest, 89
Advisory boards, 139, 220
Advisory Council to the General, 142, 150, 178
All Africa Congress, 241–42
Allemand, Edmundo, 26–28
Anderson, Ernest, 93
Argentina, early years, 26–31
Assistant to the Chief of the Staff for UK Administrative Planning, 132

B

Baird, Bramwell, 157
Bale, Malcolm, 157
Ball, Eric, 45, 81
Banks, Keith and Pauline, 126
Bearcroft, Norman, 152
Benwell, Alfred and Mathilda, 5–9
Boardman, Hubert, 88, 89
Books
 Doctrine Without Tears, 61
 How Your Corps Can Grow, 128
 Spiritual Breakthrough, 95–99
 The Man Perfectly Filled with the Spirit, 120–22
Boon, Brindley, 72
Booth, Bramwell, 5, 30, 59, 135, 181
Booth, Catherine, 36, 166, 176, 208

Booth, Evangeline, 1
Booth, Herbert, 147
Booth, William, 5, 6, 15, 133, 134, 135, 137, 149, 181, 199, 201, 206, 208, 216, 233
Booz Allen Hamilton, 148, 238
Botting, David, 81
Brengle Institute, 60
Brengle, Samuel, 64–65, 95, 99
British Commissioner, 135, 137, 141, 142
British Territory, 135
Bromley Temple Corps, 86–89, 91–92
Brown, Arnold, 92, 97, 98, 139, 140, 183
Brown, Fred, 79
Buck, Pearl, 25
Buckingham, Hillmon and Lorraine, 172
Burrows, Eva, 92, 128, 129, 131, 133, 139, 142, 145, 147, 148, 150, 151, 153, 154–55, 161
Bush, George W., 219

C

Campfield Press, 136
Carby, Mary, 126
Carpenter, George, 3, 4, 92, 139
Catford Corps, 106
Chadwick, Andrew, 196, 198
Charity Commission, 145
Chief of the Staff, 181–202

Chief of the Staff's British Council, 140

Chief Secretary, South America West Territory, 111–13

Chile, early years, 20–26

China, 5, 242–45

Christ of the Andes, 19

Churchill, Winston, 24, 54

Clark, William, 96

Clifton, Shaw and Helen, 145, 179, 200, 249

Commissioners' Conference 1958, 137–39

Commissioning day, 46

Cooper, William, 76, 84, 85

Coopers & Lybrand, 147, 148, 150, 161, 162

Copenhagen Temple Corps, 14

Core values, 165–69

Corps cadetship, growth of, 105

Cottrill, Stanley, 109

Courageous Session, 47

Coutts, Frederick, 35, 43, 46, 92, 139, 183

Coutts, Olive, 126

Covenant Day, 46

Cox, Ron and Hilda, 132, 143

Cutmore, Ian and Nancy, 154, 157

D

Dalziel, Geoffrey, 104, 159

Denmark, early years, 13–18

Disciples, making of, 230

Drury, Albert, 39

Du Plessis, Paul, 225, 226

Duggins, Norman, 182

Dumbleton, Rhys and Gladys, 47

Durman, Charles, 45

E

Ealing Corps, 81–82

Elsworth, John, 45

Elvin, Derek, 148

England, Edward, 96

European Youth Congress, 240

F

Faithful Session, 35

Farewell Salute, 246–48

Field Scene, 132, 133

Fraud, 1993, 161–63

Frederiksen, Miriam, 10, 11, 12, 17, 33, 249

G

Gaither, Israel and Eva, 179, 205, 209, 242, 246, 249

Gariepy, Henry, 131

General, 203–50

General's Consultative Council, 226, 228

Golbourn, Stan, 40

Goodwill Department, 135

Goulding, Eva, 24

Gowans, John, 71–77, 83–86, 87–88, 99–101, 102–4, 106–9, 122, 126–27, 153–54, 179, 184, 190, 192, 193, 194

Gowans, John and Gisèle, 71, 83, 202, 205, 209, 249

Granholm, Gunnar, 68, 80

Griffiths, Doris, 49

Gruer, David, 21

H

Hattersley, Roy, 206, 208
Hawkins, Peter, 143
Hay, Laurence, 209, 249
Higgins, Edward, 137, 209
High Council
   1993, 162
   1994, 170
   1999, 162, 178
   2002, 199–202
   2006, pre-conference, 245–46
Hill, Fred, 58
Hillingdon Corps, 68, 69–71
HIV/Aids, 234
Holdstock, Ray, 157
Holy Spirit renewal movement, 62, 65–68
Houghton, Ray, 152
Howarth, John, 81
Howe, Norman, 190
Hull, Walter, 97
Human trafficking, 229
Hunter, Denis, 71, 72, 73, 75, 153, 249

I

International College for Officers, 86, 133
International Conference of
   Leaders
   1988, 129
   1998, 189
   2000, 191
   2004, 229–30
International Congress
   1978, 105, 106
   1990, 152–53
   2000, 193–94
International Headquarters
   '101' building, 199
   mission statement, 186–87
   role of, 186–89
International Management Council, 149, 150, 186
International Music and Other
   Creative Ministries Forum, 230
International Officership
   Commission, 189–93
International Training College
   Cadet and Sergeant, 35–48
   House and Sectional Officer, 55–68
   Principal, 125–29
International Training College, as a
   'territory', 134, 140
Iraq, 234

J

John of the Cross, 98
Johnson, Ron and Barbara, 94
Johnstone, Patrick, 224, 226

K

Kendrick, Kathleen, 96
King, Charles, 160
Kitching, Wilfred, 137, 139, 142, 144, 145, 182, 214
Kjellgren, Hasse, 174, 200
Kragh Jensen, Henry, 14

L

Lamb, David, 150
Larsson, David, 1, 9, 11–12
Larsson, Freda, 79, 83, 93, 106, 121, 122, 125, 132–33, 157, 173, 178, 181, 202
Larsson, Karl and Anna, 1–5, 176
Larsson, Karl and Sarita, 86, 91, 111, 113–16, 125, 163, 246
Larsson, Kevin and Jacqui, 86, 91, 113–16, 125, 163, 246
Larsson, Sture and Flora, 1, 9–10, 17, 19, 25, 33, 94, 109
Leadership, consultative, 210
Lewis, C. S., 80
London University, studies, 61
Lucas, Jeff, 240

M

Magnenat, Juan, 22
Maidenhead Corps Band, 117
Makina, Amos and Rosemary, 242
Marriage, 82–83
Maxwell, Earle, 179
Men's Social Services, 134, 140
Menary, Robert and Bronwyn, 81
Metcalf, William, 105
Mingay, Albert, 39
Mitchell, Gordon, 37
Morgan, Brian, 200
Music and gospel arts, 230–33
Musicals
   Glory!, 102–4
   Hosea, 83–86
   Jesus Folk, 87–89
   Man Mark II, 126–27
   Son of Man, 120–22
   Spirit!, 89–91, 99–102
   Take-over Bid, 71–80
   The Blood of the Lamb, 106–9
   The Meeting, 153–54
   White Rose, 106

N

Nery, Jorge, 113
New Zealand, Fiji and Tonga Territory, 163–72
Nilson, Gunnar and Berit, 172
Norway Territory, 60
Nuesch, Ruben, 111, 119

O

Officership, call to, 30–32
Orr Bell, Elizabeth, 199
Orsborn, Albert, 137, 243

P

Palermo Corps, 26
Pallant, Stephen, 157
Partners in Mission scheme, 229
Peale, Norman Vincent, 23
Pender, Dinsdale, 143
Pitt, Gary, 210–12
Pope Benedict XVI, 236–38
Pope John XXIII, 237
Prayer, resource of, 229
Princess Royal, 198
Principal, International Training College, 125–26

Public Relations Department, IHQ, 134

Puerto Rico Division, 109

R

Rader, Paul, 170, 178, 190, 195
Railton, George Scott, 6, 206
Read, Harry, 38, 56, 143, 154, 158
Redhead, Robert and Gwenyth, 230
Reliance Bank, 197
Renewal, theme as General, 200–1, 222–24
Rhodes, Pam, 160
Rich, Ivor, 157
Robinson, John, 62
Russia, 2

S

Salvation Army Act 1980, 140, 143, 144, 146, 246
Salvation Army Assurance Society, 134, 140
Salvation Army Boys' Adventure Corps (SABAC), 105
Salvation Army Ceremonies, 129
Salvationist Publishing and Supplies Ltd, 76, 85, 88, 122, 134, 135, 137, 140, 153
Sandall, Robert, 207
Santiago Central Corps, 22, 112
Scotland and the Republic of Ireland, 148–49
Servants of Christ Session, 59
Slaughter and May, 144, 145, 161, 162
Smith, Peter, 145

Social Services, 140
Soldier's covenant, 128–29
Soldiers of Christ Session, 57
Spiritual development, 12–13, 14–15, 24–25, 65–68, 80, 95, 99
Springburn Corps, 93
State of the Army address, 238–39
Stead, W. T., 206
Steadman-Allen, Ray, 75
Sterling, David and Brenda, 249
Street, Robert, 121
Stubley, Ken, 49, 55
Sunderland Southwick and Washington Corps, 48–54
Sweden and Latvia Territory, 172–78
Sweden Territory, in 1938, 1
Sweden, early years, 10–13

T

Taylor, Brian, 195, 200
Taylor, Edmund, 51
Taylor, Lyndon, 97
Territorial Commander, New Zealand, Fiji and Tonga Territory, 163–72
Territorial Commander, Sweden and Latvia Territory, 172–78
Territorial Commander, United Kingdom Territory, 157–63
Territorial Executive Council, 148, 149
The Salvation Army International Trustee Company, 145, 146
The Salvation Army Trustee Company, 138, 140, 145, 146
Theinhardt, Erik, 111
Thompson, Arthur, 100, 164

Tillsley, Bramwell, 209
Tsang, Alfred, 244
Tsunami, Indian Ocean, 235–36
Turner, Freda, 82–83
Turner, Thomas and Winifred, 82, 109
Two-year training, 58

U

United Kingdom Territory with the Republic of Ireland, 145–46, 151, 157–63
Upper Norwood Corps, 31, 32

V

Van Hal, Jeanne, 209
Vis, Walter, 116–20
Vocational house parties, 88, 90–91, 100

W

Wahlström, Jarl, 99, 120, 124, 139, 141

Ward, Leo, 58
Webb, Joy, 58
Westergaard, Kaare, 47, 56, 58, 60, 92
Westergaard, Mona, 57
White, Margaret, 143, 157
Wickberg, Erik, 3, 62, 139, 140, 182, 209
Wiseman, Clarence, 68, 139, 140, 217
Women's Social Services, 134, 140
World evangelisation, 224–26, 229, 246

Y

Yoder, Stephen, 209, 215
Youth corps, Stockholm, 174–76
Youth Secretary
    British Territory, 104–5
    Scotland Territory, 93–95
Youth Year 2005, 239–40
YP Manual, 58

Z

Zonal conferences, 228–29